Preaching through

Philippians

and

Colossians

Expository sermons through the books of

Philippians and Colossians

By Pastor Paul Wallace

ISBN # 978-1-949249-03-3
Unless otherwise stated all Scripture citation is from the
HOLY BIBLE, the "English Standard Version"®.
(ESV®)Copyright © 2001 by Crossway, a publishing ministry
of Good News Publishers. All rights reserved. ESV Text
Edition: 2007
Scripture citations marked (NIV) are from the NEW
INTERNATIONAL VERSION®. Copyright ©1973, 1978, 1984,
by International Bible Society. Used by permission of
Zondervan Publishing House. All Rights Reserved. The "NIV"
and "New International Version" trademarks are registered
in the United States Patent and Trademark Office by
International Bible Society. Use of either trademark requires
the permission of International Bible Society.

Contents

Church Glue Philippians 1:1-11

Before we get into our text for today, we should do a brief review of how the church of Philippi was founded. Philippi was a town about the size of our own, around 10,000 in population, on the Via Egnatia. This was a main road connecting Rome with the eastern empire. It was on the southern edge of the European Continent. It was originally a Greek town, but because of several significant battles there, including the defeat of Brutus and Cassius by Augustus and Mark Antony, it became a Roman colony. The officials and aristocracy spoke Latin and all the city inscriptions were in Latin, but the common folks, the slaves, merchants, and tradesmen, spoke Greek.

On Paul's second missionary journey, you may recall the night vision of the man of Macedonia calling him to come. (Acts 16:9) In Acts 16, Luke records the story of Paul, Silas, and Timothy in Philippi. There was no synagogue, but there was a group of God fearing women who met to worship the God of Israel on a river bank by the city. They shared the message of Jesus with them, and a merchant woman named Lydia became a believer. (Acts 16:14-15)

Later, a woman who was possessed by a spirit, the Greek is literally a pythonic spirit, followed them around yelling out that they were servants of the most high God proclaiming the way of salvation. It was true but perhaps the spirit was trying to gain credibility for itself. Paul cast the spirit out of the girl. (Acts 16:18) The man that owned the girl saw his means of making money through her was gone and so had Paul and Silas brought before the Roman magistrate. All that the accuser needed to say was that they were Jewish troublemakers, which resulted in them being scourged and put in stocks.

Around midnight Paul and Silas were singing praises to God and an earthquake set them free. That resulted in the Centurion jailer and his family being converted and perhaps some of the prisoners as well. (Acts 16:30) Discovering that they were Roman citizens, the Roman magistrates sheepishly asked if they would please leave the town. But the damage was done! A church had been founded! Sounds like a nice homogeneous church doesn't it, a Roman soldier and family, a former fortune teller, and a merchant woman and her family?

Today we look for a church that is our kind of people with our kind of songs and preaching, in our part of town. Back then, they just wanted to praise the living Lord Jesus with anyone else that knew Him as Savior. The church is bound not by social status or culture or age or any other factor. (1Corinthians 12:13) The church is bound by our relationship with our Savior and our gratitude for what He has done for us! That's why we love each other. We share the same passion for our Savior. If we are red or yellow, black or white, or half and half, rich or poor, it's the love of Jesus that makes us what we are and binds us to one another. Everything else is insignificant compared to the one thing! (1Corinthians 2:2)

It had been some time since Paul and company founded that first European church. Paul was now in prison and writing to this church for which he seems to have great affection. He had received a gift from them to support his needs while in jail, brought by Epaphroditus. Epaphroditus is about to return and Paul is sending this letter to encourage them and to let them know that Timothy is coming to them to prepare them for the Judaizers. (Philippians 2:19)

¹ Paul and Timothy, servants of Christ Jesus, To all the saints in Christ Jesus who are at Philippi, with the overseers and deacons: Philippians 1:1 (ESV) Paul's opening to this letter is the same as most letters in some ways and different in others. Perhaps because of the affection they had for him and he for them, Paul did not mention his authority as an apostle as he did in the opening lines to most churches. (Romans 1:1)

He writes that it is from him and Timothy. Timothy was co-authoring the letter. Paul often includes co-laborers and shares the credit. That is the Christian way. The worldly will often try to retain all the glory they can for themselves. The follower of Jesus recognizes we are soldiers that have each other's back. We are in it together. We need one another. (1Corinthians 12:19) We are incomplete without one another. We are sheep in flock, parts of a body or stones that make up a building, a family. (1Corinthians 3:9) We only operate alone when it is absolutely necessary and even then constantly leaning on the Lord.

"Servants" is literally the word "slaves". When we surrender to Christ, we find great strength and joy in serving Him. We set aside our own will and take on the will of the one who knows what we need and has our best interest at heart. We walk in daily obedience to him. A slave of Jesus is a high calling. We are either a slave of self and sin or a slave of Jesus. (John 8:34) One is self-deception. The other is true liberation to be what we were created to be.

The saints are all the believers that worship together in Philippi. All believers are saints because of what Jesus did for us. (Hebrews 13:12) You don't need to be beatified first; you are already blessed! You don't need to be perfect. You are a work in progress. But God sees you as holy because you did the one work he requires, believing in Jesus. God sees you as a saint because you are *in* Christ Jesus. Amen? (John 6:29)

Paul added the mention of the overseers and deacons. We saw the role of deacon in the closing sermon on Colossians. Paul elaborates on these roles in the church in the letters to Titus and Timothy. (Titus 1:5) The Philippian church had matured to the point to where there were men in the office of elder. Overseer and elder are used interchangeably in Acts 20. (Acts 20:28; 17) Qualified, equal and accountable elders are God's plan for overseeing the church. There are so many different forms of church government today, but this is God's form. This is what He established in His word. We aren't meant to have CEOs or lone pastors who make all the decisions, nor are we to have boards of businessmen who do what they think best because of practical experience. A Biblical church will have elders, plural, who oversee the church through prayer, who teach the Word of God, and shepherd the flock. (1Peter 5:1-3)

There are also deacons. This is also a high calling of spiritual men and women who handle the practical affairs of the church. These are the only God appointed offices of the church Jesus established.

2 Grace to you and peace from God our Father and the Lord Jesus Christ. Philippians 1:2 (ESV) Every letter of the Apostle Paul has this greeting. His last letters to Timothy add the request for mercy as well. Grace *(Charis)* is the Greek greeting. Peace *(Eirene Gk. or Shalom Heb.)* is the Jewish greeting. Christianity poured new meaning into both.

Grace now meant more than beauty in life, but the loving kindness of God. Peace is no longer just life's blessing but now includes peace with God through Jesus. Paul writes that the source of grace and peace is the Father and the Lord Jesus Christ. If you don't have those glorious qualities in life, now you know where to go to get them. The only true grace and lasting peace come from God the Father and Jesus the Son. (John 14:27)

3 I thank my God in all my remembrance of you, Philippians 1:3 (ESV) Paul had some amazing testimonies about those days in Philippi. Those kind of experiences bind you together. We've been through many here. I'll never forget the Coll's transformation, or starting off Hope Cottage's fund raiser, or the radio tower in Guinea Bissau, or the Tabernacle. Even the strife that we work through binds us together. We thank God when we remember what God has done in our lives as a body of believers. And thank the Lord that there is more to come!

4 always in every prayer of mine for you all making my prayer with joy, 5 because of your partnership in the gospel from the first day until now. Philippians 1:4-5 (ESV) Paul thanked the Lord when he prayed for them. He did so with great joy because of the partnership in the gospel. Partnership is also translated fellowship *(koinonia)*. He's not talking about times they shared punch and cookies, but that from the day they came to Christ, they were earnest about praying for Paul and supporting the ministry through him. (2Corinthians 8:2-5)

This is that unity that true believers share. It's what I was speaking of earlier of being bound by our relationship with our Savior and our gratitude for what He has done for us! It is when the main thing in my life is the main thing in your life, and that is Jesus! We talked about it last week in the term "beloved brother". (Colossians 4:7) We aren't just friends. This isn't just a club. This is our life. Soldiers and first responders experience it in a slightly different sense. We have one purpose. That is how the church should be!

Some people don't know what I'm talking about because church is just a social gathering. Jesus is a side issue in their life. Deep down they long for that kind of relationship but they don't want to let go of their boundaries of self-protection. It might cost too much. But then that verse comes to mind, Jesus laid down His life for us and we ought to lay down our lives for our brothers. (1John 3:16) You have to let in the first big love before you will have the second. Love the Lord with your all and your neighbor as yourself.

This oneness and unity is only experienced when people are entirely focused on one goal. Self is set aside. Those who have experienced it long for it, because it is a source of great joy. The more we focus on Jesus and His will, the more we will experience it with our beloved brothers and sisters in Christ.

⁶ And I am sure of this, that he who began a good work in you will bring it to completion at the day of Jesus Christ. Philippians 1:6 (ESV) Oh what a great hope! We are works in progress but what God begins He completes. God wants to transform us into the image of His Son. (Romans 8:29) He wants us all to have our own unique personalities but also have the attributes of Jesus when He walked this earth. That's my definition of heaven. Imagine, if you can, a world where everyone has love and grace like that of Jesus. We are on our way. Every day is a day closer.

One man said it was supposed to have happened May 21st. I wish. As long as we're still here, there is still work to do and work to be done in us. Amen? So let's get on with the metamorphosis. (Philippians 3:13) We'll delve into the dilemma of wanting to go but still having work to be done later in this same chapter.

⁷ It is right for me to feel this way about you all, because I hold you in my heart, for you are all partakers with me of grace, both in my imprisonment and in the defense and confirmation of the gospel. ⁸ For God is my witness, how I yearn for you all with the affection of Christ Jesus. Philippians 1:7-8 (ESV) This is the heart of a pastor for those who are with him in his ministry and calling. Sometimes the pain is unbearable, but the joy is unspeakable and full of glory. Paul says they are partakers with him of grace, both in the trials of life and the proclamation of the good news of Jesus. (2Corinthians 7:3) We experience the grace of God to endure, the strength that comes through weakness, and the joy of grace that comes in the darkest of times. We know the wind of the Spirit that fills our sails when outwardly we can see no reason for it. We also know we stand together for what the Lord said and did for us. (2Timothy 2:9) The transformation of our lives confirms the truth of it. The fruits of the Holy Spirit bear witness. Praise God for a family of fellow believers! We share Jesus' love for one another.

⁹ And it is my prayer that your love may abound more and more, with knowledge and all discernment, Philippians 1:9 (ESV) Now Paul shares just how he prays for them. His first request is for an abounding increase in their love. He doesn't say whether that love is for God or for man, but he doesn't need to. Love for God results in love for one another. Without saying which, he is implying both. Look how the prepositional clause points to both. Knowledge of God and His word must refer to love for God. We can't love God unless we know from His word who He is and what He is really about. The more we know Him, the more we will love Him. (1John 4:11)

8

"All discernment" can't be toward God, but must be toward our fellow man. We love one another but we exercise discernment. Jesus didn't commit himself to man. He knew what was in man's heart. (John 2:24-25) Our love must be discerning. We can love mankind, but the kind of love we should have for the family of God must come with discernment or we will be enabling the sin of others. Our love for God must grow with knowledge and our love for one another must grow with discernment.

And why did Paul pray this for them? *10 so that you may approve what is excellent, and so be pure and blameless for the day of Christ, 11 filled with the fruit of righteousness that comes through Jesus Christ, to the glory and praise of God.* Philippians 1:10-11 (ESV) He wants them to choose not only what is good but what is excellent, the perfect will of God. He wants to see them ready for their graduation to our heavenly home. He wants to see them overflowing with the fruit of the Spirit and that comes from a relationship with Jesus, through Jesus' very life in them. (John 15:5) That love with knowledge and discernment, that holy life, is all to the glory and praise of God.

It is similar to a portion of the Colossian prayer that we have been praying. Colossians 1:9-12 (ESV) It includes discernment to walk worthy of Jesus, the knowledge of God's will, and that we be fruitful. I hope you don't get tired of praying this prayer because this is what we need. Let's pray it until we see it come to pass in our lives so that we may approve what is excellent and be pure and blameless for the day of Christ, filled with the fruit of righteousness that comes through Jesus Christ to the glory and praise of God.

Let us be bound together with the glue that held the Philippian church and Paul together, that partnership in the gospel, that priority of Jesus, that love for the family of God and desire to see God glorified in all that we do. Can we become beloved brothers and sisters to one another? Only with a great deal of surrender to the Spirit of God and a continual death to self! Only if our love abounds more and more with knowledge and all discernment! Are you willing? Will we invest the time in one another's life, to the glory and praise of God? God will help us, enable and strengthen us, if we are willing.

Questions
1 Go over the amazing stories of Acts 16.
2 Describe the first church of Philippi.
3 What is common and unusual in the greeting of this letter?
4 Why was Paul so fond of them?
5 What did Paul pray for them?
6 What are the similarities to the Colossian prayer?
7 Why is an increase in love needed?
8 What must it come with?
9 To what end is this increase in love?
10 How do we get it?

Kingdom Minded Philippians 1:12-18

What a great promise we saw in the opening of this letter. The One who began a good work in us will be faithful to complete it. (1:6) Our God is a faithful God! Amen? I cling to this promise. The more you grow the more you see how much you need to grow, but this promise keeps us from being discouraged. God will conform us to the image of His Son. (Romans 8:29) That's worthy of a Hallelujah!

Then Paul told them how he prayed. He prayed that their love would increase with knowledge and discernment so that they would be blameless and filled with the fruit of righteousness, bringing glory to God. (1:9-11) That's the plan. You don't need another one. We don't need anyone's how to lesson, or godliness in five easy steps. It's about being in Christ and living out the Great Command. (Mark 12:31-32) Do that and the Great Commission will happen naturally. Remain in Christ and you will bear fruit. (John 15:5) Grow in love and you'll walk in God's ways, filled with knowledge and discernment.

In the letter to the Colossians, we spoke of how Paul never really wrote about his situation. This letter to the Philippians is written a little later. He is definitely in Rome. (Though some believe Ephesus) The Book of Acts closes with a note of how Paul was imprisoned in his own hired house and freely proclaimed the gospel to all who came to see him. (Acts 28:30-31) Now he mentions his imprisonment, but only as it has to do with a praise report. Paul is demonstrating what he will teach later in the letter. (4:8) We are to keep our minds focused on what is praise worthy.

[12] I want you to know, brothers, that what has happened to me has really served to advance the gospel, Philippians 1:12 (ESV) Paul is kingdom minded. It doesn't really matter what happens to him as long as the kingdom of God advances. He sees the good that God is bringing out of his difficulty.

You may have a tough go of things right now, but you are free. You can come and go. You aren't chained to anyone 24/7. If Paul can see the good that God is doing in that situation and only speak praise, we can, by the grace of God, follow his example. He is turning their concern for him to praise for what God is doing, because God is always on the throne of heaven accomplishing His purposes. (Daniel 4:35)

Paul realized his imprisonment served to advance the gospel. He used a military term, "advance", (*prokope*) which means the progress of an army as it takes territory. The Good News is claiming more hearts for the kingdom of God because of Paul's imprisonment.

We don't enjoy the difficulties of life, but often they accomplish something that would never have been accomplished otherwise. David prayed, *"It is good for me that I have been afflicted that I might learn your statutes."* (Psalm 119:71) We know the end of Job, a man that suffered more than any of us ever will. He said, "I have heard of you with the ear, but now my eyes have seen you!" (Job 42:5) He ended up more blessed spiritually than he ever would have if he had not suffered. He even ended up more blessed physically, though that is not always the case. (James 5:11) Read of the saints at the end of Hebrews 11 or any issue of Voice of the Martyrs. (persecution.com)

I've never had anyone dispute the fact that we grow more spiritually when we are going through difficulty than at any other time. None of us would choose it. Even Jesus preferred not to go to the cross. (Mark 14:36) That's natural. But God cares more about our eternal good than our temporal happiness. He took Jesus to the cross because He loves us. He takes us through trials because He loves us. Not all our trials are God's perfect (intended) will, but He does permit and use each trial if we will let Him. That's a big IF. Paul was letting God use his situation to advance the kingdom.

Think about it. He was there because he was obedient to the Jerusalem leaders. If he hadn't gone to the Temple to help those brothers with their vows, he would never have been arrested. (Acts 21:23-24) I won't speculate whether or not he was in God's perfect will, but we can see that he was trying to do what was right, trying to bring unity, trying to submit to authority, and now he is suffering for it.

Some of our trials are self-induced. Others are caused by sins of others. Nevertheless, God will use each and every one if we will allow Him to do so. What is the alternative? You can pout and ignore God and have a pity party. You can wallow in your misery and the injustice of this world, but what good does that do? Paul could have said, "God, it's just not fair. I keep denying myself and serving You, and You let this happen! Isn't the thorn in my side enough?" But he didn't give in to that attitude. Instead, he looked for what God was doing. He saw the gospel marching forward like an army unit taking new territory.

He probably had no idea that we'd be reading this letter 2000 years later and be encouraged by his example. Sometimes you'll never see what God is ultimately doing, but by faith we believe that all things work together for good to those who love God and are called according to His purpose. (Romans 8:28) Decide in advance that you will look for the good in the next trial. That is God's will! Don't waiver! (4:1)

13 so that it has become known throughout the whole imperial guard and to all the rest that my imprisonment is for Christ. Philippians 1:13 (ESV) The praetorium were the personal guards of the emperor. There were 12 units of 1000 soldiers each. They were either from Rome or one of the most loyal of Roman cities. They are the ones that really wielded the power. It seems that the message of Paul's faith in Jesus had become known to them and the rest of the elites of Rome. What a strange but effective way for the gospel to reach these people who never would have otherwise heard. From slaves to the elite leadership of Rome, the gospel had advanced to every strata of society and continues to do so in the world to this day. (1Timothy 2:4)

I had someone protest that Jesus was wrong when He said the kingdom would come during the life of some of those who heard Him. I asked, "What do you call a billion people who pledge their total devotion to one King?" The Kingdom came at Pentecost when the Spirit of God took up residence in the hearts of the Jews gathered for that feast. (Acts 2:30-32) It is the Spirit that enables us to serve our King. There is definitely more to come, but to say that the advancing of the gospel to every corner of the planet is not the kingdom is to deny the obvious reality.

The King is ruling in my heart! Is He ruling in yours? Then you are a part of the kingdom. The kingdom was advancing into the very stronghold of power in Rome. Where the hordes of the Goths would fear to tread for a few more centuries, the gospel came in boldly and began invading heart after heart. God's ways are definitely higher than the ways of man. (Isaiah 55:9) Paul saw another positive outcome from his hardship. *14 And most of the brothers, having become confident in the Lord by my imprisonment, are much more bold to speak the word without fear.* Philippians 1:14 (ESV) Apparently some people were afraid that if they spoke up about their commitment to Jesus and the gospel, they would end up imprisoned. But now that they see Paul's example of being used in prison to spread the gospel, and his willingness to trust God for the outcome, they have lost their fear and proclaim the truth of the gospel with boldness.

If someone will lead the way, others will follow. I don't mean that they will follow the pattern. What pattern is there? Go get arrested in the Temple in Jerusalem? No! It is simply having the boldness to bring Jesus into the conversation, to answer honestly about why we are different. It is to proclaim the word of Christ when God gives us the opportunity without fear or hesitation. (1Peter 3:15)

There are places right now, where people are being imprisoned for Christ. Those that fellowship with them are emboldened to share Christ, and do not become more fearful. It's unexplainable. (Acts 4:31) Algeria, Iran, Morocco, and China are all experiencing increased persecution but also an increase in boldness. We need to remember them in our prayers, not that God would spare them from the persecution, but that God would use it to advance the kingdom like an army marching into the enemy's territory!

You would think that if you saw someone being beaten for their faith it would cause us to become timid. I've heard so many testimonies that the opposite is true. It gives believers courage to not fear and to lay down our sense of security and safety and trust the Lord. (Luke 12:4) I'm not saying that we invite persecution or do something that will intentionally draw persecution upon believers, but rather to be ready to see where there are receptive hearts and being willing to sacrifice all to share the truth and hope that we have in Jesus.

15 Some indeed preach Christ from envy and rivalry, but others from good will. Philippians 1:15 (ESV) Does Paul mean that even back then churches were competing with one another? We know from the letter to the Romans that there were a number of house churches in Rome. Or it may

12

have been synagogues that felt they were in competition with the churches and so preached Christ in the streets to get Paul in more trouble.

Today a church is often in competition with the church down the street. Members bounce back and forth for one reason or another. I've been told by some pastors that there are towns where pastors will intentionally do big events on the same day as another church's event so as to try to keep their own or draw others away. What an unbiblical way to see the church! (Psalm 133:1)

We are in a battle together. As long as the other church is proclaiming the gospel, the essentials of the Word, I want to pray for their success. We fight for the same cause. We may be in different parts of the battle formation, but we are on the same side. If we have a kingdom mindset, like Paul does in this letter, we just want to see the kingdom go forward. We just want to see more people liberated from darkness and have their eyes opened. No two people will agree on every doctrine. But we can be united around the fundamentals of the gospel. That is the only reason for our unity. That should cause us to encourage and hope the best for one another. (John 17:20-21)

Paul didn't even care that their motivations were envy and rivalry. He just wanted the truth of Jesus' death for sinners to be proclaimed in the streets. He didn't care if it meant more trouble for him. People were hearing the good news. Oh that we might catch that same spirit of exalting Jesus first and foremost!

16 The latter do it out of love, knowing that I am put here for the defense of the gospel. 17 The former proclaim Christ out of rivalry, not sincerely but thinking to afflict me in my imprisonment. Philippians 1:16-17 (ESV) The motivations were very different, but that didn't matter. Rivalry is all about self-advancement. The Greek word originally meant someone who did something for financial gain. Later it came to be applied to politicians. You can understand why. Perhaps these that were proclaiming Christ out of rivalry were trying to win over some of those who followed Paul's teaching. Their main motivation was to make imprisonment harder for Paul. It's hard to believe people can be so vindictive, but we see it all the time. God will deal with those who slander God's servants. We don't need to seek our own vengeance. God repays. (Romans 12:19)

18 What then? Only that in every way, whether in pretense or in truth, Christ is proclaimed, and in that I rejoice. Yes, and I will rejoice, Philippians 1:18 (ESV) "There is a lesson for us here. Paul knew nothing of personal jealousy or of personal resentment. So long as Jesus Christ was preached, he did not care who received the credit and the prestige. He did not care what other preachers said about him, or how unfriendly they were to him, or how contemptuous they were of him, or how they tried to steal his disciples. All that mattered to Paul was that Christ was preached. (1Corinthians 2:2)

"All too often we resent it when someone else gains a prominence or honor. All too often we regard a man as an enemy because he has expressed some criticism of us or of our methods. All too often we think a man can do no good because he does not do things in our way. All too often the intellectuals have no truck with the evangelicals, and the evangelicals impugn the faith of the intellectuals. All too often those who believe in the evangelism of education have no use for the evangelism of decision, and those who practice the evangelism of decision have no use for those who feel that some other approach will have more lasting effects. Paul is the great example. He lifted the matter beyond all personalities; all that mattered was that Christ was preached." Barclay's Daily Study Bible (NT – Philippians 1).

Is that all that matters to you? I must admit, I often feel the sting of criticism and have to make a great effort to keep from taking words in a persona way. Time and time again I have to remind myself that I have forgiven and that all that matters is that Christ is proclaimed. Proclaim Jesus with your witnessing program or proclaim Him with your life. Just proclaim Him. We must leave others to answer to their Master and go on about the Lord's business. (Romans 14:4)

Rejoice, the kingdom is claiming new territory! Let us follow the example of the Apostle and seek out what God is accomplishing in our difficulties and give Him the praise He deserves! After all, Paul was following the example of Jesus, who *23 When he was reviled, he did not revile in return; when he suffered, he did not threaten, but continued entrusting himself to him who judges justly.* 1 Peter 2:23 (ESV) Remember, that is the work God is completing in us, to conform us to the image of His Son. It's all about Him! Let us boldly declare Him with our life and our words. May the Lord grant us success to see the gospel advance in Sedona and around the world, whether by persecution or divine favor. Will you say amen?

Questions
1 Review the key points from the previous week.
2 What does the word "advance" mean?
3 What is condition must be met to learn from a trial?
4 What was the immediate fruit of Paul's imprisonment?
5 What was the secondary fruit?
6 What is the result of seeing Christians suffer?
7 Why is it unbiblical when churches compete?
8 What was Paul's attitude toward those trying to cause trouble for him?
9 What did Barclay see as the lesson?
10 What is the purpose of our trials?

To Live or Die Philippians 1:18b-26

As we look at our text for today, let us remember that the Apostle Paul is in prison with a possible death sentence hanging over his head. Later in the letter, he will tell them to always dwell on what is good and to always rejoice. (4:8) In our passage today and throughout this letter, Paul is practicing what he preaches. He could complain about his condition, but instead he sees the good and rejoices. Last week we read how he saw his imprisonment as an opportunity to reach the palace guard. In our current passage, he is certain of his deliverance because of the prayers of the Philippian church, but he's not so sure that is what he personally wants as we'll see in the text.

18b Yes, and I will rejoice, 19 for I know that through your prayers and the help of the Spirit of Jesus Christ this will turn out for my deliverance, How did Paul know? A few verses later he tells us that it is because the Philippian church needs more instruction from him. He had a sense that his work was not done. It's hard to explain, but something deep within says our mission is not completed.

Several military leaders had that sense. They would even stand on a front line and observe a battle with bullets whizzing by while they barked out orders. They knew they wouldn't be hit. How? They just knew in their knower they weren't done.

We are in a spiritual battle. This is a war that is as real as, and even more important than, one with bullets and bombs. (Ephesians 6:12) It is war for the souls of men. His servants often have sense of duty yet to fulfill and sometimes even a sense of when the job is done and they are ready to go. (2Timothy 4:7)

Paul knew that the Father had heard the Philippians' prayers and that the Spirit of Jesus Christ was going to see him freed to finish his work. We don't have a record of exactly how that all came about, but we do know that he was freed. At a later time, when his mission was complete, he would be tried, condemned as an enemy of the state, and beheaded. That just means an even greater deliverance (*soterian* - same word used for salvation).

There are so many times when we feel someone has died too soon. We almost always feel that way, regardless of their age. But the Scriptures tell us that our times are in God's hands. (Psalm 31:15) Two weeks ago a 13 year old boy was hit in the chest by a pitcher's ball and died. That pitcher's niece had died a week before of an asthma attack. We live in a fallen world, but we have this assurance, our days are numbered by the Lord of all. Though we most likely don't understand the whys, we do know His heart. He sees all, including the future. He knows when it is time to call a soul home and when we must linger here a little longer. Every day of our life was written in his book before we came to be. (Psalm 139:16) We can trust that His decisions come from His loving heart.

Paul's rejoicing was not that he would escape death, but rather that he had more opportunity to serve his Lord and Savior. Do you share that same passion?

20 as it is my eager expectation and hope that I will not be at all ashamed, but that with full courage now as always Christ will be honored in my body, whether by life or by death. What an expression of faith and confidence in the Lord's strength and faithfulness. Paul eagerly expected

15

that Christ would be honored in his body whether in living or in his dying. Unlike Peter's self-confidence that he would never betray the Lord (Matthew 26:33), Paul had confidence in the enabling power of the Spirit of Jesus to help him to live or die in a way that would glorify God.

Notice how he words this, "always Christ will be honored in my body". He had written to the Romans to present their bodies as living sacrifices (Romans 12:1) and to dedicate the members of their bodies to God as instruments of righteousness. (Romans 6:13) I believe he means that his mouth might honor God in his speech, that his feet may take him to where the church needs to be strengthened or where the gospel has not yet been heard, or even that as the lions devour his body in the arena that he might confidently look to God and praise him as a witness to the spectators. No wonder he prefaces that remark, "with full courage"!

We are often so weak in faith that we just pray that we won't be a bad example. How much better to eagerly expect and confidently hope that we will not be *at all* ashamed but that with full courage today and always that Christ will be honored in our body, whether by life or by death! If we are a little further along spiritually, we might just hope that would be the case. But if we have seen God do it again and again, if we know His power to enable and use us for his glory, then we have that eager expectation, along with the confident hope, that He will enable us to honor Him again. (1Samuel 17:36) That doesn't just happen on its own. We must cooperate with the Spirit and allow Him to have His way in us. He'll provide the power and direction if we will yield to his Spirit.

He could eagerly expect to glorify God in life or death because, as he stated it, *21 For to me to live is Christ, and to die is gain.* Many years before, he had encountered Christ on the road to Damascus. (Acts 9:3-6) He came to realize that all his efforts to serve and please God were not only garbage (3:8), but were achieving the opposite effect of what he hoped. That is humbling. In fact, it was this intense realization that he was incapable to doing anything for God that brought him to Jesus and an utter death to his old life. He went to the cross and died with Jesus.

Listen to how he states it in his letter to the Galatians. *20 I have been crucified with Christ. It is no longer I who live, but Christ who lives in me. And the life I now live in the flesh I live by faith in the Son of God, who loved me and gave himself for me.* Galatians 2:20 (ESV)
The old religious Paul that thought that by keeping the Law he could please God was crucified with Jesus on the cross. It is a point to which every believer in Jesus must come. It is a realization that each one of must face. Without Jesus, we can do nothing! (John 15:5) If we do anything that truly glorifies God, it is because we died with Jesus and He now lives in us. (2Timothy 2:11) We operate in this body by faith in the Son of God who loved us and gave Himself for us. His life in us is the enabling power for these physical bodies to live in a way that honors God. (Colossians 1:9-10)

Therefore, Paul could say "to live is Christ." Every day was about Jesus. Every day was under His direction, living in Him and He in Paul. If to us to live is Christ, then we will eagerly expect to glorify God in our body, come what may. Not because we are so super spiritual, on the contrary, because we died and the life that we now live we live by faith in the Son of God who loved us and gave Himself for us! To live is Christ! That gives us a reason to look forward to every single day. It gives me confidence to face the trials of life, because it isn't me facing them alone, but Christ facing them in me.

That also gives me hope of being fruitful. *22 If I am to live in the flesh, that means fruitful labor for me.* If God wills for me to keep on living, regardless of my physical abilities, since for me to live is Christ, then this day's labor will be fruitful. I may be bedridden, I may be handicapped, I may be as healthy as can be; it doesn't matter. What matters is that we are living in Christ. How can He be anything but fruitful? If Christ is our life, it is guaranteed that we will be fruitful. And that guarantee is not because I have figured out the right program or method, but because for me to live is Christ. The life I live in this body that is surrendered to Him, I live by faith in Him. I trust Him, look to Him, rely upon Him, depend on Him and love Him. How can that not mean anything but fruitful labor for me?

Sometimes we worry about whether or not we have found our calling or if we are living in our purpose. It's good to examine your faith (2Corinthians 13:5), but here is the answer to our question. Live in Jesus. Let *Him* be your life. Then your calling will come about naturally and your purpose, which is His purpose, will flow from your life and not be forced against your own desires. So Paul was saying that if God answers their prayers and he is not condemned to death then he has more opportunity to live daily in Christ which is guaranteed fruitfulness. That honors God, and that is Paul's heart, to honor God. He'll have more opportunities to lay up his treasures in heaven. (Matthew 6:20)

Yet which I shall choose I cannot tell. 23 I am hard pressed between the two. My desire is to depart and be with Christ, for that is far better. It's a tough call. Paul had a supernatural glimpse of the third heaven. (2Corinthians 12:3-4) He's seen Jesus in His glory. He knows what he has to look forward to. (2Timothy 4:6-8) He knows the work in him will be completed when he sees Jesus face to face. Even though to live is Christ, it isn't easy. Stoning, scourgings, shipwrecks, beatings and the like make you long for heaven. Even worse, betrayals and personal attacks make us long for the comfort we'll receive in heaven where every tear will be wiped from our eyes. (Isaiah 25:8) There will be no more failing Him then. It is indeed a tough call between remaining and being fruitful in a way that honors God and blesses His people, or going to see Him face to face.

I haven't suffered hardly anything compared to Paul but my desire has often been to depart and be with Christ. It is far better. Haven't you thought so at times? As I watch the elderly age, I see the same effect. God allows us to age so that as these bodies get more and more difficult to live in we begin to long for heaven. We know it is far better.

And notice that for Paul, heaven is to be with Christ. He lives in Him now, but as Paul wrote in another place, then we will know as we are known. (1Corinthians 13:12) We will see Him face to face. I long to look into those eyes and hold those feet. Mary Magdalene was told not to cling to His feet because He had not yet ascended to the Father. (John 20:17) Well, there will be no problem then. We can hold them as long as we desire and gaze at those holes that forever declare our debt is paid. I am loved. I'm accepted. Thanks be to God.

Paul adds, *24 But to remain in the flesh is more necessary on your account.* Paul would choose the sword or the lion as his ticket home, but he knows his job isn't finished. There is a need that he is meant to fill and it has to do with the Philippian church. He prays for them, writes instruction, and sends encouraging teachers to help them, and perhaps will even have a chance to visit them in person. He puts their need above his own heart's longing. What an example for the "me first" church of today!

25 Convinced of this, I know that I will remain and continue with you all, for your progress and joy in the faith, He was convinced that it was God's will for him to live and remain in touch with them. His first reason for doing so is for their progress in the faith. They needed to mature more so that they could continue in a good direction. We'll see in chapter four that there is some conflict in the church that needed to be resolved. Part of that progress is learning to work together in spite of differences, to let go of offenses and recognize that we are not competing but serving for the same cause. It is also to humbly consider others better than ourselves. (2:3) Conflict in the church is meant to strengthen and shape us if we will endure it and not run from it.

Paul's remaining in this life was also for their joy in the faith. This letter mentions joy more frequently in four chapters than any other portion of Scripture. Joy is condition of the soul that is confident in its place in the love of God. It is not related to circumstances. A Spirit filled church is a joyful church. (4:4) Our convictions in regard to who Jesus is and what He has done for us should fill us with great joy. That is our joy in the faith.

Paul wanted to remain for their progress and joy in the faith, *26 so that in me you may have ample cause to glory in Christ Jesus, because of my coming to you again.* He knew that when he visited them again, they would find reason in the rich insights Paul had of Jesus to glory in Christ Jesus. The more they saw of Jesus, the more they would glory in Him.

Someone asked how to help a loved one not be seduced away from the faith. There is only one answer. Know Jesus! Learn more of Him. Surrender your life to Him. Discover how much you are loved. Live in Him and let Him live in you. Once you experience a real and living relationship with Him, every other religion has nothing substantial to offer. Whether we live or die we are the Lord's and He is ours.

There are two issues that I want you to consider as we close this message. First I would ask the believer, "Can you say with the Apostle, to live is Christ and to die is gain?" Is your life really about Christ or all about

18

you? Have you been crucified with Jesus or is your old life still alive and well? To believe in Jesus is not just an intellectual acceptance, but a surrender of the heart. It is to accept Him as your Lord and to make Him your life.

To the unbeliever I ask? Do you know where you are going and what awaits you? Are you looking forward to it? For you, what is living? When you come to the end will it be worth it? You can find the One that makes life worthwhile and know death to be gain if you will surrender your life to the One who loves you and gave Himself for you. (Matthew 16:25)

Questions
1 Why did Paul think he would be delivered?
2 How can we find comfort when a loved one dies?
3 Where was Paul's confidence placed?
4 What was his eager expectation?
5 How can we live in a way that honors God?
6 Why can we look forward to each day?
7 Why may Paul have longed for death?
8 What is heaven to Paul?
9 Why must Paul remain?
10 How can we grow firmly in the faith?
11 Honestly fill in the blank. For me to live is _____?

Gift of Suffering Philippians 1:27-30

As we take these smaller portions of Scripture, it is important to remember the context, so let's begin with a brief review of the last three weeks. We went over the amazing things that took place to start this first European church from Acts 16. We saw how Paul had a deep appreciation for them because of their financial and prayer support. There was that beautiful promise that God would complete in us what He had begun (1:6) and Paul's prayer for their love to abound in knowledge and discernment (1:9). That is our prayer for this church as well.

In our second week in Philippians we saw that Paul cared only about advancing the Gospel. He saw two positive outcomes of his imprisonment with which he could encourage the Philippians. The Emperor's Guards were hearing the story of why Paul was imprisoned which meant they were hearing the Good News of Jesus (1:13). The brothers in Rome were emboldened to share the Gospel more freely (1:14). Paul didn't even care that some were preaching to get him in deeper trouble, as long as the Gospel was preached. We were challenged by Paul's example to be kingdom minded instead of focused on our own concerns.

Last week, we saw the conflict within Paul as he waited for his trial and sentencing. He had a difficult time deciding whether to live or die. We heard his declaration that we each long to make our own, *"For to me to live is Christ!"* We were challenged to make Christ our all in all, the reason for all we do, our very life. Paul came down on the side of remaining in this life to meet the spiritual needs of the Philippian church, though he personally would prefer to depart and be with Christ (1:23). We ended last week with Paul declaring by faith that he would be released and would come to minister to the Philippians again so that they might have ample cause to glory in Christ Jesus. (1:26)

27 Only let your manner of life be worthy of the gospel of Christ, so that whether I come and see you or am absent, I may hear of you that you are standing firm in one spirit, Paul had just set the example for what he was asking of them by saying, *"that with full courage now as always Christ will be honored in my body, whether by life or by death."* (1:20b)

So just what does it mean to live in a way that is worthy of Christ? We can never really be worthy of all He has done and continues to do for us, that is, unless *He is* our life. Even then, we all too often fall short as that old nature sneaks back in to make its demands. (1John 1:8) To say no one is perfect does not justify our failures.

Citizens of a Roman city were highly conscious of their civic duty, of living worthy to be a citizen of a Roman city. How much more should we be conscious of our heavenly duty? (Philippians 3:20) "As Philippi was a colony of Rome in Macedonia, so the church was a 'colony of heaven' in Philippi, whose members were to live as *its* citizens in Philippi." (Gordon D. Fee, *Paul's Letter to the Philippians,* p. 162)

We are a colony of heaven in Sedona, blood bought citizens of heaven, so let's live like it! Amen?

Paul elaborated on what walking worthy of Christ should look like in his letter to the Ephesians. *1 I therefore, a prisoner for the Lord, urge you to walk in a manner worthy of the calling to which you have been called, 2 with all humility and gentleness, with patience, bearing with one another in love, 3 eager to maintain the unity of the Spirit in the bond of peace.* Ephesians 4:1-3 (ESV) Whether the Lord did allow Paul to visit them or not, he wanted to hear that their testimony was one of standing firm in unity. A church body can't do that unless they walk in the fruits of the Spirit mentioned in the Ephesians passage, humility, gentleness, patience, and love.

In the letter to the Colossians, at the beginning of the prayer we've been praying, Paul prays *that you may be filled with the knowledge of his will in all spiritual wisdom and understanding, 10 so as to walk in a manner worthy of the Lord, fully pleasing to him, bearing fruit in every good work and increasing in the knowledge of God.* Colossians 1:9-10 (ESV) All three of these letters from Paul emphasized that the believers in these churches live out their Christianity in a way that honors God. That is to express the fruits of the Spirit in what we do and say. It's to walk in unity with one another. That is to stand firm in Christ and not be habitually falling into sin. When people see that gentleness, patience, love, and unity that believers have, they are drawn to Christ. When they see the opposite, which is harshness, impatience, uncaring and division, it repels them from

20

Christianity. The need hasn't changed in 2000 years. People need to see Christ in us, so we need to live in a way that is worthy of Him.

We should be standing firm *27bwith one mind striving side by side for the faith of the gospel,* "Striving side by side" literally means to wrestle together on the same team. Paul will bring up being of one mind again in just a few verses. It doesn't mean that we are all clones with only one opinion, but that we share the same conviction that the main thing is Jesus. We believe the Gospel record. We know salvation is a gift of God through faith in Jesus. That unity enables us to strive side by side for the advancement of the Gospel.

Most of the division we see in the church of America today is not so much doctrinal; that happened years ago as denominations were developing over differences in interpretation and emphasis. Today the division comes simply over having one's way, and it's usually in some matter that is insignificant in the long run. Those petty things hinder the advance of the gospel. We are told to strive side by side for the faith of the Gospel. (1Corinthians 16:13) We don't have to agree on everything, but we do have to strive side by side for the faith of the gospel.

In that unity we are to *28. ...not frightened in anything by your opponents. This is a clear sign to them of their destruction, but of your salvation, and that from God.* The word frightened here literally means "at no point swerving", like combatants engaged in a conflict. Who will turn first? When the world sees our lack of fear, our confidence in Christ, it is sign to them that Jesus will prevail. All that opposes Him will one day be defeated. (1John 3:8) It also declares that God has saved us. He is transforming us into His image. (Romans 8:29)

The testimony of some of the martyrs for Christ so boldly declares that this is true. They often pray that God will forgive those that persecute them. That is power! They often declare that death only ushers them into the presence of their Savior. As Jesus said, *28 And do not fear those who kill the body but cannot kill the soul. Rather fear him who can destroy both soul and body in hell.* Matthew 10:28 (ESV) Because we know where we are going when we die, we can be fearless, that is of course if Christ is your life. If you are living for something else that is another matter. Paul had just declared that it is much better to die and be with the Lord. (1:23)

I heard the story of one man that was arrested for evangelizing. I think the country was Iran. After the police had roughed him up they asked if he was going to quit or be beaten. He told them if he was beaten he would have a heavenly reward so go ahead. He was wiling to suffer for the cause of his Lord. They then said they could kill him. He responded, "Even better, for then I'll see Jesus face to face." They didn't know what to do with him, so they let him go. How do you scare someone who isn't afraid to suffer or die? It is sign that you are saved! It is a sign that Christ will prevail and evil will be defeated. (Revelation 20:10)

We should be fearless *29 For it has been granted to you that for the sake of Christ you should not only believe in him but also suffer for his sake,*

I'll never forget the first time I preached to slum dwellers in Bombay. The director asked me to preach on suffering. Me, a healthy, wealthy, white, have it all American, preaching on suffering to people who live in squalor. What could I share? The Word of God! This verse was my text, and I was preaching to myself more than them, but that is how all preaching should be. The Word cuts across all classes, conditions and time.

Look at what the prisoner Paul was telling the believers at Philippi. You have the gracious gift of salvation. It isn't essentially for you but for Jesus. It is all about His glory. It is an immeasurable blessing for us and we can't begin to grasp the fullness of it, yet it is *for* Christ. Salvation is a gift to us, but we are a gift from the Father to the Son. (John 17:9, 24) We could not have received a greater gift than salvation. (2Corinthians 9:15) Nothing compares. But that gift comes with another gift, one you may not be as excited to receive. It is a gracious gift of God's favor to suffer for Christ. We are given belief *for* (*huper*) Christ's sake and we also receive the gracious gift of suffering *for* (*huper*) Christ's sake. (3:10)

I don't believe that just because we are Americans we are exempt from receiving this gift. I do sometimes wonder if God looked at my physical and mental makeup and decided I couldn't make it unless I was born at this time in the USA. (Acts 17:26) In other words He saw a wimpy soul and had mercy on me.

Nevertheless, we still suffer. It is not so much physical depravation, though I have had those periods in my life. It is much more emotional. It is the catch 22s where you want to express the love of Christ but whatever choice you make, someone is hurt. You try to help someone sacrificially but are rejected and misunderstood. You submit to those in authority but know that it will hurt others. What do you do when the Scriptures seem to collide? It happens. And that's when we must look to the Lord and follow the leading of His Spirit even when we are misunderstood. God never promised a painless path.

As believers we also suffer with others because we voluntarily enter into their pain to weep with those that weep. (Romans 12:15) Some will do that for close friends or immediate family, but we do it with our entire church family and others as well. That is suffering for Christ too. It is indeed a gift, a very painful gift. When we do it for the body, we do it for Christ! (Matthew 25:40)

The pressure of Roman society upon Christians was enormous. There were civil, labor and home gods to which all were expected to offer sacrifices. To not do so was to stand out as a rebel and nonconformist. Every calamity that came upon a town, whether physical disease or economic hardship, was blamed on Christian refusal to worship the gods. That was a kind of suffering for Christ. That same sentiment is growing in the Western world today. The only difference is that the gods have been changed from stone to ideologies. But let us not look on it as a condition which we must endure, but rather, like the evangelist in Iran, a chance to share in Christ's

22

sufferings, laying up treasure in heaven, and glorifying God with our bodies. (Romans 6:13)

It is in the midst of suffering that we shine the brightest. (1 Peter 2:12) It's when people expect to see the real us, and do, in our joy and peace through it all. That makes them desire what we have in Jesus. When we suffer in a way that is worthy of the Lord, we are as persuasive as ever that Christ is the answer.

Paul wrote to the Romans that we will share in the glory of Christ if we share in His sufferings. (Romans 8:17) He went on to say that our present sufferings weren't worth comparing to the glory that will be revealed in us. (Romans 8:18) There is no comparison. It's a copper penny compared to a gold bar, a drop compared to the ocean, and those illustrations don't do it justice.

Here is another way to look at it. Jesus suffered so much for me on the cross. How can I repay Him? I can only give Him my life. (Psalm 116:12-13) I owe Him that anyway for He gave it to me. But if I am truly blessed, perhaps I'll have a chance to suffer for His sake.

A few weeks ago we talked about the fact that times of suffering are more productive for our spiritual life than any other time. It is in those times that we really grab hold of Jesus and grow in our spirit. James said we should count it all joy when we face many kinds of trials because it teaches us steadfastness (endurance). (James 1:2-4)

We suffer as we are *30 engaged in the same conflict that you saw I had and now hear that I still have.* It is a battle that is not against flesh and blood but against spiritual powers in the heavenly realms. (Ephesians 6:12) Remember Paul's early days in Philippi were met with a beating and imprisonment, but his response changed everything. We are in a conflict between our spirit and the world, the flesh and the Devil. If you are in Christ you are in the same conflict Paul had. It's not over till the trumpet sounds and we are called home. So buck up! Don't take things personal. Walk in a way that is worthy of Christ, demonstrating to the world how good He is and what He can do in a life. (Matthew 5:16)

Stand firm. This short life and God's gift of suffering will soon be over. See each trial from the heavenly perspective and know it is gaining a great reward. Remember that it is a gift for the sake of Christ just like the gift of your salvation. That will completely change your attitude. And as you learn steadfastness through the suffering ... *let steadfastness have its full effect, that you may be perfect and complete, lacking in nothing.* James 1:4

Let's go over this short passage one more time from the Message translation. *27 Meanwhile, live in such a way that you are a credit to the Message of Christ. Let nothing in your conduct hang on whether I come or not. Your conduct must be the same whether I show up to see things for myself or hear of it from a distance. Stand united, singular in vision, contending for people's trust in the Message, the good news, 28 not flinching or dodging in the slightest before the opposition. Your courage and unity will show them what they're up against: defeat for them, victory for you—*

and both because of God. ²⁹ There's far more to this life than trusting in Christ. There's also suffering for him. And the suffering is as much a gift as the trusting. ³⁰ You're involved in the same kind of struggle you saw me go through, on which you are now getting an updated report in this letter. Philippians 1:27-30 (MSG)

I want to close by doing something unusual. Let us go the outer aisles and arm in arm declare that we will by the grace of God live out this passage. "By the grace of God, I will live as a citizen of heaven, worthy of Jesus, standing firm in one spirit, of one conviction, striving side by side for the sake of the Gospel, not being frightened, receiving the gracious gifts of believing and suffering, engaged in the conflict. So help me God!"

¹⁴ May the grace of the Lord Jesus Christ, and the love of God, and the fellowship of the Holy Spirit be with you all. 2 Corinthians 13:14 (NIV)

Questions
1 Review the letter to this point.
2 How can we live worthy of Christ?
3 What is the description in Eph. 4?
4 What is the description in Col. 1?
5 How is our united effort described?
6 What does our lack of fear say?
7 What two gifts have we received?
8 What is the most common suffering for Christ in the USA?
9 When do we shine the brightest?
10 What is the connection of suffering and glory?
11 How should we look at suffering?
12 Re-read the MSG translation.

How We Were Meant To Be

The Apostle Paul is painting a picture of what we, as believers that make up the body of Christ, should look like. It's how we live out the previous command to walk worthy of the gospel. (1:27) It's a picture of the perfect church. Though it doesn't exist, it is to be our aim. When we have problems as a church body, we can come back and look at the picture and see where we don't line up. Next week we'll see how Jesus exemplified this and the glorious results.

Our short passage for today is just one sentence in Greek. It begins with the word "so", which means the author is drawing a conclusion from what was just said. SO let's begin by reading what was just said. Remember, Paul has decided he will go on living to serve the believers. He'd rather go home to Christ but there is still work to be done. (1:24-25) And then he writes, *²⁷ Only let your manner of life be worthy of the gospel of Christ, so that whether I come and see you or am absent, I may hear of you that you are standing firm in one spirit, with one mind striving side by side for the faith of the gospel, ²⁸ and not frightened in anything by your opponents. This is a clear sign to them of their destruction, but of your salvation, and that from God. ²⁹ For it has been granted to you that for the sake of Christ you should not only believe in him but also suffer for his sake, ³⁰ engaged in the same conflict that you saw I had and now hear that I still have.* Philippians 1:27-30 (ESV)

So, since we should live in manner worthy of Christ, since he's asking them to be of one mind standing side by side for the faith of the gospel, since they have received the gift of belief and of suffering for Christ, and are engaged in this spiritual conflict that spills over into this physical world, he makes the following points.

He begins by reminding them of what they have in Christ as a body of believers. *¹ So if there is any encouragement in Christ, any comfort from love, any participation in the Spirit, any affection and sympathy,* Paul is making some understatements in the form of a question to emphasize what we have and what it should mean to us. This should motivate us to do what he is about to ask of us.

Is there any encouragement in Christ? Well, is there? I'd say being made right before our holy Creator is pretty encouraging. When you get a clearer picture of who God is and who we are it is extremely encouraging! Knowing that God loves us enough to send His only Son to redeem us is pretty encouraging, wouldn't you say? (John 3:17) Knowing that the One who planned the future is living in me and directing me can be pretty encouraging. (Isaiah 30:21) The encouraging thing I keep sharing with you and that we read in verse 6 is that if we are in Christ, the work He began in us He will complete and that means being made into the image of Jesus. (3:21) That is very encouraging to me. So, is there any encouragement in Christ?

How many stories come to mind of when Jesus supernaturally got you through a difficult time? His Word came alive or a song said what you needed to hear. He prompted someone to call or send a card, or even when suddenly without explanation the darkness lifted and the burden was gone. That is the encouragement and strengthening believers experience throughout their life. (Hebrews 11:25)

Is there any comfort from love? Paul doesn't qualify who or where this love is from, but it is the word *agape.* That kind of love is from God or God's love through our fellow believers. (1John 4:7) It's the love that isn't looking for something in return, but simply loves for the value it sees in the one that is loved. The cross tells me the only limit to God's love for me is my willingness to receive it. (Revelation 22:17) The thief on one side received it while the thief on the other was unwilling and rejected it. (Luke 23:41-43) Isn't it comforting to know that the only limit is within you?

That same love flows through others that have received God's love, and that is the unique quality of a follower of Jesus. It is unselfish love. One of our dear sisters took a brother and me to breakfast for Father's Day. Why? We are a family and she saw us as her spiritual fathers and spent her limited resources to show her loving appreciation. Another person spends their valuable time week after week with someone who is going through a difficult time. They don't have anything in common in the natural realm, but the love of Christ is flowing through them and they are blessed by letting it flow. Someone else gives their finances to help another in need. No one asked; it was just the love of Christ perceiving the need. That comforts the one that gave and the one that received. (1John 3:17) Is there any comfort from love?

Is there any participation in the Spirit? When we are given a direction by the Holy Spirit we all come together in wonderful unity of purpose through the Holy Spirit. We saw it in the Tabernacle and other projects that God has given us. The word "participation" is the Greek word *koinonia* that we usually translate fellowship. We talked about it a few weeks ago when we were looking at 1:5. There we used the word "partnership". That is the unity we enter into when we are truly one in Christ. (1Corinthians 12:13) We have one vision and one goal. It's that deep sense of commitment to one another bound by something much stronger than mere blood relations. We love the same Lord. We have the same priority in life. And even when we don't agree on the details or have totally different interests, we can set differences aside for we are motivated by the same Spirit working in each of us. You can't explain it in the natural. It is truly supernatural. (Ephesians 4:5-7)

Do we have affection and sympathy? Does our heart go out to one another and are we willing to overlook faults? These are the work of the Spirit in us knowing that others are overlooking our own weaknesses and shortcomings. (Ephesians 4:32) Affection is a heart for one another. Sympathy is a merciful attitude. If we are filled with the Spirit, then those qualities will certainly be in us.

So Paul asks in a rhetorical way if these qualities that are in a Spirit filled church exist among the Philippians. Since the answer is clear and should be acknowledged by all to be their daily experience, Paul makes a request based on those realities. *2 complete my joy by being of the same mind, having the same love, being in full accord and of one mind.* Paul is telling the Philippians the evidence of Christ that he has seen in their fellowship but now asks them to go further. He says that if they will do so it will complete his joy. He had joy in their partnership with him in the gospel (1:4-5) but it would make his joy complete to see them of the same mind, having the same love, in full accord of one mind.

Something had sprung up within this good fellowship that had brought a division of mind, and a difference in love. That means that people were taking sides on an issue and not having the *agape* love of Christ. It had disturbed the usual unity of this church.

Paul does a very wise thing in not entering into the trivial details of the debate and not coming down on one side or the other. We don't even know what it was about. It certainly was not some heretical issue or Paul would have clarified the gospel. He would not enter into some minor dispute, and most disputes are over a minor issue when you get down to it. It dampened Paul's joy when he saw them divided over a trivial issue. Paul used the opportunity to teach a more important lesson, unity.

He has just given them five ways to maintain unity: 1 Value the encouragement of Jesus. A believer's relationship with his brothers and sisters is a reflection of his or her relationship with God. 2 Revel in the comfort of love. Our bonds of love should be ever deeper as we sacrifice for one another. When differences come, we will look past them because of the foundation of love we have in Christ. Love never fails. (1Corinthians 13:8) 3 Recognize the same Spirit is in us. (Ephesians 1:13-14) Our calling and minor convictions may be different, but as we see the unique calling in each person, we should rejoice. The Spirit empowers us to love one another. We can say as a matter of fact that the unloving do not have the Spirit. (1John 2:11) 4 Affection – genuine concern and caring for one another brings unity. 5 Sympathy - if someone is in disunity we need to feel what they are going through and help them through it. That is what Jesus does for us! (Hebrews 4:15-16) All five of these gifts should be present even when you are undergoing strife within the body. Perhaps we should say especially when you are in disagreement. We should draw from these gifts until we are in full accord and become of one mind.

This doesn't mean we walk in lock step and agree on every minor issue. It does mean we are all focused on the gospel (mentioned 5 times in chapter 1) and united in our understanding of its importance in our life. Together we strive to walk worthy of the gospel. (1:27)

The verse that follows warns them of how to avoid this disunity and lack of love and keep it from entering into a congregation. *³ Do nothing from rivalry or conceit, but in humility count others more significant than yourselves.* Disunity and lack of love comes from pride and arrogance. It begins when someone decides they are competing with, instead of serving alongside, another. The other party may sense this and up the ante. Soon a power struggle develops and people start to choose sides. If it isn't checked it will develop into gossip and slander and eventually a church split.

Why does this happen? Someone thought they heard from the Lord more clearly than someone else. Someone thought they had the answer and everyone needed to get on board. Their issue may sound like a worthy cause, but the root is conceit. Humility considers others more significant. (Psalm 25:9)

How unlike the world that is always trying to prove oneself superior to others in any way one can. Brockmuehl describes godly humility in his commentary, *The Epistle To The Philippians* (pg 110-111). "The biblical view of humility is precisely *not* feigned or groveling, nor a sanctimonious or pathetic lack of self-esteem, but rather a mark of moral strength and integrity. It involves an unadorned acknowledgement of one's own creaturely inadequacies and entrusting one's fortunes to God rather than to one's own abilities or resources."

What does the humble person do when they have a difference of opinion on how something should be done? They yield to the other person considering them more significant. They trust that if God was not leading in the way that person insisted on going that it will soon become clear and corrections will be made. The conceited, however, demand to have their way or else they will leave and take with them those that are willing to listen to their petty complaints. (Proverbs 21:2)

I've seen it happen over and over since I was a young teen. The complaints range from too many evangelistic messages, not enough sensitivity to the Spirit, too many contemporary songs or hymns whichever the case may be, to build or not to build, not enough emphasis on this or that but always something other than the central issue of who Jesus is and what he has done for us. It goes directly against the prayer that Jesus prayed for unity among believers. (John 17:21) It ignores the five points that Paul reminded us as the source of our unity.

Paul went on to give another tip in how to not fall into this divisive trap. *4 Let each of you look not only to his own interests, but also to the interests of others.* We all have a unique gift and calling. (1Corinthains 12:4-7) We each have our personal interests. Sometimes we get so enthusiastic about our calling that we think it should be everyone's emphasis. We can even make people feel guilty that they don't have our calling or gifts. The worst case scenario is that we try to form a group that believes we should all have the same interest and that those that don't just aren't in the Spirit. It's usually a very Scriptural thing; it's just not the only Scriptural calling.

This last verse in our passage today tells us that we should expand our interests by looking at others' interests. That broadens our appreciation for all that the body is doing. That will avoid an overly strong emphasis that would split a church, not only by appreciating that person's calling so they don't feel they must go elsewhere, but by seeing that your interest is just one of many.

There is even a movement today to appreciate the different callings in the various denominations. Each has an emphasis and many of them are godly. With one it is a clear understanding of Scripture, with another the leading of the Holy Spirit, with another reaching out to widows and orphans and the least in our world in need and with another the historical traditions of the church. Each is important and has a place. We are more well-rounded believers when get familiar with Scriptural interests other than our own favorite one. The true church of Jesus will have diversity in non-essentials, unity in essentials, and in all things love. The true church will adhere to the Word of God and focus on glorifying God.

So what about your church? Do we have the encouragement of being in Christ? Do we have comfort from the love of God and one another? Do we experience participation with the Spirit, and do we have affection and compassion for one another? We can always grow in these areas, but Paul asked, "Is there any?" If there is then we can grow from there in unity to become of one mind, having the same love and being in full accord to the glory of God and the joy of your leaders. That is how we are meant to be.

28

That is God's desire for us. It is a picture of a spiritually mature church, because it is Christ like.

Questions
1 Why does the passage begin with "so"?
2 What encouragement do you have in Christ?
3 Do you have any comfort from love?
4 Is there any participation with the Spirit?
5 Is there any affection and compassion?
6 What brings a shepherd complete joy?
7 What is source of disunity?
8 How can we avoid it? (vs3)
9 What's another way to avoid it? (vs4)
10 Does your church have the 5 qualities?

Step Down Philippians 2:5-11

We have come to one of the most important passages in the letters of Paul. It was written in the form of a poem. We don't know if he composed it on the spot or if it was perhaps a poem or song of the early church. The exact meaning is debated, but the overall message is very clear. The first four verses of this chapter were a call to humility and a preference for others' interests. It was a challenge to be gentle and kind in the way we relate and work together so that the body of Christ could be of one mind and express a unity that is supernatural. It was really a picture of what the individuals of a perfect church should be like. But then Paul pointed to the perfect example to help them understand exactly what he meant.

5 Have this mind among yourselves, which is yours in Christ Jesus, Some translators add this phrase on to the previous sentence and some connect it with the following sentence. It all flows together in the original language so we should not think of it just one way or the other. *4 Let each of you look not only to his own interests, but also to the interests of others. 5 Have this mind among yourselves, which is yours in Christ Jesus, 6 who, though he was in the form of God, did not count equality with God a thing to be grasped,* Philippians 2:4-6 (ESV) That humble attitude of putting others first, is the mindset we should have and do have in Christ who demonstrated it for us while he walked as a man on this earth.

Paul is referring to a way of thinking. In verse 2 he used the word for "think" twice, asking them to have the same thinking. Now he's explaining just what that kind of thinking looks like. It is the way Jesus' thought about life. I'll call it "the Jesus mindset". (Ephesians 4:22-24)

I like the way the ESV says this mindset is ours in Christ Jesus. (1Corinthain 2:16) That is true but perhaps not exactly the way the Greek is worded. "This mindset is in you and in Christ", is more literal. It's that mindset of thinking of other's interests. The Message translation words "thinking of others' interest" in this way, *4 Don't be obsessed with getting*

your own advantage. Forget yourselves long enough to lend a helping hand.
Philippians 2:4 (MSG) Jesus was certainly not obsessed with gaining his own advantage. He continually put others first for their good, whether teaching or healing or washing their feet. (John 13:3-5) But the greatest example is in his very willingness to be incarnate as one of us.

He had the glory of heaven. He was fully satisfied in His relationship with the Father. But He had this mindset of looking out for others and helping them. (John 13:15-17) So though he was in essence (form of) God, he didn't cling to that equality. It is a difficult verse to interpret. *6 who, though he was in the form of God, did not count equality with God a thing to be grasped,* We'll see in the following verse that this is regarding His choice to be human. This is not saying that Jesus didn't see Himself equal to God, just the opposite. He did not count equality as something to cling to. Even though He was in essence God, He was willing to let go of equality with God to be in human form. (Ephesians 4:10)

The Christmas miracle is as great as the resurrection miracle, perhaps even greater, in that one who is in essence God would become a baby within the womb of a human woman. (Isaiah 7:14) The Creator entered into His own creation. "Thou art my Son. This day have I begotten Thee," the psalmist wrote. (Psalm 2:7) "Unto us a child is born; unto us a Son is given," predicted the Spirit through Isaiah. (Isaiah 9:6)

The Apostle Paul is pointing out that though Jesus knew He was infinitely superior to His creation, for our sake He was willing to come down to our level of humble condition to relate to us in a way that would help meet our greatest need. That is the example we are to follow. That is what we must do if we are to have unity in a church and model Christ likeness to the world. If Jesus could take such a huge step down, then can't we take a little tiny step down for one another?

Let's look at what an enormous step down he took for us. *7 but made himself nothing, taking the form of a servant, being born in the likeness of men.* He stepped down from His glorious throne and entered into this fallen world. It is beyond my ability to describe. Bill Gates giving away all his wealth to live in a slum in Bangladesh wouldn't begin to come close to an equivalent step. Jesus stepped down from holy glory surrounded by worshiping seraphim and millions of servant angels (Revelation 5:11) into this fallen morass of selfish and sin sick humanity.

Don't lose the context. Yes it was for our salvation, but the context is that it was to help us in our need. We must follow this example of humbling ourselves to help one another.
He made Himself nothing. There is much debate over the expression. Of what did He empty Himself? The passage cannot mean that he was literally "nothing". It means He poured Himself out or emptied Himself. This is often referred to as the Emptying Passage *(ekenosen).*

What did He empty Himself of? I've wrestled with the Scriptures in regards to this, and personally believe He emptied Himself of His glory along with all power, knowledge and universal presence He had before the incarnation. For example, He did not know the hour of His return. (Matthew 24:36) He was limited in His location. Satan's temptation to command the stones to become bread was an attempt to get Him to pray selfishly, to use His personal relationship with the Father for His own gain. (Matthew 4:3) He grew in wisdom and stature. (Luke 2:52)

You might ask, how then did He perform miracles? I believe He did them through the power of the Holy Spirit just as any man can do them at the leading of the Spirit. Think about it, He looked to God to multiply the loaves (Matthew 14:19), to raise Lazarus (John 11:41), etc. His touch healed because He was sinless, utterly holy, but not because He was all powerful. (Exodus 29:37) When others asked Him why they could not do a miracle, He told them it took prayer. (Mark 9:29) He didn't say it was because they didn't have the power of God. He spoke of the power of God as something the Sadducees did not know personally and were therefore wrong in their understanding. That implies that they as men could know that power and then draw a right conclusion. See Mark 12:24. Jesus operated out of prayer and obtained the power of God through the Spirit.

Please understand that Jesus was no less God, but that to be human He had to set aside those all-powerful abilities or He could not have been our example in all things. He accessed the power of God to do God's will in the same way we do, through prayer and obedience to the Holy Spirit. He rebuked Satan the same way that you and I do, with the Word. (Luke 4:12) Everything He did we can do if it is at the leading of the Holy Spirit. In fact, He said we would do greater things because He was going to the Father. (John 14:12)

Jesus took the form of a servant. Angels and men are made to be the servants of the living God. (Psalm 103:20) Paul, and many of the Old Testament prophets took it as a title of honor to be the servants of God. (Romans 1:1) It meant that they were walking in God's will. Jesus went from being the One that gave the orders (in love and for our good), to only taking orders from His Father in heaven. He could say that He did not come to be served but to serve and to give His life a ransom for many. (Mark 10:45) He could say the greatest was the servant of all because in serving God He served all of humanity. (Matthew 23:11)

Is this your mindset? Is this the way you think? Is obedience to God a way to serve everyone and the way that you picture true greatness? Kingdom thinking is completely unlike worldly thinking.

8 And being found in human form, he humbled himself by becoming obedient to the point of death, even death on a cross. I've wondered when Jesus consciously became aware that He was God emptied and now in human form. Remember Satan's temptation, "If you are the Son of God, then…" (Matthew 4:6) But even at the age of 12 He said He had to be in His Father's house. (Luke 2:49) Whenever that moment came, He realized the frailty of the human form. (Psalm 103:14) He knew the only hope of anyone living in a human body was to humble oneself and become completely obedient to the Father. Humility comes before obedience can follow.

Man is the most undeservedly prideful creature that was ever created. It was pride in the Garden that tempted Eve to desire to be as God. (Genesis 3:5) It was pride that welcomed Satan's lie. It was wounded pride that was behind the first murder (Genesis 4:8), and pride that motivated the first great ruler, Nimrod. (Genesis 10:8-10) It was pride that caused the nation of Israel to murmur against God, their Deliverer and Redeemer. (Exodus 16:8) It was pride that rejected and crucified Jesus. (John 18:40) It is pride today that refuses to subject oneself to God's ordained leadership whether secular (Romans 13:1) or of faith. It is pride that was bringing division to the church at Philippi and there was one solution; humble yourself as Christ humbled Himself. He came down so far for us; can't we come down a tiny bit for one another?

Jesus became humbly obedient even to death on the cross. What does it cost you to die to yourself a little to let another have his or her way? Not nearly what it cost Christ to be obedient to the Father. His obedience took Him all the way to the cross, but look at what it accomplished for all who will receive it! Humble obedience produces great fruit. It may not be obvious at first, but it will come in its time.

And now, look how God rewards humble obedience. *⁹ Therefore God has highly exalted him and bestowed on him the name that is above every name,* He is LORD! Do you remember Jesus' instruction to the Pharisees that were invited to be guests? He told them to take the lowest seat, for then the host may invite them to sit up at a more honored position. (Luke 14:10-11) True humility is rewarded with exaltation.

Jesus now has the highest title, the most exalted name. That is another indication that He is one with the Father when you consider what the psalmist wrote. *¹³ Let them praise the name of the LORD, for his name alone is exalted; his majesty is above earth and heaven.* Psalm 148:13 (ESV)

Jesus humbled Himself and now He has returned to the equality He had with the Father from before the world began. (John 17:5) He went from an exalted position to humility and back to exaltation again. It is one thing to go from humility to exaltation, but it is a far greater thing to go from exaltation to true humility for the sake of others.

We need to grasp this "Jesus mindset". If you are truly humble you will look to God for direction. God instructs us for the greater good of man made in His image. When we obey we serve the greater good. That is true greatness. Jesus' humility led Him to trust and obey God even to the cross and that led to the greatest good for all who will receive Him. That is why He is the greatest of all! That is the pattern we must follow. That is why we take up our cross and follow Him. Humility – obedience – greatness – exaltation, all for the glory of God!

¹⁰ so that at the name of Jesus every knee should bow, in heaven and on earth and under the earth, Paul takes a quote from the Old Testament prophet Isaiah and applies it to Jesus, but look at the original context and you will get a clearer picture of what Paul was really saying. *²¹ᵇ …there is no other god besides me, a righteous God and a Savior; there is none besides me. 22 "Turn to me and be saved, all the ends of the earth! For I am God, and there is no other. 23 By myself I have sworn; from my mouth has gone out in righteousness a word that shall not return: 'To me every knee shall bow, every tongue shall swear allegiance.'* Isaiah 45:21-23 (ESV)

By quoting the passage, Paul is declaring that Jesus is our righteous God and Savior. There is none besides Him. Turn to Him and be saved from wherever you live on this earth. He is God and there is no other. Every knee will bow to Jesus. Every tongue will swear allegiance to Him. That was the reward to Jesus for His great humility and great obedience.

And what of you and me? If we will humble ourselves and submit to the Lord will He not greatly exalt us? In fact, the One who modeled it for us made us that very promise. *12 Whoever exalts himself will be humbled, and whoever humbles himself will be exalted.* Matthew 23:12 (ESV)

11 and every tongue confess that Jesus Christ is Lord, to the glory of God the Father. "And every tongue shall confess to God" was the Greek (LXX) ending of Isaiah's prediction. In place of "God", the devout Jewish believer, Paul, inserted that our confession would be that Jesus Christ is Lord, to the glory of God the Father. Paul had complete conviction that this passage from Isaiah that is about God our Savior was specifically about Jesus our Lord.

What a lofty poem Paul has set before us. It has taken us into the heavenly realms with wonder and awe and showed us Jesus in glory, humbling Himself to serve us through the incarnation, ending life in His obedient death, then to be highly exalted. There is no greater call to humility and service in all of Scripture, but let us not lose Paul's reason behind sharing this. It is so that we might emulate Jesus by humbling ourselves just a portion of the way Jesus did so that we might live together in love and unity.

The petty divisions that had sprung up in Philippi were being shamed by Jesus' awesome example. Our petty jealousies and divisions and disagreements are shamed by Jesus' awesome example that is recorded in this beautiful poem. It shames us and challenges us, but it also lays before us an amazing promise.

Humility comes before exaltation. The farther the step down, the greater the step up. Who will take up this challenge? You will know them by their love! (John 13:35)

Questions
1 What is the call of the first 4 verses of Philippians 2?
2 Does verse 5 go with verse 4 or 6?
3 What does verse 6 tell us?
4 How great was Jesus step down?
5 What did Jesus empty Himself of?
6 How did Jesus perform miracles?
7 What did Jesus do when He realized He was God incarnate? Why?
8 What is man's great weakness?

9 What is the reward for humility?

10 What was the name Jesus was given?

11 What passage was Paul quoting and what does it declare?

Shining Stars Philippians 2:12-18

Let us begin with a brief review so that we take our passage today in the context in which it is written. Paul is writing to this church that he is very fond of to encourage them to return to unity they once had. He's told them the basis for that unity is the encouragement we have in Christ, the comfort we receive from His love, the participation of the Holy Spirit in our lives, and the affection and sympathy He gives us for one another.

Then Paul shared a rich poem of how Christ demonstrated this attitude for us by emptying himself to become a man and by humbling himself to completely surrender His will to the Father. That dependence and trust took Jesus to the cross, but it didn't stop there. His perfect example of humility and trust were rewarded with the greatest exaltation ever given to one that walked the earth. His name is now the name above all names. In refusing to cling to his power and rights, He was given full authority to rightfully possess them.

And now we know what the following "therefore" is there for. *12 Therefore, my beloved, as you have always obeyed, so now, not only as in my presence but much more in my absence, work out your own salvation with fear and trembling,* Paul is calling on these believers who he loves so dearly to obey his request to live in a way that is worthy of the gospel. (1:27)That is to humbly obey the Father like Jesus did, serving one another in love. It is to take the low place and die to self that we might consider others interests but especially the will of the Father. (2:3-4) That is the way to overcome the division they were experiencing.

Paul is not referring to good works to save our soul. (Romans 5:8) He is adamantly opposed to the idea of earning salvation and teaches that it is unrelated to works. (Ephesians 2:8-9) He is referring to living out or expressing what is already ours. We can add nothing to what Jesus did, but we must with concerted effort cooperate with what He has done in us. (Ephesians 4:3) We often refer to this as the process of sanctification. The words "work out" (*katergazomai)* can also be translated to do or perform. In other words Paul is asking them to live out what God has done within. If you are a new creation, live like it!

That's a main ingredient in half the sermons you will hear. If we've been redeemed, if we have a new heart, then we should live a Christ like life. (2Corinthians 5:17) The fruits of the Spirit should be demonstrated in all that we do. (Galatians 5:22-23) We should humbly serve one another and our Lord every day. That's what it means to live in Christ and for Him to live in you. And why is it that we need to hear it again and again? You guessed it, the old zombie called the flesh would love to rise from the dead and take back over your life. (Galatians 5:16)

That is why Paul says to perform your salvation with "fear and trembling". Paul used the combination of these two words to describe how he carries out his ministry. (1Corinthians 2:3) Paul knew he did not have the power within himself to deliver the life changing Word of God without any element of self, exalting God alone. He needed to carefully carry out his calling.

It is the same with our daily life. Can you in your own power live as a representative of Jesus? And since you are called by His name, Christian, you and I need to live every day in performing the life of Christ with fear and trembling. I looked up those words, *(phobos kai tromos)* and they mean fear and trembling. But wait a minute, aren't we supposed to be free from fear and confident in the Lord?

Paul just explained what he meant with his example of Jesus. Jesus found himself in human form and so became totally obedient to the Father. (2:8) The implication is that we as humans are weak and prone to error. Even when we are in Christ, even when Paul could say that for him to live is Christ (1:21), we still have the enormous potential to get on a pride trip or justify giving in to some temptation. When influential Christian leaders fall it is because they lost the sense of fear and trembling and became self – confident.

So while we know that the Good Shepherd can keep his sheep (John 10:29), we also know how prone we are to sin and how powerful the allure of the flesh can be. We don't fear the enemy, for greater is he that is in us. (1John 4:4) We do fear our weak, sin prone nature and how easily we slip back into it. We tremble at the thought of stumbling someone and turning them away from Christ through our poor testimony. The more we realize the destructive power of sin the more we will fear and tremble to live out our salvation.

Paul is probably alluding to the language of Psalm 2:11 (ESV) *[11] Serve the LORD with fear, and rejoice with trembling.* Everyone will stand before the glorified Christ and give an account to Him. He is the final judge of all mankind. That is why we should work out our salvation with fear and trembling so that we may know where we stand. Live it every day!

The Message translation puts it like this, "Be energetic in your life of salvation, reverent and sensitive before God." I want to catch those checks in the Spirit that tell me not to go some direction. I want to sense that tap on the shoulder that says to check my motives. Paul is asking them, and the Spirit is asking us, to live in daily awareness of the battle that rages around us for our soul and the souls of all men and women. The Living Bible says it like this, *"...be even more careful to do the good things that result from being saved, obeying God with deep reverence, shrinking back from all that might displease him."* We should know our own weaknesses and be on guard.

[13] for it is God who works in you, both to will and to work for his good pleasure. Why should we live out our salvation with a serious concerted effort? It's because God is at work in us to do so. Cooperate with

Him! He's giving you the will power. He's empowering your ministry. He hasn't given you an impossible task. What He asks of you He is helping you to do. He is the life giving sap that produces the fruit on the vine. (John 15:5) But we must allow that sap to flow. We must obey with deep reverence, because His good pleasure is all that matters. His good pleasure is what is best for you and me. His good pleasure is so much more than all we can ask or imagine. But even more, His good pleasure is what is right and holy and just. Get caught up in going the other direction and it quickly spirals into the ugly destruction of sin and death. That is why we live out our salvation with fear and trembling. (James 5:20)

Paul goes on to give them the manner in which we obey the Lord. *14 Do all things without grumbling or questioning,* No whining! If we learn anything from Israel in the wilderness, we should realize how self-destructive it is to murmur against God and His goodness in our life. (Numbers 14:29) It is the old nature that wants to wallow in complaint instead of living in praise. Did you hear that? Complaining draws toward the old nature like a magnet and pulls our thoughts and speech in an ungodly direction. We focus on what we perceive to be bad when in fact the circumstance is often God at work waking us up for our eternal good.

Complaining about God's goodness is a dangerous way of dealing with difficulty in your life. It may mean God has to allow things to become even more difficult for us so that we turn from the direction we are taking. Complaining is a way of declaring our lack of faith and lack of trust in God. It is one way we declare that we don't believe in Romans 8:28, That is that all things are for our good.

Paul included this important imperative command because grumbling is often the source of discord within the church body. Someone doesn't like this thing or the way that is done. Then they seek to draw others to agree with them so they can have enough voices to demand change and have their way. It is the opposite of the humble, serving attitude that Christ exemplified.

We are also not to question everything, or as the NIV translates it, argue. By this I believe Paul meant to question or argue with what God has allowed. It can also be translated disputing or debating. The general idea is an attitude of vocal discontent. Together, the whining and arguing show a person to have a spirit of ingratitude. The flesh is disappointed because it is not having its way and everyone needs to know it because you are the self-appointed arbitrator of what should be done. The body of Christ should be a "NO WHINING ZONE". Instead we should be thanking God for His goodness and considering what is praiseworthy. What a different attitude will fill a church when it turns from whining to praise! This does not mean that we ignore real problems or relationships that are at odds, but that we look for positive solutions and expect God's intervention.

Obediently cooperate with the work of God in you without complaining and arguing so *15 that you may be blameless and innocent, children of God without blemish in the midst of a crooked and twisted generation, among whom you shine as lights in the world,* The goal of our cooperation with the Spirit, our Christ like expression of humility and service, our lack of grumbling and arguing is so that we might shine in this dark world. If we express the salvation that is ours in Christ, we will be blameless and innocent children of God living in unity. There won't be anything the world can point to that discredits our testimony. God will be glorified.

The world of the first century was just as twisted and perverted as the world today. In fact, the Christian faith has illuminated much of the darkness that was in the world of the first century. That has brought prosperity which is the natural outcome when evil is suppressed. But the cycle of man goes from prosperity to a turning away from God which results in an increase of the darkness which is followed by a desperation that once again seeks revival out of desperation. The West is heading down that path from prosperity to an increase in darkness.

If we will shine with the life of Christ, like stars in a dark night sky, we'll slow that descent into darkness and offer hope to those who are already in desperation. But how do we shine? We shine by doing what Paul has just instructed, expressing our salvation with fear and trembling, obediently cooperating with the Spirit, without grumbling and arguing. (Matthew 5:14) The world notices people that are at peace and filled with gratitude. The life of Christ in us is what shines. (John 8:12) As long as He is coming through, people can see the light in us. It leads them to Him.

We must therefore be *16 holding fast to the word of life, so that in the day of Christ I may be proud that I did not run in vain or labor in vain.* The word of life is something we must cling to. Do you know the Scriptures? Do you hide them in your heart (Psalm 119:11), meditating upon them (Psalm 1:2) and letting them guide you? They will strengthen us and renew our mind so that we don't give in to those temptations. They show us the devices of the enemy of our soul so that we know what to watch for. (2Corinthians 2:11)

Everyone is running through life, chasing something. What are you chasing? Paul writes that he will cling to the word of life so that when he gets to the end of the race he won't find he ran in vain. Life is an effort. You might as well make it an effort to serve the God who loves us and will richly reward us for our faithfulness. We might as well serve a God that modeled for us the way to live and showed the great reward for humble obedience.

How many will end up finding they worked all their life for religion and hear God say He never knew them? (Matthew 7:23) How many will enter heaven because they trust Christ but find they never worked out their salvation with fear and trembling and have nothing to show for this life they were given? (1Corinthians 3:15) Are you running in vain? The only way to know for sure is by clinging to the sure Word of God, the word of life. (2Peter 1:19)

Paul had said he was confident that God would answer their prayers and that he would be released (1:19), but he now writes, *17 Even if I am to be poured out as a drink offering upon the sacrificial offering of your faith, I am glad and rejoice with you all.* If the church at Philippi will just do these things so that it will shine in this dark and twisted world, Paul would be joyful even if he is to be martyred for his faith. He compares his eventual death to a drink offering that the priests poured out on the altar.

The end of the race has us standing before the heavenly Judge who rewards the winners. Paul's mind shifts to the potential end of his earthly life. The daily sacrifices that the Jewish priests performed were offered with a drink offering. After the lamb was slain and placed on the altar, a quarter hin of wine was poured out to the Lord. (Exodus 29:40-41)

Greeks also had a daily tradition. Before and after a meal, they would pour out a cup of wine in gratitude to the gods. Paul is saying that he is glad to be the wine the Philippians pour out in gratitude to the true God. Whether it is the Hebrew or Greek custom, the idea is the same. Paul is glad that his life can be an offering to God.

18 Likewise you also should be glad and rejoice with me. Precious in the sight of the Lord is the death of His saints. The home going of a believer is a time to be glad and rejoice for them. We weep for ourselves that we no longer have their fellowship, but we should be glad and rejoice with them. Two weeks ago our brother Robert Hornby finished his race. He clung to the word of life. His life was poured out like a drink offering in gratitude to God. We'll miss him, but our parting is not a goodbye, but a "see you soon". That is why we should be glad and rejoice with him.

May I ask you the destination of your run? Are you clinging to the word of life or are you running in vain? Will those you leave behind rejoice and be glad with you because your life gave evidence that Jesus was your life? Will they be able to say that your gratitude and peace shone like a light in the darkness of this world leading others to all we have in Christ?

Questions
1 What is verse 12 "therefore" there for?
2 What does "work out" mean in 12?
3 To what "salvation" was Paul referring?
4 Why with "fear and trembling"?
5 Who helps us will and work?
6 What is God's good pleasure?
7 What are the negative commands here?
8 What does complaining say about us?
9 Instead of whining we should be ____?
10 How do we shine?
11 Why do we shine?
12 What are the cycles of man?

Faithful Brothers Philippians 2:19-30

Before we begin to look at the passage, I have something that God stirred in my heart this week to share with you. I was very convicted that I do not expect more from you, and have not challenged you to be more engaged with the passages we study. So let me tell you what I believe the Lord desires of this congregation.

Each week we work our way through the book of the Bible we are studying. If you believe that God is sovereignly in charge of where we are studying, as we have seen so many times in the past, then you can expect He has something to speak to you in that passage. Listen with that kind of expectation. Take it home and go over it. Meditate on it. Download it and re-read it. Look up the cross-references. Finally, apply it to your life. Let it transform the way you think and act.

Then look at the passage for the next Sunday. Guess how many verses I'll go over. See beforehand what you believe to be the main points. Read a commentary or two on the passage. Talk to others about the passage and share what you are seeing in it and listen to what they are learning from it.

Is that asking too much? If we believe in a sovereign God who loves us and wants to transform us into the image of His Son through His powerful Word, what could be more important? We act on what we believe. What do you believe? I'm not preaching to entertain you. There are a lot more entertaining pastors than me. I'm preaching the Word so that we all might be changed. Will you take the challenge?

In the preceding passage, the Apostle had challenged the Philippians to be more like Jesus in preferring one another through genuine humility. (2:3) Jesus' example shames those who cause division through insistence on having their way. Instead of expressing the old nature, Paul encouraged them to work out what God had worked in them. (2:12)

One preacher (Tony Evans) describes it as popcorn Christianity. When you heat up a kernel of corn, the little bit of water inside the kernel begins to boil, turns to steam, expands and BOOM! The whiteness that was on the inside is suddenly on the outside. The self-sacrificial life of Christ in the spirit of the believer suddenly starts to be expressed outwardly. The heat is the Word applied by the Spirit. The Apostle challenged them to shine like luminaries in the darkness of this fallen world. (2:15) Let that new life come bursting forth so that the little grievances would be swallowed up in the all-encompassing love for Jesus and for one another.

Our passage for today is more of a personal note about two men Paul was sending to the Philippians. It's one from which we can draw a number of lessons. *¹⁹ I hope in the Lord Jesus to send Timothy to you soon, so that I too may be cheered by news of you.* Paul had met Timothy on a missionary journey to Lystra. (Acts 16:1) He was the son of a Jewish mother and Greek father. His grandmother, Lois, had taught him the Scriptures. (2Timothy 1:5) Paul saw something special in this young man and brought him along to mentor him. He soon became Paul's representative to the churches. When Paul was concerned about a church, Timothy would go and minister there and bring back a report. (1Thessalonians 3:2; 1Corinthians 4:17) Paul was concerned that the animosity between two of the sisters in Philippi may be growing into something far worse. Sometimes the voice of someone not immediately involved can clarify the issues and help a local church to see the big picture and move forward.

This is another indication that Paul believed that through the prayers of the believers he would be freed and continue his ministry because of the great need to get the churches soundly established. He trusted in his Lord, Jesus, that Timothy would no longer be needed to help him in prison so he could go and help the church and then bring back good news. Paul had a positive outlook, but it was because of his faith in his Lord.

20 For I have no one like him, who will be genuinely concerned for your welfare. Paul was declaring that Timothy shared his heart for them. He was likeminded with Paul in his love and concern. What a word of recommendation. If you really want to encourage a group to trust the leading of someone, tell them the person genuinely cares for them. Paul probably discerned this care in Timothy's heart through the prayers of Timothy. Remember that Timothy was there with Paul and Silas when the church began in Acts 16. The experiences there were probably a great step in his spiritual growth. God had endeared them to his heart. But there was a greater reason for Timothy's genuine concern.

21 For they all seek their own interests, not those of Jesus Christ. Paul usually spoke quite highly of his fellow workers, but after some time in prison, he has seen how few are really sold out for the gospel. If Paul walked into our church today, I think we'd be uncomfortable with how fanatical he is. He doesn't even care about his own life. All he wants to do is see the gospel advance and he's not impressed with those who don't share that passion.

Timothy had been growing in Christ. Though he had a very different demeanor than Paul, his heart was growing to be like Paul's heart which is because they were both growing more like the heart of their Savior. Paul had admonished the church at Philippi to look on others' interests and not just their own. (2:4) He held up Jesus as an example of how that is lived out. Now he is saying that Timothy models that as well.

Instead of putting his own interests and desires first, Timothy puts the interests of Jesus first. That is where his genuine concern originated. Jesus cared about the church in Philippi. Timothy shared Jesus' genuine concern.

Do you think that perhaps Jesus is concerned about this church? What about the other churches in the community with genuine believers? Doesn't He care about them? So the question we must ask ourselves is this, do we share Jesus' genuine concern for fellow believers, or are we like the bulk of the people that Paul referred to that seek their own interests? (1Corinthian 10:24) Just as the ultimate example of Jesus was set before them, Timothy was used as an example of putting self last. Sometimes we think only Jesus could do it because He's special. Then we see one of those rare examples of the life of Christ in a person and realize we don't have an excuse. (1:21)

More of Christ and less of me,
This I pray so solemnly.
Crucified I long to be,
Christ's alone eternally.

22 But you know Timothy's proven worth, how as a son with a father he has served with me in the gospel. 23 I hope therefore to send him just as soon as I see how it will go with me, 24 and I trust in the Lord that shortly I myself will come also. They knew Timothy had proved himself in service to the gospel with Paul. The word for "proved" was used for the testing of metal to see if it is fit for coinage. Timothy had been through the fire and come out purified of his own desires. He had genuine value. He was like a son to Paul. (1Corinthians 4:17)

There is a fellowship that sold out believers have that is deeper than family relationship, because it is a fellowship of the heart that is focused on the same thing. We share the same passion. We understand the other's longing because it is our own.

Paul was going to send his dear son in the Lord to them as soon as he learned of the verdict. He was confident that he would be released and also have an opportunity to see them.

Servants of the Lord never know where they will be tomorrow. Jesus said everyone that is born of the Spirit is like the wind. (John 3:8) You can't tell where they are going. Every day is open to the leading of the Spirit. Will the cloud lift off the tabernacle and guide me on? We don't know. We just wait and watch.

25 I have thought it necessary to send to you Epaphroditus my brother and fellow worker and fellow soldier, and your messenger and minister to my need, Meanwhile, until Timothy is sent, Paul will send Epaphrodites. The divisiveness needed immediate attention. Paul realized the destructive power of division. Jesus had taught that a kingdom divided against itself could not stand. (Matthew 12:25) It was urgent that someone go and help them work through this.

Look at the three descriptions of Epaphroditus. First, Paul calls him his brother. There once again we see the family of God. Timothy is a son, growing up under Paul as a spiritual father, but Epaphroditus is a brother, an equal, mature, under the same Father. (2Corinthians 3:13)

Secondly, he is a co-worker or fellow laborer. Paul uses this term for a number of people in his letters. (1Corinthians 3:9; Philemon 1:1) Though Paul was an apostle by God's divine appointment, he saw others that were ministering as equals who worked side by side. Paul recognized the Spirit of God in us makes us all equals serving for one glorious goal, that the gospel of Christ advance in the world. We must recognize authority in the church knowing that God does call some to lead (Romans 12:8), and yet others have the same Holy Spirit working in them. We are fellow laborers.

Thirdly, he is a fellow soldier. This was another term that Paul liked to use. (2Timothy 2:3-4; Philemon 2) Paul recognized that we are in a great battle over the souls of men. God is not willing that any perish (2Peter 3:9), while Satan is determined that all will perish. (John 10:10) Mankind stands on the battlefield with the gift of free will. Satan's weapon of choice is lies and deception. God's weapon is truth. Satan lies about what is of value and the soldier of Jesus swings the sword of the Word and hacks the lies to pieces. (Ephesians 6:14-18)

A brother that came to Christ last week had fallen for those lies all his life. Once he heard the truth in his heart, he chose the truth. He declared that he wants to live the rest of his life as a soldier for Jesus. That is why we sing that classic hymn, Stand Up, Stand Up For Jesus, to remind us of the heart cry when we were first saved.

Stand up, stand up for Jesus, Stand in His strength alone; The arm of flesh will fail you, Ye dare not trust your own, Put on the gospel armour, Each piece put on with prayer; Where duty calls or danger, Be never wanting there.

Stand up, stand up for Jesus, The strife will not be long; This day the noise of battle, The next the victor's song. To Him that overcometh A crown of life shall be; He with the King of glory Shall reign eternally.

Epaphrodites had come from the Philippian church with a gift for Paul's support. (4:18) Paul is now sending him back. Paul called him their apostle (messenger) which was the common use of the word, not the official title.

26 for he has been longing for you all and has been distressed because you heard that he was ill. 27 Indeed he was ill, near to death. But God had mercy on him, and not only on him but on me also, lest I should have sorrow upon sorrow. Epaphrodites was concerned for the church because they had heard he was seriously ill. He wanted to get back to them to let them know he had recovered. Paul says his recovery was the mercy of God on Epaphrodites and on him as well. It would have added to the sorrow that Paul was experiencing, sorrow on sorrow. What was the sorrow? It wasn't imprisonment. Paul praised God for that because the Imperial Guard was hearing the gospel. (1:12-13) His sorrow was the news of the division within the Philippian church. If Epaphrodites, who was one of their stronger brothers, died, it would be even more difficult for the church to overcome their present trial.

28 I am the more eager to send him, therefore, that you may rejoice at seeing him again, and that I may be less anxious. The church's common love for this man and the joy of his return will be a factor in their moving forward. When they see him they'll remember what is really important. His presence and instruction along with this letter from Paul will help them. I think the translation of "anxious" is unfortunate here. The word is usually

42

translated sorrow. It is the same root as the words for sorrow in the last verse. Paul is literally saying his sorrow will decrease.

In a few chapters he will order them to be anxious for nothing. (4:6) That is a completely different word. Paul was sure that the Epaphrodites arrival and the letter would help them work through their struggle, so he would have less sorrow about their spiritual condition. It's the same idea he mentioned earlier about fulfilling his joy by being likeminded. (2:2) Paul wasn't having an anxiety attack. He was sharing the Lord's concern for this body of believers that he dearly loved.

29 So receive him in the Lord with all joy, and honor such men, 30 for he nearly died for the work of Christ, risking his life to complete what was lacking in your service to me. The language sounds like a scolding, but that is not the spirit of the letter. It means they could not be there physically to help him so they sent Epaphrodites. The Philippian church was one of the few that supported Paul's ministry.

There are those who risk their lives for the sake of the gospel or to minister to those that do. We are to hold them in high esteem, not because they are any more special than any other part of the body (1Corinthians 12:7), but because they model for the rest of us complete devotion to Jesus, putting Him first above everything in their life, even life itself. We should respect all who live this way.

Brother Sam, in a country I won't name, was severely beaten a week ago. He survived and is out of the hospital. He won't stop ministering the truth to those who are under the lies of Satan. I have the utmost respect for him! Those who live like he does challenge us to let go of petty things and be all out for Jesus. What will really matter when we are looking back from eternity?

In our passage today, we've been given an introduction to two soldiers of the cross. We know of others, like Sam. Their interests are those of Jesus Christ. They are focused on His concerns and not their own. They are 100%. I'm not trying to make you feel guilty or manipulate you. I'm just asking what is your relationship with Jesus Christ? Is He your free ticket to heaven or your Lord? I'm not here to judge where your walk is with Jesus, but I know one day we'll look back with joy that we followed Him or with sorrow that we were so wrapped up in pleasing ourselves.

Timothy, Epaphrodites, and Paul are in that grandstand in the sky, cheering us on, pointing us to Jesus. (Hebrews 12:1) They're yelling, "Run! Give it all you've got! He's worthy!" We hear them through their testimonies recorded in the Word. We hear it through the reports of the martyrs like Sam. How can we be apathetic when we have such great examples as these? Let's get serious about the transformation God desires.

Questions
1 What is the popcorn analogy?
2 Why was Paul sending Timothy?
3 What was Timothy's great asset?

4 Is Jesus concerned about Wayside? RU?
5 What were Paul's 3 descriptions of Epaphrodites?
6 Describe the weapons of the cosmic battle.
7 What makes one a soldier of Jesus?
8 What is sorrow on sorrow in vs 27?
9 Who do we honor and why?
10 What matters in light of eternity?

Found In Him Philippians 3:1-9

Paul had just told the Philippians that even if he was poured out like a drink offering, he wanted them to be glad and rejoice with him. He knew where he was going when his time on earth was done. He knew a reward for his service was waiting for him. But most of all, he knew he was going to be with Jesus forever. Yet, his conviction was that the Lord was going to give him more time to strengthen the church. In the meantime, he was sending Timothy and Epaphrodites to encourage the Philippians' faith.

We see in this chapter that one reason behind sending Timothy is that some of the Jewish Christians were trying to get the Gentiles to obey the ritual laws of Moses. This sect was referred to as the Judaizers. These people came from a life and culture that depended on keeping rules to feel they were in good standing with God. It was so engrained in their way of thinking that even when they accepted Jesus as their Messiah, they could not break free from thinking that their rule keeping was somehow making them acceptable to God. So of course, they thought Gentiles that trusted Jesus needed to keep the rules too. (Acts 15:1)

Paul had the revelation that it was never about works, but about faith in Jesus that saves us. (Ephesians 2:8-9) The Law was there to show us our need for a savior, to show that it is God's work to save our souls, as their Scriptures express it, "the God of our salvation" (Psalm 18:6; 25:5; Micah 7:7), and "I am the LORD who sanctifies you". (Leviticus 20:8; 21:8,15; 22:32)

Chapter three begins with another of Paul's imperative commands. *1 Finally, my brothers, rejoice in the Lord. To write the same things to you is no trouble to me and is safe for you.* Rejoice in the Lord. We have one great reason to be the most joyful people on earth. We are *in* the Lord! He has accepted us as his own. We are clothed in Christ. He is our life. (Colossians 3:4) We are made right with God, and what God began He will bring to completion. (1:6) Rejoice! It's not just to make an effort to smile and be happy. It is realizing all that we have in Jesus.

Sometimes we need to stop and take account of what has been done for us and all that we have in Christ. If after doing that you are not rejoicing, there is something seriously wrong that needs to be addressed. Your debt has been paid by the only One that could afford to do it. His payment for your sin debt shows you how much your Creator loves you. He has great plans for you. He will glorify Himself through you and then reward you for yielding to His work in you. He is working in you to will and do His good pleasure. (2:13) Eternity with Him is more awesome than your best earthly experience multiplied a thousand times over. (1Corinthians 2:9) Rejoice!

Paul is repeating himself in telling them to rejoice, and he'll say it again before he closes the letter. (4:4) He may be referring to repeating points from a previous letter. (possibly Ephesians or some lost letter) We need to hear the truth and these God glorifying instructions again and again. The world bombards us with its way of thinking. We need to encourage one another with godly thinking and reminders of spiritual realities. (Hebrews 10:25) We need to encourage one another with Scriptural instruction. Amen?

Now Paul begins the warning. *2 Look out for the dogs, look out for the evildoers, look out for those who mutilate the flesh.* He is speaking of the Judaizers that would try to teach the Philippians that to please God you must keep the Laws of the Old Covenant. That covenant came through Moses to the nation of Israel. (Acts 7:38) There were moral laws, community or civil laws, and ritual worship laws. What the Judaizers did not grasp was that the New Covenant was written on the heart. (Jeremiah 31:31-33) It was not about keeping the letter of the law but of the Spirit of the Law filling the heart. Now that the Spirit of God had come upon every believer because of the work of Christ, instead of obeying written rules to please God, the believer goes directly to the Lord and takes their instruction from Him. (2Corinthians 3:6) Instead of an outward religion, it had become an inward relationship which was always the intent. Many Old Covenant believers realized they could not keep the rules. They then discovered that their faith in God's willingness to accept their repentance along with their faith in the goodness of God was the only way for them to be justified. Without realizing it, they were looking forward to the cross.

The Judaizers still looked to rules of religion instead of the wonder and joy of a relationship with the living God. Paul uses language here that indicates that they never had such a relationship.
Each of these descriptions started with the Greek letter kappa so that they could be remembered. The term "dogs" was a way of saying a self-centered, evil person. (Psalm 22:16; Isaiah 56:10; Revelation 22:15) Dogs ate dead animals which was an unclean thing to the Jews. So while the Judaizers prided themselves in eating kosher, Paul is saying they've eaten of false doctrine, such as salvation by works.

"Evildoer" was a term to describe those who refused to try to keep the law. Once again Paul is making the point that what they boast in is actually contrary to the Law. By demanding others keep the letter they have missed the Spirit.

"Mutilate the flesh" was a pun in Greek. These people were insisting that Gentile Christian men needed to be circumcised. The word for circumcise and mutilate sounds very similar in Greek. The pun is saying: "If you have nothing to show but circumcision of the flesh, you are not really circumcised; you are only mutilated. Real circumcision is devotion of heart, mind, and life to God." (Barclay's Daily Study Bible (NT)) The Old

Covenant declared as much when it spoke of the circumcision of the heart. (Deuteronomy 30:6) It is very similar to the concept of baptism. Circumcision of the flesh was a sign that your heart was made sensitive to God. Baptism is an outward sign of an inward act of death, burial and resurrection to newness of life.

3 For we are the circumcision, who worship by the Spirit of God and glory in Christ Jesus and put no confidence in the flesh – Note the three signs of circumcision of the heart, that is, the new life in Christ. First, we worship by the Spirit of God. Remember when Jesus told the woman at the well that the day was coming when true worshipers would worship not in a special designated location, but in Spirit and truth. (John 4:24) That day came at Pentecost. If you have been born again you worship by the Spirit of God. You don't just sing a song or pray a prayer. The Spirit of God stirs you to worship with your whole heart. He leads you in worship, as you commune with Him heart to heart.

The second sign is glorying in Christ Jesus. The truly born-again soul gives Jesus the credit for every good work and testimony. We know it is all by His grace and power. We know that without Him we can do nothing! (John 15:5) Our constant pointing to Jesus irritates some, but we can't do otherwise.

The third sign is related to the second. If we glorify Christ alone, we put no confidence in the flesh, but like Jesus, we humble ourselves and become obedient. (2:8) We know our best thinking, our natural talent, and our greatest efforts are nothing unless they are empowered by the Spirit at His leading. We want to join God in what He is doing, not come up with a good idea with no eternal effect. So Paul is implying that the Judaizers really aren't born again and have nothing to assist us in our walk of faith.

Now Paul goes on to say that he knows what he's writing about from personal experience. He was once the Judaizer of Judaizers. *4 though I myself have reason for confidence in the flesh also. If anyone else thinks he has reason for confidence in the flesh, I have more:* Paul is being obviously sarcastic here. He puts no confidence in his flesh. But since these people do, Paul suggests they line up their best efforts with his. He had surpassed them all and yet found it was unhelpful, but even more than that, it was a hindrance!

He was *5 circumcised on the eighth day, of the people of Israel, of the tribe of Benjamin, a Hebrew of Hebrews; as to the law, a Pharisee;* He is a descendant of Abraham and was circumcised exactly according to the Law. (Leviticus 12:3) He can trace his Jewish lineage to one of the few tribes that remained faithful to God when the nation split. (1Kings 12:21) Hebrew of Hebrews probably implies that he retained the Hebrew language and was able to study the Scriptures in their original language. (Acts 21:40) He was a Pharisee. That means he was one of only a few thousand in all of Israel that kept the minutia of the written and oral law. They were the separated ones, highly respected by their people for dedicating themselves totally to God. Very few of the Judaizers could claim such obedience to the Law.

6 as to zeal, a persecutor of the church; as to righteousness under the law, blameless. The Jewish leadership considered Christianity a perversion of the true faith. Just like some of the men in the Old Testament who in their zeal slew those who turned from the faith (Numbers 25:11-13; Psalm 69:9), Paul saw himself as a guardian of true Judaism. He led "witch hunts", bringing Christians to trial and even putting them to death. (Acts 26:10) He could say that under the rules of the law he was blameless. No one could find fault in Paul's rule keeping or performance of what the Law required. (Note that Paul did not say he was sinless, but rather that he saw himself as a sinner that was keeping the rules of the Law.) There was probably not a single Judaizer who could make all of these claims.

7 But whatever gain I had, I counted as loss for the sake of Christ. Paul was a super religious person. It was hard to top his religious activity. But he declared it to be a detriment. Instead of a credit with God, it was putting him in greater deficit. Why? Because the more he did the more self-righteous and self-confident he became. The more he accomplished the more he thought he deserved God's favor. While at the time he thought he was pleasing God, he was actually sinning against God by his pride and self-reliance. All that religious zeal and dogmatic obedience to what he was taught ended with him killing God's true children! He put to death those who were living in a loving relationship with God. He was doing what God calls sticking his finger in God's eye. (Zechariah 2:8)

The temptation of the world is the one great hindrance we see to spiritual life, but I think Paul would put on par with that, the temptation of religiosity. When we ignore a personal relationship with God and get wrapped up in the ritual, rules, and performance, and programs, we can be just as sinful or more so than the most worldly person on earth. We stop worshiping by the Spirit. We stop glorying in Christ and we begin putting confidence in the flesh. That is the opposite of a true believer. So Paul says all that he worked for all his life he now sees as a detriment. He forsook it all for the sake of Christ. (Luke 14:33) He went from being the most likely to succeed in the eyes of his respected peers, to being the most despised traitor. Paul's conversion and life afterward are a great testimony to the love and grace of God and to the truth and power of the gospel that leads to a personal relationship with Jesus.

8 Indeed, I count everything as loss because of the surpassing worth of knowing Christ Jesus my Lord. For his sake I have suffered the loss of all things and count them as rubbish, in order that I may gain Christ. Verses 8 through 10 are some of the more powerful verses of this letter that we should commit to memory. Jesus said that if we want to be his disciples we must forsake everything. (Luke 14:33) Paul was a true disciple. Nothing held sway in his heart other than his desire to know Jesus. He gave up all his life of learning and obedience to religion and everything else he valued. Compared to Jesus, he counted it as waste. The word means that which is thrown to the dogs as no longer good for human use. Medically speaking, it means excrement.

I'm telling you, this guy Paul is a radical! Nothing else matters to him. Jesus is all he can think about. Jesus is all he cares about. He doesn't even care if he dies or not (Acts 20:24), as long as he is serving Him. He loves Jesus and just wants to know Him more. It sounds to me like he is madly in love, and I mean mad as in crazy! And how I want to be like him! (2Timothy 1:13)

⁹ and be found in him, not having a righteousness of my own that comes from the law, but that which comes through faith in Christ, the righteousness from God that depends on faith -- All Paul wants is to be found in Christ. His hope is that when people see him they see Jesus. He doesn't want them to see the perfect rule keeper, or Mr. Religiosity, but a person whose hope and faith are completely dependent on Jesus. If he is in Christ then he is credited with the righteousness of Christ. Clothed in Jesus, God sees Paul with the very righteousness of Christ. How is that even possible? It's by faith, pure and simple. Cast yourself on the Lord and trust in Him just like Abraham (Romans 4:22-25), like King David (Psalm 32:1-2), like Paul the Apostle.

Paul's point is not just for a church in Southern Europe 2000 years ago. People today will tell you some variation of this as well: Jesus plus something. Some will teach Jesus plus this program or that action if you really want to be spiritual. Religiosity is tempting because it's easier to do than to be. It's easier to bow to Mecca 5 times a day and give alms than it is to have a relationship with the living God who will tell you to do something you don't naturally desire or not do something you do desire. It's even easier to go to church on Sunday, Bible study during the week, 15 minutes of devotion every morning and prayer every night than to let Jesus be your all in all, the Lord of your life.

Don't you want to be found in Him? Do you want to know Him, to gain Him? I want to have the mindset of Paul. I want to consider everything that would lure me away from Jesus as leftovers for the dogs. *Then* we can live rejoicing every day because we can say without hesitation, *"I am my Beloved's and my Beloved is mine."* (Song of Songs 6:3)

Questions
1 Has the way of salvation ever changed?
2 Why should we obey his command to rejoice?
3 Why do we need reminders of Scriptural instruction?
4 What was the pun Paul used about Judaizers?
5 What are the three signs of true circumcision?
6 Why did Paul bring up his religious standing?
7 How does Paul see his past now?
8 What did Paul give up?
9 What does the word "rubbish" mean?
10 Why did Paul count all loss?

To Know Him Philippians 3:7-11

Paul had quite a resume in the Jewish religious community. He was the poster boy for orthodoxy. If righteousness could come through obedience to the Law, he was as righteous as anyone could be. (3:6) Yet, after meeting Jesus on the road to Damascus (Acts 9:5-6), he understood that all that was a hindrance, not a help. It hadn't really brought him any closer to knowing God. His heart was never changed. Though he knew what God expected of him, his best efforts weren't getting him any closer to being that person. (Romans 7:18) At least he could say he did a better job of living up to the Law's demands than the next guy. But after meeting the risen Jesus, he knew it wasn't enough.

Paul's keeping the letter of the Law to the best of his ability ended in him killing the family of faith! No wonder he later wrote that the Letter kills but the Spirit gives life. He personally experienced the Letter without the Spirit.

The Law didn't change. His understanding of the Law did. Now, instead of trying to please God by keeping the rules of the Law, he trusted in what the Messiah had done for him. (Galatians 2:20) All his education, all his fastidious efforts to do everything in the Law, the respect he had earned among his peers was suddenly seen as a detriment and not a help. He wrote, *7 But whatever gain I had, I counted as loss for the sake of Christ.*

In fact, nothing mattered anymore, religious or secular, inherited or earned. He let it *all* go. *8 Indeed, I count everything as loss because of the surpassing worth of knowing Christ Jesus my Lord. For his sake I have suffered the loss of all things and count them as rubbish, in order that I may gain Christ* He realized the longing of his heart was to know his Messiah. All his efforts were just getting in the way. He had found something of surpassing worth, Christ Jesus! He was living the parable Jesus told about the man who found a treasure in field or a pearl of great price (Matthew 13:44-46), who, once he found the thing of surpassing worth, sold everything to obtain the treasure.

Paul's eyes were opened on the road to Damascus. They were opened to begin to see the surpassing worth of Jesus. Later, he will write that God did that for him because he was acting in ignorance. (1Timothy 1:13) He was sincerely doing what he believed was right, but was sincerely wrong. God had mercy on him, revealed Jesus to him, and he was never the same. The zeal he had for God then turned from protecting the religion as defined by his teachers to personally knowing the Messiah as his Savior.

At this point, I think we should stop for a moment to consider whether we may be chasing something of inferior worth. Has God revealed to you that Jesus is the great treasure of such surpassing worth for which we'd be foolish not to give up everything and count *all else* loss? (2Samuel 7:22)

I think that many of our faith struggles come from a lack of seeing the surpassing worth of knowing Jesus. When the value of something, whether a physical possession, or prestige, or a relationship, holds our heart back from commitment to Jesus, we probably haven't seen the surpassing worth of knowing Him.

For Paul, it wasn't just the revelation on the road to Damascus, which was the beginning. It was the continual dawning of the Scripture's unveiling of the heart of Messiah and the plan of God. Sometimes it overflowed from Paul's pen in bursts of praise. *33 Oh, the depth of the riches and wisdom and knowledge of God! How unsearchable are his judgments and how inscrutable his ways!* Romans 11:33 (ESV)

3 Praise be to the God and Father of our Lord Jesus Christ, who has blessed us in the heavenly realms with every spiritual blessing in Christ. Ephesians 1:3 (NIV)

17 He is before all things, and in him all things hold together. 18 And he is the head of the body, the church; he is the beginning and the firstborn from among the dead, so that in everything he might have the supremacy. 19 For God was pleased to have all his fullness dwell in him, Colossians 1:17-19 (NIV)

You don't have to have a Damascus Road experience. You just need to let the Spirit reveal Jesus through the Scriptures. That is what deepened Paul's sense of the worth of his Savior.

With Paul, the great sense of mercy and forgiveness was also a factor. (1Timothy 1:15) It should be for us as well. Maybe you didn't help to put Christians to death, but before you knew Jesus you were alienated from God in your mind. (Ephesians 2:3) You inherited the fallen nature of Adam. (1Corinthians 15:22) Any good works you did can be put in the same category as Paul's religiosity. They were a hindrance, not a help, because it blinded us to our need.

How many times have you heard someone say they think they are good enough to get into heaven? That just means they know nothing of the holiness of God. The clearer we see how depraved we are without Jesus, the more we appreciate what He has done and the plans He has for us. The more we see the judgment we deserve, the more we see the surpassing worth of Jesus.

But it is even more than what He has done. It is also who He is. A love that would die for us while we were still sinners came from an amazing heart of love. (Romans 5:8) We all long to be loved unconditionally. We crave the love that will not let us go regardless of how long it takes to change us. The only place we will find it is in Jesus. He's it! Paul realized that and so he could say that everything else is left behind. (3:8)

He just wants more of Jesus, *9 and be found in him, not having a righteousness of my own that comes from the law, but that which comes through faith in Christ, the righteousness from God that depends on faith --* Be found in Him. In other words to moment by moment experience the life

50

of Christ in the depths of his being. He wants to continually be clothed in Christ. (Galatians 3:27)

Regardless of your occupation, you can do that job the way Jesus would do it if it were His job, that is of course, if you are found in Him. Do whatever you do as unto the Lord (Ephesians 6:5-6), representing Him to those you come in contact. Best of all, when we go to our heavenly home and stand before the judge, we'll have a righteousness that comes through faith in Christ. God will look on our soul and see the righteousness of Jesus… if we are found in Him. (2Corinthians 5:21)

Then it is as if the passage breaks and Paul's thought goes to a higher plane. It is definitely connected with his experience of considering all things loss to know Jesus, but it sounds like a mission statement right out of Paul's heart. *10 that I may know him and the power of his resurrection, and may share his sufferings, becoming like him in his death,*

There are four things of Jesus that Paul desires. First and foremost is to know Him. The Greek word is used here in the Hebrew sense of relationship (Heb -*yada* – Genesis 4:1). In 1Corinthians 8:3, Paul uses this word in the sense of God being in relationship with us. *3 But if anyone loves God, he is known by God.* Paul wants to deepen his love relationship with Jesus. He sees the surpassing worth of Jesus, but he knows there is even more. He desires a greater revelation of Jesus. The more he sees of Him, the more he loves Him. In Ephesians 4:13 Paul related knowing Jesus to spiritual maturity. Knowing Christ intimately leads to spiritual maturity. Are you increasing in the knowledge of the Son of God?

That is the first half of our purpose statement as well, "To know Christ…" We increase in that intimate knowledge of Him as we study the Word, letting it speak to our hearts.

A number of you contacted me during the week and said you were taking up this call to read the passage before Sunday and meditate on it and then to take home what the Spirit spoke to your heart on Sunday and apply it, making it a part of your life each day. You've said you do want to know Him and what He would say to our hearts through His word each week. And then there are your own devotional times in the word as well. As we live out what He is showing us, we experience His power in our lives. When we face a situation or a conversation and we are found in Him, we know Him by experience.

The second thing Paul desired was to know the power of His resurrection. In Ephesians 1:19-20 Paul prayed that the church of Ephesus would know the power of the resurrection in their own lives. Paul knows that to carry out his mission he needs that power in his own life. He wants to daily experience the power that can take a person who has been crucified with Christ and make him tool in the hands of Almighty God. He wants to be a weapon that can utter the powerful word of God and break through the darkness and set captives free for the glory of God.

Here is how he put it in the letter to the Romans. *11 If the Spirit of him who raised Jesus from the dead dwells in you, he who raised Christ*

Jesus from the dead will also give life to your mortal bodies through his Spirit who dwells in you. Romans 8:11 (ESV) The Spirit of life gives us life in the resurrected Lord. It is resurrection life in these mortal bodies, right now! Not someday when we die. He'll write about that in the next verse. Paul is talking about presently experiencing resurrection power.

When the Spirit of God is behind your speech, you are experiencing resurrection power. When you have joy in the midst of the loss of the things of this world, you are experiencing resurrection power. Whenever you react to life in a way that the world cannot comprehend because of the Spirit that raised Jesus from the dead living in you... yes!

Paul experienced it over and over but he wants more. He was literally raised from the dead. (Acts 14:19-20) He was made bold before kings and rulers. He raised the dead and preached the word in demonstration of the Spirit and of power. (1Corinthians 2:4) Still he wanted more of Jesus. Do you want more? Then pray, "More Lord! I want to know You! I want to know Your resurrection power!"

> More of Christ and less of me,
> To know You intimately.
> Resurrection power divine,
> Take me Savior, make me Thine!

The third request is the one we saw in 1:29. Paul wanted to share in Christ's sufferings. What does that mean? It means that this world is ruled by the prince of the air, the spirit that is now at work in those who are disobedient (Ephesians 2:2), the unholy spirit. A soldier for Jesus is going to have some battle scars. Epaphrodites almost died. Brother Sam almost died. Paul was waiting for his sentence and would one day be decapitated. Paul loves Jesus so much and the truth that Jesus is, that he is not only willing to suffer with Jesus for that truth, but finds fellowship with Christ in it. That is the Greek word used in the passage, to fellowship in His sufferings. Paul wrote that all that live godly in Christ Jesus will suffer persecution. (2Timothy 3:12)

I'd like to think that was for another time and another place. My flesh would just like to get along with everyone and try to find common ground. But when you stand with Christ, you stand against the world, and the world will make you pay one way or the other. I don't believe you can know Christ and have the resurrection power in your life and not also, in some form, fellowship with Him in His sufferings. (Acts 14:22)

Finally, Paul was becoming like Jesus in his death. This is an ongoing present tense, "becoming". Paul desired to live every moment like Jesus died. He died forgiving, encouraging, witnessing the love of God, quoting Scripture and once and for all triumphant! And He did it in the midst of great suffering. It's as if the thought of fellowship with Christ in His sufferings brought to mind the awesome demonstration of victorious life that Jesus demonstrated on the cross.

I'll be honest with you. I want the first two. I want to know Jesus. I want to experience resurrection power. I'm not too excited about suffering with Jesus and being like Him in His death. But I think the more the first two work in us, the more we'll begin to long for the last two as well.

Paul follows this purpose statement with a vision statement. *11 that by any means possible I may attain the resurrection from the dead.* It sounds as if he's saying that these desires of his may earn him the right to be worthy of resurrection, but that cannot be the case. In a few verses he will confidently say that we are already citizens of heaven who will be transformed into the image of Christ. (3:20-21) Paul was sure of his resurrection and he writes about it in other letters. (1Corinthians 15:51-52; 1Thessalonians 4:16-17)

We should take this as an expression of Paul's humility. He speaks of persevering to the end (1Timothy 4:16) and has seen others fall. (1Timothy 4:10) Considering his past, he doesn't want to be overconfident in himself, but rather he places all confidence in Christ and His sacrifice to "somehow" make it possible for him to experience the final resurrection.

Why is physical resurrection such an important goal? It's not just about eternal life, or his heavenly rewards, or even his new heavenly body. What he's really looking forward to is the unhindered presence of Christ, and of knowing Him even as we are known. (1Corinthians 13:12) That is what Paul lives for daily and hopes for in the future. (1:21)

How about you? If you can't say that you are long to be in the presence of Jesus, then you need a vision of His surpassing worth. We see that greatness in the Scriptures, in how He lived, in the words He spoke, in the way He died, and in His victory over death. Is Jesus worth losing everything else, even this earthly life? Absolutely! Do you want to know Him more? Do you want to experience in His resurrection power? How about fellowshipping with Him in His suffering and being conformed to His death? We're not able, but are you willing? Then pray as Paul did to know Jesus, his resurrection power, the fellowship of His suffering, becoming like Him in His death.

Questions

1 Why did Paul count everything loss?
2 Paul was living which parables?
3 How did Paul come to know the surpassing greatness of Christ?
4 How can we…?
5 What does Paul mean by knowing Him?
6 What is the second thing Paul desired? What is its application to your life?
7 What does Romans 8:11 mean?
8 What is the third thing Paul desired?
9 Why would he want that?
10 What is the fourth?
11 What does verse 11 mean?
12 Will you make these four desires of Paul your own? Is Jesus worth it?

The Prize Philippians 3:12-16

Paul had just written that he had given up everything he once valued for the surpassing worth of knowing Christ. Everything else was a detriment, and considered worthless. His goal is to be found in Christ Jesus, living in resurrection power, sharing in Christ's suffering, and becoming like Jesus in His death. (3:10) Paul wanted to know that on the day the last trumpet sounds and the dead in Christ rise, he'd be right there with all the other saints, receiving his new body, perfected, forever with the Lord. (1Corinthians 15:52-53)

We have to know what he had just said to understand the next passage. *12 Not that I have already obtained this or am already perfect, but I press on to make it my own, because Christ Jesus has made me his own.* It's not that he does not already know Christ, but that he knows there is so much more to know. He knows that we now see through a glass darkly but then we'll see Him face to face and know Him as we are known. (1Corinthians 13:12) Meanwhile, he wants to keep pressing into Christ, living to know Him more each day. He wants to be found in Him as he walks through this life facing all the opportunities and the suffering that God allows to come our way. (Matthew 11:12) He knows there is more of Jesus for him to experience in this life.

Think about it! If the great Apostle Paul who saw the glorified Jesus, who was caught up to the third heaven (2Corinthians 12:2), who raised the dead and cast out demons, who founded numerous churches and wrote a good part of the theology of the New Testament said he had more to take hold of, what about us?

If you think you've arrived, and you are comfortable with your knowledge of Jesus, you've settled for a lot less than He has for you! Your vision is too limited. Your understanding of what Jesus wants to do in and through you is way too small. We'll return to this thought at the end of our passage for today.

There is a branch of the church that teaches entire sanctification. (1Thessalonians 5:23) If by that they mean they are holy in the sight of God because of what Jesus did for them, then I agree. But often the term is interpreted as being sinless. I can't agree with that. If Paul knew he hadn't arrived, I don't know why anyone would think they had.

D.L. Moody was approached by a man who made the claim. Moody shot down the whole idea with his quick witted response. "Can I talk to your wife about that?" It was great response on several levels. Those closest to us see the real person, warts and all. On a deeper level, the man who came up with the doctrine, though a great evangelist, sadly, neglected his wife. He failed to keep the command for husbands to love their wives as Christ loves the church, giving Himself up for her. (Ephesians 5:25)

When Paul said he was not perfect, he didn't even mean perfect in the way we think of perfection. Perfect *(teleios)* is used in scripture and in that day in a number of ways. It was used of a mature believer as opposed to one that was still learning the basics of the faith. We see that in our last verse for today. It was used of someone who thoroughly knew their subject as opposed to a student. And in the case of offerings, it meant an unblemished sacrifice. It could mean a fully developed adult as opposed to a growing child. There are so many different uses, but you get the idea that it means to have arrived at maturity.

Paul was saying that he was still a growing Christian. The early Christians referred to martyrs as having been perfected by the sword and the day of their death as the day of their perfecting. (Barclay's Daily Study Bible (NT) Philippians) This is in line with Paul's theology. But that doesn't mean Paul just sits back and waits for the day of his death. He knows that he can know more or Jesus every day. He presses on to experience Jesus to a greater extent. He wants to lay hold of Christ because Christ had laid hold of him on the road to Damascus and turned his life right side up. (Acts 9:4-6)

In Paul's mind and heart, Christ is a treasure to be possessed, a treasure of surpassing worth. (3:8) All he desires is to know and love Jesus more each day. We don't need another blessing from some anointed minister, some impartation that tingles our spine. We need to know and love Jesus more and let Him have His way in us.

13 Brothers, I do not consider that I have made it my own. But one thing I do: forgetting what lies behind and straining forward to what lies ahead, Paul had not arrived. God wasn't done with him. He was still a work in progress. It was Jesus that took hold of him. He had nothing to do with his conversion. It was all God. But now that God had taken hold of him, he exerted an effort. That one effort was to forget about the past and strain forward to what God had for him that day and the next. This is not a psychological instruction to think positive, but to be passionate about living for Jesus. (Romans 12:1)

The past is past. You can't change it. You can learn from it, but take the lesson and leave the past in the past. No matter how much you think about it, it won't change what happened. Paul had poked his finger in God's eye by killing believers. (Zechariah 2:8) He can't change that. God still had mercy on him. Should I have done this or should I have avoided that? It doesn't matter now, as it is in the past. What matters now is what God has for you today.

I'll bet you struggle with this like I do. Yesterday haunts us. But it is too late to change it now. The only time to change direction is as you go forward. (Isaiah 30:21)

Paul used a sports term here of a runner stretching to the finish line. He doesn't rest on yesterday's victories or dwell on past failures; he strains forward to what God has for him today. And just like a runner, you can't look back and stay focused. He wants to make the right choice and yield to the life of Christ in him this time around. He has told us in a previous letter that God has good works prepared in advance for us to do (Ephesians 2:10), and he longs to do them because he experiences more of Christ when he does.

We don't know what lies ahead, but we do know that whatever it is, we can experience the life of Christ going through it. We can be found in Him or we can face it in our flesh. The grace of God is always there, but are we straining toward that finish line? God does His part, but are we cooperating? Lack of cooperation is called rebellion. Paul says he gives it all he's got to cooperate with the Spirit (Galatians 5:24-25). He's watching for those opportunities. He's sensitive to the Spirit. He's listening for the still small voice.

14 I press on toward the goal for the prize of the upward call of God in Christ Jesus. I believe Paul is saying that the goal line is the last trumpet. The prize is the upward call. That is when we get our transformed body. He mentions that in the coming passage. (3:21) He wants to hear, "Well done good and faithful servant. Enter into the joy of the Lord!" (Matthew 25:23) That's quite a goal. Jesus is the way, but am I walking in it? Am I pressing forward to make it my own?

The more I study the New Testament, the more I find this seeming contradiction of our salvation being all a work of God and yet we are to give our all. I believe Paul is telling us that God does it all, but then we better be sure we received it by giving it our all. (1Corinthians 15:10) He's very clear that that his deeds have nothing to do with meriting salvation, but rather are a result of our salvation. And if the Apostle Paul wanted to give it all he had to be sure he wasn't fooling himself, then I certainly want to do the same.

Are you pressing toward the goal for the prize of the upward call of God in Christ Jesus? Paul tells us how careful he is in this pursuit of being in Christ. *26 So I do not run aimlessly; I do not box as one beating the air. 27 But I discipline my body and keep it under control, lest after preaching to others I myself should be disqualified.* 1 Corinthians 9:26-27 (ESV) This is about personal discipline of the body and soul like an athlete training their body because of a love for Jesus and the desire to be found in Him. Paul wants to know that the prize of the upward call is indeed his, that he has obtained it by faith and will one day experience the reality of it. You see, if you miss the resurrection of the justified, than you will rise at the Great White Throne judgment. (Revelation 20:11) You'll be justified in Christ or condemned by your own words and life lived in rebellion toward God. (Matthew 12:37)

Another way to look at what he is saying is through the teaching of Jesus. You know a tree by its fruit. (Matthew 7:20) If a person thinks they are a peach tree but only grow thorns, someone is wishful thinking. Paul wants to bear the fruit of the righteous to walk worthy of the Lord to the end because of all Jesus did for him.

15 Let those of us who are mature think this way, and if in anything you think otherwise, God will reveal that also to you. He's using the same word he just said he had not achieved, but obviously in one of the other uses. He's not already perfected/matured. Let those of us who are mature/perfected think this way. The first is the sense of God's work in him being completed. The second is of a mature believer. If you are a grown up Christian, then you should recognize how far you have yet to go.

To what way of thinking is Paul referring? He means Christ is of surpassing worth. He is the prize, to be found in Him and destined for the resurrection of the just. (Luke 14:14) It's to be looking forward each day to what God has for us, straining forward to do His will each day as we are on our way to that resurrection day.

To think otherwise would be to consider something in this world of value. Instead of just repeating his point or telling them to see what hasn't yet been revealed to them, he just writes that "if in anything you think otherwise, God will reveal that also to you." If there is something in your life that you think is as important as Jesus, if you don't see the need to stretch forward each day to the finish line, God will show you.

God loves His children. If there is some idol, some worthless thing, something that gets in the way of our total dedication to God, then God will reveal it. I can point it out to you, but you probably won't receive it from me. When God shows you, it sticks. No argument is needed. His conviction isn't just an opinion; it's the way it is.

I have found great comfort in this verse. When you see someone compromising, one of the flock under the wrong influence, but you truly believe they are God's child, you don't have to intervene unless led to do so. (James 5:20) You can warn them but then trust that God will bring conviction. He'll reveal it to them. The Holy Spirit brings conviction. I just bring my judgment and opinions, unless of course I'm acting at the leading of the Holy Spirit.

When the Spirit reveals the surpassing worth of Jesus, you don't have to tell the person to let go of garbage. They will do it on their own because of the great value they have found in Jesus. They may need some advice and encouragement on how to let go, but the desire will be their own. Too often we see young Christians' lives and want to go and tell them all the things they should give up and end up discouraging them. The Spirit will convict them and they will choose to give it up on their own. Then it will be from a heart of love for their Savior not obedience to your instruction. It will come from the heart and not the head.

16 Only let us hold true to what we have attained. God will show us all where we have other affections that are not Christ, but keep living up to what *has* been revealed to you. Don't slide backward. (Luke 9:62) We are accountable for what we know and have seen. While we are learning and seeing more don't let go of the ground you have covered. Do what you know to be the will of God. (Ephesians 4:27)

People often ask about God's will in a given situation. If God hasn't revealed to you what you should do, just keep doing what you know to do. Keep reading the Word. Keep praying. Stay in fellowship. Keep yourself pure. Keep being a witness where God has you at the present time. Here is God's will for now, "hold true to what you have attained."

Let me read the passage to you again, this time in the New Century Version. *12 I do not mean that I am already as God wants me to be. I have not yet reached that goal, but I continue trying to reach it and to make it mine. Christ wants me to do that, which is the reason he made me his. 13 Brothers and sisters, I know that I have not yet reached that goal, but there is one thing I always do. Forgetting the past and straining toward what is ahead, 14 I keep trying to reach the goal and get the prize for which God called me through Christ to the life above. 15 All of us who are spiritually mature should think this way, too. And if there are things you do not agree with, God will make them clear to you. 16 But we should continue following the truth we already have.* Philippians 3:12-16 (NCV)

We aren't yet experiencing all God has for us. We haven't reached the goal. But are we making every effort to reach the goal, forgetting the past, straining forward to reach the goal and to possess the prize for which Christ has called us to life above? If you are spiritually mature, that will be your mindset. If not, God will make it clear to you. But whatever place we are at spiritually, we should live up to the truth we already have. Amen? What a passion Paul had for Jesus! Will you dare to pray to have the same?

Questions
1 What is the context for this passage?
2 If Paul wanted more of Jesus then…
3 Are you entirely sanctified?
4 What are the various meanings of "perfect"?
5 What effort does Paul exert?
6 What is Paul's goal?
7 Which resurrection are you aiming for?
8 What is the second use of the word "perfect"?
9 How do mature believers think?
10 What if someone doesn't?
11 What do we do in the meantime?

Citizens of Heaven Philippians 3:17-21

Last week we read about the zeal of the Apostle Paul as he chose to forget what was in the past and strained forward for the prize of the upward call of God in Christ. His hope was that, by the grace of God, he would serve Christ each day doing what his Lord instructed him until the day he was called home to heaven. To those who were not as devoted, he trusted that God would reveal that it was the only way to live. We ended with the challenge to live up to what has already been revealed to us.

The next paragraph picks right up with this previous thought of giving our best to the Master. Paul points to himself as an example. *17 Brothers, join in imitating me, and keep your eyes on those who walk according to the example you have in us.* Paul did not hesitate to use himself as an example. He'll do it again before the letter concludes. (4:9) He said the same to the Corinthian church. (1Corinthians 4:16)

I remember years ago reading this expression of Paul and being a bit taken back by it. How could any human urge others to follow them? In 1Corinthians 11:1 Paul exhorted the Corinthian church to follow him as he follows Christ. We have to remember that he just wrote that he had not yet reached his goal. He humbly gave an accurate assessment of his spiritual life and he encourages others to do the same. *³ For by the grace given to me I say to everyone among you not to think of himself more highly than he ought to think, but to think with sober judgment, each according to the measure of faith that God has assigned.* Romans 12:3 (ESV) We should avoid an overestimation of our self, knowing that Jesus is the example. But neither should we underestimate the gifts and spiritual maturity with which God has graced us. (1Corinthians 7:17) Excessive humility is as uncomely as pride. The verses that followed this invitation to judge ourselves are about spiritual gifts.

My discomfort from reading the verse was that I was not at peace with where I was spiritually. There were things in my life I knew that still needed to change. I couldn't say, "Brothers, join in imitating me." I don't even think that I would be comfortable with being one of the ones that Paul was pointing to as examples to watch. I had to forsake some habits, change some priorities, and take up as my goal the prize of the upward call of God. As the Apostle said in the previous passage, *"...if in anything you think otherwise, God will reveal that also to you."* Philippians 3:15b (ESV) He revealed it to me and the changes became my priority in response to the love of Christ.

Would you be comfortable with a brother living with you and observing your life on a daily basis? Could you say, "Brothers, follow my example"? And if not, why not? What needs to change? In what area are you refusing to follow Christ? That is the assessment that Paul encouraged, to think with sober judgment.

There is an interesting word that Paul uses in this exhortation, "the example". It is sometimes translated pattern (NIV). There are certain habits that are a part of the mature believer's life. These disciples don't make a person mature, but the mature engage with them because they have matured spiritually. The changes I had to make in my life were a part of becoming mature. The changes didn't make me mature. We pray because we desire communion with God, not to as a ritual that merits reward. (Hebrews 5:14)

Paul doesn't give a full list of the examples they observed in him, but he does list more of these disciplines in other letters. He has just told them one, forgetting what is behind and straining forward for the prize. (3:13) He has also pointed to rejoicing in the Lord. (3:1) In the next chapter he'll also instruct them to think in a godly way. (4:8) In other letters he mentions continual prayer (1Thessalonians 5:17), study of the word (2Timothy 2:15), yielding to the Spirit (Ephesians 4:30), speaking truthfully, not unnecessarily offending, sharing with those in need, encouraging others, and being hospitable to name a few.

We could make a long list, but it's easier to sum it up in saying that Paul loved God with his all and his neighbor as himself. Though not perfect, his conscience was clear (Acts 24:16) and the pattern of his life was on target, heaven directed, and an example for all to imitate. By the grace of God may our lives become examples as well! Amen? In the meantime, watch those that are examples and learn from them. The spiritual life is more caught than it is taught. The rabbi disciple relationship is still the best way to learn.

Paul gave himself and his team as examples in contrast to the bad examples influencing the Philippian church. *18 For many, of whom I have often told you and now tell you even with tears, walk as enemies of the cross of Christ.* The contrast was made between Paul's way of sacrifice and those who live for the flesh. They may have been Gnostics who intellectualized Christianity and used grace as a justification for indulgence. Their reasoning went something like this: "My flesh is evil, but I am saved by grace. God has saved my soul but my flesh is beyond hope, so I'll indulge it to appreciate the grace I have received." (Romans 6:1)

It was a false idea that still permeates the church today. People mistakenly see sin as a thing of the body. When God finished creating man, He declared all was good. (Genesis 1:31) When man fell it was not because his body was evil, but because in the freewill of his soul (mind, will and emotion), he turned from God. The corruption of the soul is behind the misuse of the body not the other way around. The salvation of the soul results in a right use of the body for the glory of God. Hedonism is an expression of a depraved soul. Righteous living is the expression of a redeemed soul. (Proverbs 20:7)

Paul wept over those who refused to die to themselves and follow Jesus. He could see the future consequences and it broke his heart. (Acts 20:31)

"Enemies of the cross" took on a special meaning in the first century. The Romans often mocked Christians for worshiping a condemned criminal that was executed in such a humiliating way. (1Corinthians 1:18) Some churches would downplay the cross because of this cultural issue, but it is the great difference between the Greek or Roman gods and the God of the Bible. Their gods would never humble themselves to serve their subjects because they have no love for them. The God of the Bible loves us and was willing to humiliate Himself to pay the price we could never pay. (Philippians 2:8)

That message was hard to communicate then as it is now because it implies that we imitate Christ in taking up our cross daily. (Luke 9:23) We become friends of the cross, while they become enemies of the cross. We embrace sacrifice and service to others while they indulge in selfishness.

And the reason for Paul's tears and ours as well is we know that *19 Their end is destruction, their god is their belly, and they glory in their shame, with minds set on earthly things.* The decision of the soul that results in that lifestyle not only is destructive here but will be eternally judged. (2Thessalonians 1:9) They live for their sensual appetites. Living for the belly did not simply mean for food, but for everything they physically desired. (Romans 16:18) Selfish gratification of the body of a depraved soul is self-destructive now and forever, for it is not just the body that is in rebellion but the very soul of the person. The forbidden bodily pleasures become enslaving to the soul and body. Paul says of this depravity that they lose all sensitivity and continually lust for more. (Ephesians 4:19) They are gratified but never fully satisfied. And what do they boast of? Their shameful acts!

Perhaps the worst consequence is their minds become enslaved by their worldly desires so that they only think of sin. (Romans 8:5) That is why it is so important to guard our thoughts, something Paul will exhort in the next chapter. God has given us all things to richly enjoy, but when the things of this world become our goal and are abused to try to fill the void in our hearts, what was meant for good becomes the means of our own destruction. Then to justify their lifestyle, they justify their actions and encourage others to join them. (2Peter 2:3)

This is why Paul told them to follow his example. His zeal for the things of God, his love for others, his daily carrying his cross was a contrast to the self-indulgent. His joy shouted the message that Jesus is worth it! His forward-looking life declared that there is more than this world has to offer. (Hebrews 11:26)

[20] *But our citizenship is in heaven, and from it we await a Savior, the Lord Jesus Christ,* We've come to two more great verses to memorize and hide in your heart. The desire of a transformed believer is Jesus! His presence is where our heart is at home. The world holds no lasting appeal to us. We would gladly leave it behind to be with our Savior. Our eyes are on Him, waiting for His return.

Philippi was a Roman colony. After 21 years of military service as a soldier to Rome you would receive citizenship and could retire to a colony somewhere in the world. Regardless of the culture around them, they dressed like Romans, spoke Latin, had Roman magistrates, morals, and were proud of it. Philippians knew what it meant to be a citizen in a colony surrounded by another culture. It was a Greek city taken over by Rome.

The word "citizenship" is also used of a community that has its own laws within a surrounding culture with different laws. It was used of a Jewish community in a Romans city. We are strangers and aliens here, just passing through. We're from another place and one day we're going home. (Hebrews 11:13) But while we are in this foreign land, we invite all who will listen to join our community. You will be seen as different. You will have new boundaries placed on your life. You won't fit in like you did before, but we have a destination and a hope. (1Corinthians 15:19)

The Caesars of that day were referred to as saviors. They came into a territory and having conquered it, established order and the peace of Rome.

That often meant cultural and practical improvements as well as a more orderly life.

We should be waiting for our Savior to come. We have lost the expectation of the early church that at any moment the Lord will appear in the eastern sky and we will be caught up to meet Him in the air. (1Thessalonians 4:16-17) I think we need to restore that fervor, gazing occasionally to the eastern sky with expectant longing as we imagine the scene of Jesus bursting through the clouds, more radiant than the sun, with eyes of fire, welcoming us home. (Matthew 24:29-31 Are you expectantly waiting for your Lord and Savior?

The King from our homeland is coming to take over. The improvements He will make are out of this world. The first great improvement is to these corruptible bodies. As good as they are, they are perishable and made for this temporal existence. (Psalm 139:14) The king is coming, *²¹ who will transform our lowly body to be like his glorious body, by the power that enables him even to subject all things to himself.*

Jesus already transformed the souls of those who have received the salvation He offers. That is what made us citizens of heaven. But we still have these fallen bodies that have degenerated over the millennia to the state we now experience. I realize some in the church believe they should have perfect health and I can see where they get that idea from Scripture, but I also see that all God's servants (with a couple of notable exceptions) eventually died. Paul had a thorn in the flesh. (2Corinthians 12:7) John the Beloved died of old age. And when the rest of the Apostles were martyred, they were not raised from the dead. Some people want to stay here forever. Not me!

Last week there was a special TV program about people that had near death experiences. The ones that had a little taste of heaven were disappointed to have had to return. They say they'd much rather be there. I'm filling out my DNR! If God wants me back here because He has more for me to do, fine, but otherwise let me go.

1 Corinthians 15 tells us that at the last trumpet, Jesus will clothe us with immortality. We will be changed in the twinkling of an eye. In the Philippian passage, Paul says that Jesus will do it with the power by which everything is subject to him. Jesus speaks and it is. (Matthew 8:8) He is all powerful.

Our bodies right now are quite lowly compared to the glorious body into which he will change them. He writes that they will be like the Lord's glorious body. We know from Luke that after the Lord rose He could walk into a locked room. (Luke 24:42-43) He could eat. He had flesh and bone. (Luke 24:39) He was tangible. But other than that we only have the awesome description of John in Revelation chapter one. (Revelation 1:13-16) From other descriptions we know that we will be recognizable as the person we were on earth. And when talking about this moment when the dead are raised and the living are caught up to meet the Lord in the air, Paul says we should comfort one another with these words. (1Thessalonians 4:18)

Here is the great contrast that Paul was pointing out. Some were living for the gratification of their body in destructive lifestyles and choices, justifying it and trying to lead others to do the same. Paul tells the church that they should follow his example of pressing forward for the upward call. Why aim for destruction when you can aim for glory? All the hedonists have is temporary gratification of the flesh that leaves them wanting more. They will never attain the lasting joy that we have found.

We are headed toward the wonderful goal of being in the presence of Christ forever. We taste it now (Ephesians 1:14) as he transforms our soul and enjoy this world in legitimate ways (Ecclesiastes 8:15), but we are ultimately looking forward to that day when we will get our heavenly body. Then we can enjoy the presence of Christ unhindered. (Revelation 1:17) Then we will experience all that God has for us to the fullest extent. Those who have had just a glimpse struggle to find words to describe it.

Let's follow Paul's example of aiming for the upward call. Let's forget what is behind and strain forward toward the prize.

A Chinese Communist, who delivered many Christians to their execution, came to a pastor and reportedly said: "I've seen many of you die. The Christians die differently. What is their secret?" I don't know what the pastor said, but I know what I would have answered. "We're going home. Where are you going?"

Questions
1 Would you urge others to imitate you?
2 What is a sober judgment of oneself?
3 What is the pattern? Who had it?
4 Who were the enemies of the cross?
5 Where does evil reside?
6 What was the shame of the cross?
7 What is their god?
8 Describe the contrasting examples?
9 What does heavenly citizen imply?
10 What are we waiting for?
11 What will Jesus do first?
12 What will our bodies be like?

Unity, Joy, and Peace Philippians 4:1-7

This week we are returning to our study in Philippians. I have heard of several other fellowships just concluded their study in Philippians as well. We shouldn't be surprised that God has us on the same page as we are the body of Christ. Many of us are in need of the same instruction at a particular point in time. We should see how the passage applies to us as the church at large, to our particular fellowship, and to us individually.

The closing chapter begins with a transitional verse. It is a concluding passage for the previous thought about being citizens of heaven and having our eye on the prize of the upward call, as we forget what is behind and strain forward to the finish line. *¹Therefore, my brothers, whom I love and long for, my joy and crown, stand firm thus in the Lord, my beloved.*

We see that concern and love Paul had for this church. (1:7-8) He called them his joy and his crown. He knew that they were the fruit of his ministry and would carry on when he went home to be with the Lord. They are the one thing he will have in heaven with him, the wonderful relationship of brothers and sisters in Christ and the joys in Christ that we share with one another.

He is telling them to follow his example and stand firm in the Lord to the end. Continue to seek a greater revelation of the surpassing worth of Christ. He ends the verse by repeating the term, beloved *(agapetoi)*. All these endearing terms show us the love of Christ for this family of believers was very real in Paul's heart. (John 13:34-35)

Now we come to one of the main purposes for which he wrote this letter. *² I entreat Euodia and I entreat Syntyche to agree in the Lord.* Apparently there were two women in the fellowship that were at odds with one another. We don't know what their issue was. It probably wasn't that important. More than likely it started over something small, and then escalated. I've seen it happen numerous times. It's often over an issue that is very dear to someone, but not so important to someone else. They voice their differences, but then it begins to become personal. (Proverbs 10:12) They start to criticize one another for other things. They start telling their side of the story to others to "have them pray for the other person". It's only out of loving concern, of course. Then others begin to join one side or the other and before you know it there are two factions in the church. And in the terms of the body of Christ, the nose revolts against the eye. (1Corinthians 12:16-17)

This makes the body unable to function properly. It becomes handicapped. Either the issue is ignored and resentment sets in, or there is continual conflict until there is forgiveness and a restoration of brotherly love. (Proverbs 17:9)

If you've been in church a long time, you've probably seen a thriving church decimated by this kind of problem. Some have tried to avoid it by giving the pastor more authority, like a CEO of a corporation, but that is not God's solution.

Paul appeals to each of these two sisters to agree in the Lord. He has told the church that to be worthy of the Lord they should be of one spirit and one mind. (1:27) He also told them it would fulfill his joy if they would be of the same mind and in full accord. (2:2) If our love for one another is one of the main witnesses that we belong to Christ, the lack of that love severely handicaps our witness.

It seems to me that all through this letter, this conflict has been a factor behind much of what Paul has written. He's told them to think more highly of others than you do of yourself. (2:3) He's given us Christ's example of humble obedience. He's warned not to grumble or complain

(2:14), and to forget what is behind and press forward to the upward call of God in Christ. (3:13)

This is a great letter for personality clashes within the church. It is full of good, sound, practical advice to check oneself to see if we are walking in the Spirit and following Jesus' example or living in our flesh.

I don't believe the single-mindedness that Paul is asking means to completely agree on the issue at hand. As we read in the previous passage, sometimes we allow the differences of opinion, trusting that God will show the one who is in error. (3:15) Our single-mindedness and agreement is that Jesus is everything! He's the One we live for and serve daily. He is the One we passionately love. Our unity is in who He is and what He has done for us. These sisters need to get their focus on Christ. What they need to agree on is that it is all about Jesus. In Him, we love and serve one another. (Galatians 5:13)

³ Yes, I ask you also, true companion, help these women, who have labored side by side with me in the gospel together with Clement and the rest of my fellow workers, whose names are in the book of life. This verse has been a challenge for translators. It is impossible to tell if Paul is writing to a loyal person named Sysygos or to an individual he referred to as loyal yoke-fellow. We do know the one he's asking for help is one man (singular masculine). Paul and company were assisted by these two women, Euodia and Syntyche. They labored along with Paul's team for the advancement of the gospel. But now they are at odds over something. So Paul asks either the loyal elder Sysygos or someone he called "loyal yokefellow" to help them get over it. (James 5:19-20)

We know some have been blessed with the ability to help others resolve conflict. It is good to seek them out. We have some among us with that gift. The wrong third party can actually make things worse. The mediator should be completely neutral as they come to hear about the issue at hand but with heart for the Lord first and foremost and grounded in God's word. If you really want the Lord's will in a matter, seek those that have that gift. Those who would bring in someone that is already on their side as a third party, or that already has a bias, are really not seeking resolution but victory for themselves. A Sysygos is an asset to any church and should be a valued part of the body of Christ. (Matthew 5:9)

⁴ Rejoice in the Lord always; again I will say, Rejoice. Paul reiterates his command to rejoice! (2:18) I don't think it is coincidental that he repeats the command after exhorting these two women to focus on Jesus. If you are filled with joy over the same thing about which someone else is filled with joy, you have an instant bond that overcomes differences, the joy bond.

I'm always amazed at the joy of those who suffer for their faith. (2Corinthains 6:10) I find an instant connection with them. They love the One I love! Their hearts are thrilled with the same One that thrills my heart. To rejoice in the same One is unity! (John 17:20-21)

Rejoicing in the Lord, as we often do in song, fills the heart and helps us focus on what really matters. Our differences melt away as we are caught up in the wonder of who Jesus is. It is a taste of heaven where we'll join with those Seraphim rejoicing in the holiness of our awesome God. (Isaiah 6:3)

So shouldn't we do it all the time? The verse does say "always", does it not? What a difference in our work day, in our conversations, in our home life, in our leisure if we are found rejoicing in the Lord! Can you think of any reason we should stop rejoicing in the Lord? And how attractive would that make Jesus to the world?

⁵ Let your reasonableness be known to everyone. The Lord is at hand; Whatever the difference was, reasonableness was probably the answer. It is often the answer to disputes. We should always seek the Lord's heart, and His answer is always reasonable. It may seem unreasonable to the unreasonable, but to those with the mind of Christ (1Corinthians 2:16), it will always be reasonable. The body of Christ should not seem unreasonable to the world. Our testimony should be of doing our best to be at peace with a generous spirit. The word can also be translated "gentle", as in "let your gentleness be known to everyone", and is applied to our Lord. (2Corinthians 10:1)

"The Lord is at hand" may have been somewhat of a warning. Jesus could appear at any moment. The Lord is at hand, literally means He is near. (James 5:8) He is the silent observer of our actions and attitudes. And yes, before we know it, the trumpet will sound. Will he be pleased with your attitude toward your brothers and sisters?

The Apostle wrote this almost 2000 years ago, but whether Jesus comes in the clouds in our lifetime, or we die of natural causes, this life is a vapor that disappears in a moment. (James 4:14) Then we will forever be with the Lord. Are we living for that day? Are we investing in eternity? Paul had just declared that he was. He was waiting for the transformation of his body. He was pressing toward the upward call. What are the little differences we experience in the light of that soon coming event? The Lord is always near! Are we living as if He is standing beside us?

⁶ do not be anxious about anything, but in everything by prayer and supplication with thanksgiving let your requests be made known to God. In the light of the brevity of life, and the faithfulness of God, there is no need to be anxious about anything. (Matthew 6:25, 31, 34) You can't be filled with anxiety and rejoicing at the same time. You have to release your anxiety to truly rejoice. In fact, the opportunity to release our anxiety is one of the reasons we rejoice. God is fully capable of dealing with our problems. He has planned our days. (Psalm 139:16) So when anxiety is felt in our heart and mind, we know what to do. We take it to the Lord in prayer.

I wonder if this verse was the inspiration for the song, *What A Friend We Have in Jesus*? The last verse of that song may not be familiar to you.

Blessed Savior, Thou hast promised
Thou wilt all our burdens bear;
May we ever, Lord, be bringing
All to Thee in earnest prayer.
Soon in glory bright, unclouded,
There will be no need for prayer—
Rapture, praise, and endless worship
Will be our sweet portion there.

When our burdens are unloaded on those greatest of all shoulders, those of our Lord, then we have a reason to rejoice. Things may not go as we desire, but they will be for the best. Those in love with Jesus can rest assured of that. (Romans 8:28) Our undistracted rejoicing unites our hearts. This was Paul's longing for the church at Philippi and the church at large.

We think of this passage applying personally and that is where we should start. We should never be that sour puss, long in the face, down in the mouth so called Christian. We should ever be those glowing, rejoicing, believers with a positive outlook and hope in our Savior for today and all eternity. We take our anxieties and burdens to the throne of God with thankful hearts and are assured that they are in the most capable and loving hands. (Hebrews 4:16)

Can we apply this verse as a church body of believers? I don't see why not. If we have concerns as a church body, we take them to God in prayer. We are a house of prayer. (Isaiah 56:7) This year we've been asking for us as a church to be filled with the knowledge of his will in all spiritual wisdom and understanding, so as to walk in a manner worthy of the Lord, fully pleasing to him, bearing fruit in every good work and increasing in the knowledge of God. We ask to be strengthened with all power, according to his glorious might, for all endurance and patience with joy, giving thanks to the Father... Colossians 1:9-12a (ESV)

We are even invited as a nation to take our requests to the Lord. (Isaiah 65:1) With humility and repentance we lift our nation up as a concern of our heart to the Lord.

And the results of this continual casting of our burdens and anxieties upon the Lord is the following verse. *7 And the peace of God, which surpasses all understanding, will guard your hearts and your minds in Christ Jesus.* Our dependency upon God brings us the peace of God. It is not peace like the world experiences, a peace that is absent of conflict. It is much greater than that. It is the peace that can remain through any storm, even in the middle of it. It is God's own peace. (John 14:27)
God inhabits the Eternal Now, present in every moment of time, involved in it all at once. He knows the future like it was the past. He's always experiencing it. If He says it will be then you can be certain that it will be. Talk about surpassing our understanding, it puts me in awe to just talk about it.

This peace is the very presence of the Lord in our life assuring us that He has it all under control. It will all turn out to be a blessing in the end. We can't see how. We don't need to. All we need to know is that it's in His hands and those hands are all-powerful. (Daniel 4:35)

That is the peace that will keep, or guard, our minds. You see, it is the turmoil of the mind that pulls us out of that peace. We start to imagine scenarios. We entertain fear. We dwell on past conflicts. All of these are dealt with when we take it to the Lord in prayer. The peace that God gives guards our mind from the turmoil that keeps us from rejoicing. (Acts 16:25)

We started this morning with unity. We moved to the topic of rejoicing, and have concluded with the peace that comes when we take our anxiety to the Lord in prayer. They are completely interconnected with the situation that was happening with the Philippian church. They needed to rejoice in the Lord to get focused on the eternal. They then needed to cast on the Lord the concern for the differences that sprang up. (1Peter 5:7) With the joy of the Lord in their hearts and His peace in their minds, there is bound to be unity, one Spirit, and one mind.

This is the true unity God desires for the church. Not that we all are forced to think the same. We don't need to be brainwashed. We need the mind of Christ. We need to see things as they really are. We need to focus on the One that matters, our Savior. Rejoicing in the Lord and prayer that brings the peace of God is the path to that unity that overrides minor differences that so often plague the church.

May we as individuals and as a church live out this passage in the years to come. May we be known as the joyful church because we are always rejoicing in the Lord, and because Jesus has become our sole focus. May we be the ones that have a peace that comes from continually letting our requests be known to God in prayer, experiencing His own divine peace. And may our joy and peace result in a holy unity that attracts others to our Lord and Savior Jesus!

Questions
1 What do you get to take to heaven?
2 How do factions form in church?
3 What does "agree in the Lord" mean?
4 What does this say about a woman's role in the church?
5 What gift is needed in times of conflict?
6 Why do we rejoice? How does this bring unity?
7 Why shouldn't we be anxious about anything?
8 What do we do with anxiety?
9 What is the result?
10 How does peace guard our mind?
11 How does joy and peace result in unity?

Thought Life Philippians 4:8-9

Paul had just entreated two important women in the church to get past their differences. Euodia and Syntyche needed to agree in the Lord to keep division from infiltrating the church. Paul went on to exhort the whole church to rejoice in the Lord. He told them to take their concerns to the Lord in prayer and allow God's peace to guard their hearts and minds in Christ. Our passage today continues with the thought of guarding our hearts and minds in Christ. It is another of the great passages in this letter that is well worth memorizing! *⁸ Finally, brothers, whatever is true, whatever is honorable, whatever is just, whatever is pure, whatever is lovely, whatever is commendable, if there is any excellence, if there is anything worthy of praise, think about these things.* Philippians 4:8 (ESV)

This simple instruction is the way to be the joyful believer that Paul is instructing us to be. The great majority of our struggles with attitude come from not taking charge of our thought life.

When I approached the time to prepare this sermon, I had just come back from vacation. My mind had been wandering to some painful broken relationships and how hard it was when faced with an ultimatum to compromise convictions or end a relationship. I had just enjoyed a blessed time with my family and should have been overflowing with joy, but instead, I was becoming depressed. I wasn't practicing what Paul said was his one important action, to forget what is behind and strain toward the prize, the upward calling of Christ in God. (3:13) But then I looked at this passage and realized what was happening. I was allowing myself to be spiritually defeated when the victory was mine if I would just make one simple choice, to think on what is good.

Suddenly, I did what we call in wrestling, a reversal. The enemy had me in a hold and I turned it around and put him in one. When speaking of spiritual warfare, Paul told the Corinthians to *take every thought captive to obey Christ,* 2 Corinthians 10:5b (ESV) I took my thoughts captive and my attitude went from depression to joy, from whining to praise, from defeat to victory.

It's not always that easy. Sometimes we go through unexplainable hardship that is so painful that it seems to be impossible to take our thoughts captive. The battle goes on for a much longer time; but if we will endure, the victory will be ours. The longer the battle the greater the lessons learned and the more our faith will grow. The vast majority of the time it is as simple as just choosing to dwell on what is good.

Paul starts his list with another "finally". If you recall, he used that word at the beginning of chapter 3. This time he really is wrapping things up, and he does so with this list of things to think about. Let's examine each expression.

Think on *whatever is true*... The Word of God is truth. (Psalm 119:160; Proverbs 30:5) The words of Jesus are true. Jesus said that He came to testify to the truth and that everyone on the side of truth listens to

Him. (John 18:37) God cannot lie. (Numbers 23:19) His word will always prove true. I may think it has failed, but that is because I am so limited in my understanding. When I apply the Word that comes with a promise, I should expect to see the promise come to pass in God's time. If I find my thinking in contradiction to the Word of truth, then I must adjust my thinking. It is not ignoring reality, but rather conforming my thinking to the reality of the Word, the ultimate reality. I guarantee you that if you apply the Word with its proper meaning in its context, then you will see that it is true.

Much of our mindset and attitude depend on our interpretation of events. It is amazing how two people can see the same event and come up with a completely different perspective. When we went through Mexican security at the airport, they took away Kaiden's favorite toy, little rubber missiles that you dive for in a pool. His dad saw an unreasonable request. I would too if I were Kaiden's daddy. I saw God teaching Kaiden to hold on to things of this world lightly. Ed saw the potential of Kaiden being untrusting of people in uniform.

Think in terms of the truth of the Word. Is there a Scripture that applies? "Submit to those in authority." (Romans 13:1) If I see my submission to authority as obedience to God who I love, my whole attitude toward the situation changes. It becomes a teaching opportunity for my grandson. It may be too difficult to understand at the moment, but the Word of God has brought truth to the situation and changed our attitude and guided our thoughts. Interpret your situations in life through the lens of the Word of God, and you will be thinking on what is true.

Think on *whatever is honorable...* NIV uses the word "noble". I believe this should be in consideration of our own behavior and also to notice that which is honorable around us. In relationship to our own behavior, we should ask ourselves how we can act in a way that honors God. (Romans 13:13-14) Peter exhorted the church to *12 Keep your conduct among the Gentiles honorable, so that when they speak against you as evildoers, they may see your good deeds and glorify God on the day of visitation.* 1Peter 2:12 (ESV) Because we represent Christ, we should be honorable in everything we do. If we are not, because of some cost to us, those who feel cheated will point to our faith and either say that it does not have the power to change lives or that it a false belief. Our witness is sullied.

Doing what is right does not mean being a doormat, but rather being honest no matter the cost.

The world is rarely honest in its dealings. I could give you a dozen examples, but Paul just told us not to think on those things, so I'll refuse the temptation. Don't we just love to go over injustices, as if we were somehow getting even?

When people are dishonest with us we have the tendency to play it again and again in our mind. The result is a poisonous bitterness that only hurts us. They have most likely forgotten the deed and gone on to be dishonest with someone else. We only hurt ourselves when we think on the dishonesty of others. We can certainly learn a lesson and not be fooled twice, but refuse to dwell on the dishonest act.

Instead look for noble actions and think about those. Think about the time when others went out of their way to be kind to you. Think of those who stand their ground for Christ even when it costs them a great deal. Think about the testimonies of great men and women of God who lived nobly. (Titus 2:7; Philippians 2:29)

Think about *whatever is just*... This means to be a person who deals equitably with others. Sometimes the word is translated "righteous" or "upright". This is a qualification for elders. (Titus 1:8) Once again this applies to our own behavior and when thinking of others' behavior. It is similar to the word honorable, but more along the lines of being holy. (Luke 2:25) What would God think of your action? You can be honest but not be righteous. This means we must be sure our hearts are open to God's direction and correction. We should think about whether our behavior and attitude is pleasing to God or not. (Colossians 1:10)

When we see holiness in others, a heart that is sensitive to being obedient to the Holy Spirit, we should take note of it. We should contemplate the fruit of that life and observe how they cultivate that sensitivity. Think on the righteous acts of others. Paul already encouraged them to do this in the last chapter. (Philippians 3:17)

Think about *whatever is pure*... Our world is fallen and therefor filled with the impure. If we dwell on evil for long, or even that which infiltrates the good and corrupts, we will soon be discouraged. But we know that what is pure will endure. What is pure will prevail in the end.

The enemy of your soul wants to engulf your thoughts with the impure. Pornography is one of his favorite weapons in our time. If he can fill your mind with idols that promise satisfaction but are only a cheap counterfeit, he can keep you from dwelling on the pure word of God which is your weapon to defeat him. (Hebrews 4:12; Ephesians 6:17)

This battle for the high ground of the mind is one that takes constant vigilance. If we let down our guard for a moment, our thoughts can be overwhelmed and thoughts become patterns that eventually spill over into behavior.

Instead, fill your thoughts with the pure word of God. (Psalm 19:8) The Word helps you see what is real and lasting. It unmasks the deceit of temptation. It strengthens you for the battle and arms you. Watch what you watch, but even more importantly, guard what you dwell on. Be sure it is pure. (Titus 2:14) Develop a habit of rejecting impure thoughts.

Think about *whatever is lovely*... Used only here in the New Testament, this is a compound word that means "brotherly love toward". So rather than to think of an object like a lovely flower, we should think in terms of loving acts. How can we show love? Jesus told us we are to love one another. (John 13:35) It would then behoove us to think about how we can do that. It would be good to note those acts in others. If the church is anything, it is to be about love for God and for one another. If we don't have that we are not a church of Jesus Christ. We need to think about how we can accept the love of God for one another.

Think about *whatever is commendable...* There is obviously some overlap with these terms, and yet each is bringing out a subtle difference. All the previous qualities are commendable, but now Paul is saying to think on anything commendable. It doesn't have to fall into one of the other categories. It may not be a noble or righteous act, or an act of love, but it is a good thing that you should imitate or encourage in others. It is commendable to examine our hearts. It is commendable to read the Word. It is commendable to help a neighbor or to forgive an offense. Think about what you could do that is an example for others to follow.

Instead of dwelling on acts that others should not follow, dwell on the good acts of others that you might demonstrate in your own life as well. We can dwell on that bad driver that cut you off, or we can drive courteously. Which is going to be more joyful? Which will put you in the right frame of mind?

These are the things we should dwell on. These are the qualities we should nurture and encourage in one another. These are the guidelines for our thought life. Paul adds, *if there is any excellence, if there is anything worthy of praise, think about these things.* If we see some excellent or virtuous thing, or something worthy of praise, we should grab hold of that action or thought and dwell on it. What a joy filled, thankful example we will become to others when we apply this instruction!

Can you picture a church filled with people that only think on excellent, praiseworthy things? What an attractive group of people we would be. Can we do it? If God asks it of us, He will surely provide the power and help to see it come to pass in our lives, if we are willing to let Him reign in us.

Our problem is we are so used to the worlds' way of dwelling on the negative that we must make a concerted effort to allow God to have His way in our thought life. We are here to let the Word of God challenge and transform us. I want to challenge all of us to memorize verses 4 through 8 and make a concerted effort to live them. In the weeks to come, if you have a testimony of how it turned around your attitude and actions, please let me know.

We have one big problem – our thought life! I'm concerned that the church today is so caught up in passing politics and opinions of minor doctrine and even being accepted by our peers in the world that we don't stand out as the joyful example God means us to be.

All of these virtues we've looked at describe Jesus. He is the One that's true! He is entirely honorable, always just, completely pure, altogether lovely. He alone is excellent and worthy of all our praise! Turn your eyes upon Jesus! If the world is going to see Him, they need to see Him in us who claim that He lives in us. Let's let God change it so we can be a witness of our awesome Lord who is our life. (Colossians 3:2-4)

I know we can do it because Paul did it. That is what Paul is saying in the next verse. You saw it lived out in me. Now you do it. If a former Christian killer can do it, by the grace of God, you can too! *9 What you have learned and received and heard and seen in me—practice these things, and the God of peace will be with you.* Philippians 4:9 (ESV) Paul not only taught it, but he lived it. He promises that if you do, that great promise that God gave to Moses (Exodus 3:12) and Joshua (Joshua 1:5) will be yours as well. The God of peace will be with you.

Now who doesn't want to live in perfect, unshakeable peace? I know I want it! So what do we have to do? Think on, take account of, the things that are true, just, honorable, pure, lovely, commendable, all virtuous and excellent things! Take control of your thought life and watch your attitude change and the peace of God take over.

All of us struggle with concerns and anxiety to some extent, but this message is especially for those of us who allow worry to overwhelm our life! You don't need to live a life of worry and dread. God has peace for you if you will discipline your thought life to remain in the boundaries Paul has described for us here. He isn't saying to ignore the problems. In the previous verses he told us to take them to God. It isn't that you pretend there aren't deadlines and problems, but rather that you dwell on the good and not the problems. God's peace is waiting for you to enter in each and every moment of each and every day. It's your choice.

Don't allow your thought life run wild. Tame it with the Word of God. Take your anxieties to the Lord, think on what is good, and be at peace!

Questions
1 How did the chapter begin?
2 What is the benefit of a long struggle?
3 List the things we are to contemplate and a short definition of each:
4 What do all these describe?
5 What is the promise if we do this?
6 Is it really possible?
7 Will you let God's Word change you?

Contentment Philippians 4:10-13

I would like to remind you of the challenge to memorize and apply Philippians 4:4-8 to your life on a constant basis. When we read the Word of God, one of the techniques we should employ is to be watching for eternal truth that we can apply to our lives. We are to think on what is true. These are principles and promises that apply to everyone in every age. They are timeless words of wisdom that when applied bring the promised results. The world says there are no absolutes. The very statement is silly because it contradicts its own claim. It is claiming there is one absolute, that there are none, and if there are none, then it is not one. The world is rapidly losing its sense of reason.

In the verses I challenged you to memorize, we saw a promise of God. If you refuse to let anxiety take hold of your heart and mind by taking your requests to God, then the peace of God will guard your heart and mind! That is truth! Do you believe it? Even if you don't, if you diligently apply it, you'll discover that it is true!

Paul goes on to explain that we should capture our thought life (2Corinthains 10:5) and think on what is true, honorable, just, pure, lovely, commendable, excellent and praiseworthy. He tells them to follow the pattern of life they saw in him, which I understand to be what he has just described, and repeats the promise. (4:9) The God of peace will be with you. Do you believe it? If you really do, and you desire to live a life free of anxiety, abiding in the peace of God, then you will, by the Holy Spirit's enabling power, live what Paul taught and exemplified.

You certainly can't do it on your own. You must be surrendered to Jesus and willing to obey the leading of His Holy Spirit. (Romans 8:13) The world tries through sheer grit and determination to think positive thoughts. That is helpful, but it doesn't bring the peace of God. It may settle a disturbed mind for a time, but it doesn't invite the God of peace to be with them. Paul told us in the letter to the Romans that we are controlled by the flesh or by the Spirit. If you are controlled by the Spirit, you are a son of God and the power that raised Christ from the dead gives life to your mortal body! (3:10) He goes on to say that because we have this power of the Spirit we can put to death the misdeeds of the body. (Romans 8:9-11) We can, if we will to do so, because we have been enabled to do it. That is the declaration of Romans 8. Do you believe it?

So, let me ask, can you have the peace of God? "Well, Pastor, you don't understand, I have this and that and a long litany of things that are exactly what Philippians 4:8 tells me not to think about… and I take it to God in prayer but I just don't have peace." What that tells me is that you refuse to leave it with God, for the promise is that if you do then you will have His peace. Could it be that in those times we trust self more than we trust God? After all, it shows we feel the need to continue to worry about it instead of letting God deal with it. Believe the Word of God! It is His love letter to you! It will guide your steps and give you life! It never fails. (Proverbs 30:5)

The passage for today follows along with the same thought about living in the peace of God, following Paul's example. It speaks to every believer since it was written. *10 I rejoiced in the Lord greatly that now at length you have revived your concern for me. You were indeed concerned for me, but you had no opportunity.* The Philippian church was a source of support for Paul's ministry. Epaphroditus had brought the financial gift to where Paul was incarcerated because people who Rome imprisoned had to pay for their own food. Paul rented the house where he was held prisoner. (Acts 28:30)

In the letter to the Corinthians, chapter nine, he explains that those in fulltime ministry should be supported by those to whom they minister. (1Corinthians 9:11) Yet, in the case of the Corinthian church, he felt it would stumble the Corinthians. So, he refused to let them help him financially. Instead, he worked while in Corinth to support himself. (9:12) Paul's trade was tent making. He received support from some of the churches he founded because he had apparently spent his family's wealth financing his own missionary journeys. (2Corinthians 8:1-5)

We are a mission minded church and help to support a number of mission works. The Connors in Mongolia are just about to finish their translation of a Bible study from Genesis to Revelation. (Firm Foundations by New Tribes Missions) They have also provided gers (Mongolian house tent) for needy families. Ken Holcomb told us last week of his efforts helping Spanish speaking churches reach out as short term missionaries. The India Evangelical Mission is one of my favorites. It has a free Bible College to train native Indians from the various states of India to be pastors and evangelists. It also has a childrens' home of 150. We help support someone who came from this church that leads part time missions around the world, Clair Loungevan, as well as a pastor of a small Canadian church. We also give to the Walker's mission in Botswana that trains up local missionaries and oversees their outreach to unreached villages. We give to Wycliffe translators who are trying to finish translating the Bible into every dialect by the year 2025. In addition we give locally to Sonshine Rescue Mission outreach to the homeless in Flagstaff, Young Life's outreach to the Jr. and Sr. High locally, and Pastor Ed's work of chaplain for the police department and counseling those who cannot afford to pay.

All of these mission endeavors are reaching people with the good news of Jesus Christ. As the Philippians partnered with Paul to make his ministry possible, so we partner with all of these different ministries, to advance the kingdom of God locally and around the world. By sharing in their support, we make what they do possible, and that means sharing in the heavenly reward. We look for opportunities to help where our financial support can do the most to advance God's kingdom and show the love of God around the world. That means occasionally adjusting whom we support and one-time special gifts where there is a need or opportunity, like our recent gift to get Bibles into a country closed to the Gospel.

Paul goes on to say, *11 Not that I am speaking of being in need, for I have learned in whatever situation I am to be content.* Paul wasn't joyful merely because he had the finances to pay for his expenses, but for the fact that it showed their love for him and spiritual health. (4:17) He was content as he was.

Paul write in another passage, *6 Now there is great gain in godliness with contentment, 7 for we brought nothing into the world, and we cannot take anything out of the world. 8 But if we have food and clothing, with these we will be content.* 1 Timothy 6:6-8 (ESV) Paul learned the secret of contentment. Sometimes he had nothing and even went hungry. Sometimes he had a large gift to take to others in need. Either way, he trusted in God for His physical necessities and found his heart's longing, and need for security, met in Christ. (2Corinthians 11:24-27)

There is one main reason for the discontent we see in the world around us and in our own hearts. It comes from trying to fill the void in our heart with something other than Jesus. When we haven't found a deep and satisfying relationship with Jesus that fills our hearts with joy like a fountain that never stops gushing, we will look for something else to fill the emptiness. Nothing else will. Everything else leaves us in a state of discontent. (Hebrews 12:1-2)

The problem was stated clearly by Jesus. If any man will save his life, he will lose it, but whoever loses his life for my sake, will find it. (Matthew 16:25) That relationship begins with abandoning yourself to Jesus. We give up control of our life and surrender to Him. It is a death to the old self and self-rule. It's a leap of faith. But you can't remain lord of your life and accept Him as Lord too. No man can serve two masters. (Matthew 6:24) And so we writhe in this state of discontent, trying to fill our hearts with the creation rather than the Creator. Every man and woman's heart will be discontent without the presence of the Creator.

Even believers that have known the life of Christ within can experience a lack of contentment. The world keeps telling us we need this thing or that thing and we start to focus on those things to the neglect of our relationship with Jesus. Just like a couple that can grow apart because busyness, or lack of expressions of love and times of intimacy, so believers can grow apart from God. (Ephesians 5:32) The solution is the same in both cases. Repent and restore what has been neglected.

Some believers even allow a sense of discontent to sneak in because of the particular calling God has given them. Numerical success is a worldly standard. We hear testimonies of "successful" believers and wonder why we aren't used to accomplish more. I think the vast majority of pastors struggle with the size of their congregation. We want to be successful and respected for our efforts, but what we need to realize is God's version of success is faithfulness, not numbers. Fruitfulness is not measured in numbers.

The Stoics of Paul's day boasted of contentment but it was contentment of independence rather than total dependence. They would have never been content with humiliation, which was first on their list of things to avoid. (See Kent Hughes, *Preaching the Word*, Chapter 21 Content in Christ) But Paul could say that he, like Christ, could be content in humiliation. (2:8)

Independence is taking things into our own hands instead of trusting God. Faith is all about dependence upon God. It doesn't matter what type of job you are given, work can be worship. (Play the video clip – Work as Worship) When we are experiencing a deep and abiding relationship with God we trust that, our station in life, our particular calling, our relationship with others, is all in God's hands. He can change it or direct us clearly to something else if He chooses.

We are content in Him, knowing that success is faithfulness to Him. By faithfulness I don't just mean doing what He asks, which is part of it, but also faithful as in the faithfulness of a wedded partner to love Him alone.

12 I know how to be brought low, and I know how to abound. In any and every circumstance, I have learned the secret of facing plenty and hunger, abundance and need. Paul trusted God completely for the circumstances in His life. He could be bobbing in the ocean for a day and a night, beaten and in stocks in a prison dungeon, carrying a large financial gift to the needy in Jerusalem, or seeing a church form in a place that never heard the Gospel. As long as he knew He was being faithful to the lover of his soul, he was content.

If anyone had the right to question God's dealings and wonder why God didn't intervene, it was Paul. He was stoned and left for dead. His most effective years for the kingdom were in prison where he wrote these letters that are encouraging us. But even there he saw the situation through God's eyes and saw the opportunity to reach the palace guard. (1:12-14) He could be content because he looked for what God was doing, and even when he didn't understand, he trusted God. He trusted right up to the day of his beheading and at that moment he saw the One he had seen once before on the road to Damascus, the risen Lord, saying, "Well done good and faithful servant. Enter into the joy of the Lord."

He could say from personal experience, *13 I can do all things through him who strengthens me.* This is one of those verses that we use out of context quite frequently. It's not that it doesn't apply to other things God calls us to do, but here it is specifically about going through anything God allows to come our way. It is recognizing that whatever life throws at us is really what God has allowed for our good. So instead of whining about it, he looked for what God was doing through it and took it as being from the hand of God. He received the power of God to face each situation. (Colossians 1:28-29)

Why could he face all the things that we cringe at just reading about? Someone strengthened him. (2Corinthians 12:9-10) That power I spoke of earlier, that he had written about, was not some abstract theological idea but a reality in his life. Resurrection power was enabling him to face the abundance and the depravation with contentment. (2Corinthians 6:4-5) God always gave him food and clothing, and we are promised that as well, if we seek first the kingdom of God. (Matthew 6:33-34) He faced times of hunger, but God always came through or we wouldn't have this letter. (1Corinthians 4:11-13)

Food and clothing are all a physical body really needs, right? That is a profound thought! What else to you really need? Our body needs food and clothes and our soul needs Jesus. So can you be content with that? Food and clothes for the body and Jesus for the soul is the sum total of our needs. Most of us have so much more. How generous we should be?

Just as important as contentment in poverty is contentment in abundance. It may be even more difficult to experience contentment that doesn't demand the abundance continue but can just enjoy it as a temporary physical gift of God. It takes the power of God to not let abundance capture our hearts.

Now, so that you don't misunderstand the message, I'm not criticizing profitable business or savings or insurance. How else do we have the finances to help the missions like those who helped Paul. I'm not saying that becoming wealthy is evil. It is all a matter of the heart. (1 Timothy 6:9-10; Psalm 62:10)) Some are called to be successful financially so that they can give. We are all called to work to support our family and to give to those who have needs. (Ephesians 4:28) We are told to look to the state of our herds and consider the ant that stores up for winter. (Proverbs 27:23; 6:6) The issue is whether or not we are trying to make those physical things our security and the source of our contentment. (Ecclesiastes 5:10)

The physical will never satisfy the heart. People have spent their whole life trying and die unfulfilled. Drugs only provide a temporary counterfeit feeling. Some realize it is a spiritual need and begin seeking out a spiritual path. Jesus said, "I am the way." He's the way to God who fills that longing in our heart. He put that longing there to lead us to Him. The secret to contentment is abandoning ourselves in love to our Savior and being faithful in our relationship to Him. Then, it doesn't matter what comes our way, what happens to our society, whether we have millions or are penniless, our heart will be content.

Buddhists call it the lack of all desire, but for Christians it is being engulfed in one great desire, to know Jesus more intimately today than yesterday. We long to see His face and hear His voice say to us, "Well done, good and faithful servant. Enter into my joy!"

Questions
1 What should we look for when we read the Bible? Why?
2 Why was Paul grateful to the Philippians?
3 How do we do the same?
4 What was Paul's secret?
5 Why are we discontent?
6 How did Jesus state the problem?
7 What is the difference between Stoic contentment and Biblical contentment?
8 Why do believer lack contentment?
9 What is Paul's example of contentment?
10 Is wealth evil? What's the focus?
11 Are you content?

Partnership Philippians 4:14-23

Last week we looked at the previous passage and found that the phrase, "I can do all things through Christ who strengthens me", does not mean we can bench press 500 pounds. Nor does it mean that we can resolve any conflict. The context was in regards to being content in poverty or abundance because of the strength we have in Christ. (4:12) We can face any situation in life through Christ's enabling power. That makes all the difference in our current economic downturn. Believers who are in Christ have the strength to go through their situation with contentment. There is a peace and joy that is a witness to the world of the difference we have in Christ.

Our secret is not just knowing Christ, but being *in* Christ. (1:1) We can know Christ and yet be in our old nature. We can respond to our circumstances in the Spirit (which is in Christ) or in our carnal nature. (Romans 8:13) The believer gets to choose. The unbeliever only has the old nature to rely on. The old nature can grin and bear it only so long. It has no external power source to turn to. The believer turns to Christ and is empowered with the strength and joy He gives. The situation is not necessarily changed, but our attitude certainly is. That is the noticeable difference that those who are controlled by the Spirit exhibit to the world. (Romans 8:9)

In today's passage Paul continues his words of thanks to the Philippians for the gift that they sent. Paul had just thanked them, but added that he was content even without their financial support. *14 Yet it was kind of you to share my trouble.* He appreciated the kindness of these brothers and sisters in Christ as much as the gift. It was an expression of their love. (2Corinthians 8:3-5) We often hear the phrase that it is the thought that counts. Sometimes the thought behind the gift is more heartwarming than the gift itself.

An expanded translation of the Greek is that they partnered or shared with him in the pressure of his imprisonment. The presence of Epaphras was as much a participation in the pressure as the financial gift, nevertheless, he did have a financial need to pay for his food and the housing.

The next verses tells us that the Philippians had been generous like this before.*15 And you Philippians yourselves know that in the beginning of the gospel, when I left Macedonia, no church entered into partnership with me in giving and receiving, except you only. 16 Even in Thessalonica you sent me help for my needs once and again.* When the church first began there in Philippi, they saw the need to support Paul's ministry. Paul had told the Corinthian church that it was only right that the laborer receive wages. The one who plants eats of the crops. If he had sown spiritually into their lives then it was only right that he be rewarded with his physical necessities. (1Corinthians 9:11-12) The workman is worthy of his wages. In other words, he earns his wages because of the labor he exerts. (Luke 10:7)

That is not to excuse those who would be rich from their particular ministry. Paul was speaking of his necessities, food, clothing, and shelter. He even refused to receive support from the Corinthian church because he knew some would be offended by it. (1Corinthians 9:12) The advancement of the Gospel was far more important to Paul than his physical comfort or financial support. He was daily dying to self to fulfill his calling. (1Corinthians 15:31) Those who use ministry simply to enrich themselves will answer to God. (2Peter 2:3)

Paul used a word in this verse that he just used in the last verse, partnership. He considered their financial gift a partnership with him. It comes from that word we are familiar with, *koinonea*. They fellowship with him through their giving. Missionaries often use the term when raising support. They ask if you will partner with them. It is very Scriptural to express financial support in those terms.

Last week I shared with you the various ministries we partner with. Don't downplay the importance of being a financial partner. We make works like Young Life and Sonshine Rescue Mission possible. The souls they win to Christ, the lives they see transformed are a part of your giving ministry. We team up with them and make it possible. Long ago I thought it was a compromise to tell people that not everyone was called to be a missionary, but that they could   participate in the Great Commission by giving. That we actually do partner with the evangelist or missionary is evident by the wording in this verse.

That does not mean that we don't need to share Christ with those God places in our life. Our joy and peace should be so evident that people ask why we are different. We are to always be prepared to tell them of the hope within us. (1Peter 3:15) We should actively watch and pray for opportunities to share.

You have faithfully partnered with me in giving and receiving just as they did with the Apostle Paul. In providing my necessities you enable me to study and pray about what to share each week. You are a partner in the ministry of my books and web site that reach out to thousands every month. We will share our heavenly reward because of our partnership in the Gospel. (Matthew 10:41-42) Thank you! How generous and faithful you have been. Some have worried about a downturn in the finances of the church because of the economic situation, but you have been so faithful that we have never lacked!

Just last week the board decided to do some significant repairs to the parking and painting. The office needed to update the computer. It amounted to a significant sum, and before we could spend it, more than that amount was donated. Praise God! Thank you for your willingness to partner with Wayside Bible Chapel in its many ministries. Our goal is to partner with others where the finances will be used most efficiently in advancing the Gospel both here and around the world.

17 Not that I seek the gift, but I seek the fruit that increases to your credit. Paul wanted to make sure that they understand that it isn't the money that thrills his heart. Their partnership with him makes it possible for him to reach more and increases their heavenly reward. God is just. He keeps track of every act and gift and will reward what is done at the leading of the Spirit. (Matthew 6:19-20) We don't give to get a reward, but God promises He will reward our Spirit directed giving. It may not be in this life, though I've found it true that you can't out give God. The reward is even better if it is in eternity. The interest accrued is much better there. We give because we love Him and in obedience to the gentle prompting of His Spirit. It is a joy to give, and really, we are just giving back, for everything comes from Him. (1Corinthians 4:7) Still, God graciously promises to credit our heavenly account. He's the best! (Luke 6:38)

In a practical sense, Paul needed financial support, but he sought fruit that increases to their credit. Every mentor understands this priority. We are thrilled when we see spiritual growth in those with whom we've been sharing. It is incomparably more encouraging than any gift we might receive from them for the investment of our time.

18 I have received full payment, and more. I am well supplied, having received from Epaphroditus the gifts you sent, a fragrant offering, a sacrifice acceptable and pleasing to God. I can say the same. Wasn't it great to hear the Holcombs say they were fully funded and didn't want an offering to go to them but the children's mission in Mexicalli? That just thrilled my heart!

Epaphrus had brought a financial sum. There were some wealthy people in the church, like the merchant Lydia and the centurion that kept the prison. It was probably a sizable gift. Some had probably sacrificed to give even to the point of lacking their own necessities. Paul called it a fragrant offering. The Jews had certain offerings prescribed in the Old Testament as the burnt offering or fragrant offerings. (Exodus 29:18) Paul saw these financial gifts in a similar way, sacrificial giving that was not only acceptable, but pleasing to God.

Have you sensed God's pleasure in something you did, or in giving? (Romans 12:1) I sense it most when I find myself doing something I would rather not do, but deny myself and do it because I know God wants me to. Oh what a feeling! I think that feeling is part of the reward. (Hebrews 13:16) The work that we do because of guilt or arm twisting doesn't give us that same sense of God's pleasure. It just wears us out. But when we sense God's pleasure we are energized!

Now we come to one of those famous Philippian verses that so many have committed to memory but is so often used in a way that is separated from the context of the passage. *19 And my God will supply every need of yours according to his riches in glory in Christ Jesus.* Besides a doxology and greeting, this is Paul's closing thought. When the church denies self to give sacrificially to partner in advancing the Kingdom of God in obedience to the leading of the Holy Spirit, God will supply our every need.

Just like verse 13 is misused to say I can do anything I set my mind to, so this verse is used to say Christians will never suffer lack. Yet Paul tells us several times in his letters that he went hungry and was homeless. (1Corinthians 4:11) It does not change the fact that the Lord is our Shepherd. (Psalm 23:1), or that He is able to provide our needs. (2Corinthians 9:8) Paul did not starve or die of exposure. Remember, food and clothes is all we need to be physically content.

There is a big difference between need and want. God doesn't promise to give us what we want. (James 4:3) That would often be detrimental to our eternal good. If we need a time of hunger, he'll provide it. If we need a time of rest, He can provide that as well. This is the life of complete trust in God. We should certainly do all that we can to live within our means and work so that we have something to share with those in need, and to give to the work of the Lord. (Ephesians 4:28) But we should not trust in those riches. (1Timothy 6:17) And when the work is not available, nothing changes, for we are still trusting in God who is our provider, our Jehovah Jireh.

I can tell you story after story of miraculous provision in my own life and the lives of friends. Mac recently told me about running out of money and food on the mission field in Botswana and being invited the next day to a wedding which is an all-day feast. When we give sacrificially to the work of the Lord, Paul declares that all our need will be met in Christ Jesus. Jesus told us that the world worries about food and clothes, but we are to remember that He clothes the flowers of the field and feeds the birds of the air. (Matthew 6:30-33) He promised that if you seek the Kingdom of God first, then those necessities will be given to you.

One of the missionaries we sponsor is brother Binu in India. We give him about $90 a month for his family. I think we should raise it quite a bit next year. I can tell you that when I see him, he is always filled with joy. How is that possible? He has all he needs in Christ Jesus!

There is another way to read this verse that we tend to overlook. All our need is met in Jesus. Need is singular. Our one need is Jesus. In Him is all. He is the great necessity of life. He is our provider. He is where we find God's riches in glory. He is what our spirit, soul, and body needs. He should be everything to us. Giving as He leads should be a wonderful privilege. We do not worry about whether we have enough or not, because if He leads us to give then He knows what is coming. It's by faith because we can't see it yet, but we know He does.

I know many of you are very concerned about the economic future of our nation. We certainly are in a mess because we have ignored some very basic Biblical principles. But you have no need to worry about tomorrow. If you are putting the Kingdom of God first in your life, if you are generous in giving as God leads, then all your need will be met in Jesus. You may have nothing, but all your need will be met. You may have the opportunity to fast, but all your need will be met in Jesus. Be at peace in Him.

Sometimes I'm asked why I don't preach on tithing. When we get to a passage, I preach on that passage. 10% is a great guideline, but don't let it keep you from being led by the Spirit to joyfully partner with ministries and receive fruit credited to your account. Give as the Lord leads.

Here is Paul's simple benediction to close this letter. *20 To our God and Father be glory forever and ever. Amen.* This is what this world and our life is all about, the glory of our God and Father. Every blessing we receive is because of His glory. The whole earth is filled with His glory. Eternity is filled with His glory! His glory is the outshining of His attributes.

Then Paul adds a final greeting from the family of God in Rome to the brother and sisters in Philippi. *21 Greet every saint in Christ Jesus. The brothers who are with me greet you. 22 All the saints greet you, especially those of Caesar's household.* As Paul had said in the beginning of the letter, he did not want them to feel bad about his imprisonment, for the Word was going out to the Palace Guard. (1:13) Caesar's household had believers in Jesus. We are one huge family that now covers the planet. We love one another because we are the family of God that loves our Savior, Jesus.

And one more line of benediction, *23 The grace of the Lord Jesus Christ be with your spirit.* If there is grace in your spirit, then there can be grace in your soul and body. The Christian that walks in the spirit is directed (controlled) by the Spirit of God within their spirit. (Romans 8:14) That is our source of direction and discernment. It is where our joy and peace reside, and from there it overflows into the rest of our being.

What an awesome letter! Let me conclude as Paul did. Because of your partnership with God's ministers, my God will supply all your need according to His riches in glory in Christ Jesus. To our God and Father be glory forever and ever. The grace of the Lord Jesus Christ be with your spirit. Amen!

Questions
1 What's our secret?
2 How was Paul supported?
3 What is implied by "partnership"?
4 What does it mean in heaven?
5 Have you sensed God's pleasure?
6 What is the context for verse 19?
7 What does verse 19 mean?
8 Might a time of hunger be a need?
9 Why should we be at peace if we are in Jesus?
10 What is all eternity about?

Philippian Highlights

Many of you have heard of the Air Force study that concluded that within 72 hours of a lecture, the students have forgotten 90% of what they heard. That is why our Sunday morning Bible study is reviewing the sermon from the previous week. That is why the message today is a review of this inspiring letter to the Philippian church. We want to retain and practice the eternal truths we found in it.

We saw that the glue that held the church together was their common love for Jesus and that includes His body, your fellow believers. (Ephesians 5:30) Paul had founded this church in a town of 10,000 when a vision sent him to Macedonia. (Acts 16:9) He met a group of women worshiping by the river and after sharing Christ with them, Lydia became the first believer. (Acts 16:14) Then after the miraculous jail shaking, the Philippian jailor was converted with his whole house. (Acts 16:34) The church that was formed partnered with Paul in his ministry by sending financial support to him via the hands of Epaphrodites.

The first golden nugget we came across was the promise in 1:6 that God will complete the work he has begun in us. *6 And I am sure of this, that he who began a good work in you will bring it to completion at the day of Jesus Christ.* 1:6 (ESV) The letter holds in tension the dual reality that we are already citizens of heaven, and yet the work in us is not complete. Everyone that has ever had a conflict with a fellow believer should say, "Amen!" But our hope is in this promise that we will be complete. If God can complete the work in me, then He can do it in every believer, because I need as much work as anyone! Part of the joy of heaven is that the work in everyone there will be completed. Everyone will be Christ like. (1Corinthians 1:8)

Then Paul shared his prayer for them. *9 And it is my prayer that your love may abound more and more, with knowledge and all discernment, 10 so that you may approve what is excellent, and so be pure and blameless for the day of Christ, 11 filled with the fruit of righteousness that comes through Jesus Christ, to the glory and praise of God.* 1:9-11 (ESV) His first request is for an abounding increase in their love, the glue that held the church together. He doesn't say whether that love is for God or for man, but he doesn't need to. Love for God results in love for one another. Without saying which, he implied both.

Knowledge of God and His word refer to how we practice our love for God. We can't love God unless we know from His word, who He is, and what He is really about. The more we know Him, the more we will love Him. (1John 4:11) The more we love Him, the more we will love those made in His image even though that image is not yet restored. His love in us compels us to love one another.

He wanted their love to abound with knowledge and discernment so they would choose what was excellent in God's eyes. Love that comes with knowledge and discernment turns us away from what is evil and selfish and to what is pure and blameless. The fruit of righteousness brings glory to God. God is about the work of restoring His image in us, finishing that work He started. We often get wrapped up in working *for* God when God's priority is working on us. (Romans 12:1-2)

The first message from Philippians challenged us to become a family of God that partners together to know Jesus and be changed by His word. We need to abound in love with all knowledge and discernment as much or more than the Philippians.

We saw Paul's great example that, while chained to Roman soldier and with others preaching Christ in the streets to get Paul in deeper trouble, Paul was grateful that the Kingdom of God was advancing. (1:18) Instead of viewing his situation as a detriment, he saw God using it to proclaim the Gospel to the Palace Guard and embolden the church of Rome to share Christ with others. He saw his situation from God's perspective.

He had a hard time deciding whether he wanted to be sentenced to death or remain alive to serve the Lord. That brings us to one of our favorite verses. *²¹ For to me to live is Christ, and to die is gain.* His conclusion was that through their prayers he would remain because he still needed to minister to them. (1:24) His call from God was not completed. Whether he lived or died, he just wanted his life to glorify God. (1:20) If to us to live is Christ, then we will eagerly expect to glorify God in our body, come what may. If Jesus is our very life, how can that mean anything but fruitful labor for us?

Paul closed that first chapter with an exhortation for them to stand firm in their faith and not be frightened by the opposition. We should be fearless *²⁹ For it has been granted to you that for the sake of Christ you should not only believe in him but also suffer for his sake,* This isn't a favorite verse of very many people, but it is one of my favorites. It tells us that suffering for Christ is a gift, just like the gift of believing. We will suffer in this life, regardless of the path we choose. The path of a believer includes suffering for being committed to Jesus. It sometimes means the loss of friends and the distancing of family members. It means we share in one another's burdens to a deeper extent than the world. We care because Christ in us cares, and so we weep with those that weep. (Romans 12:15) In some places in the world it means physical pain of persecution. We should suffer with them in prayer. (Hebrews 13:3) The gift of belief and the gift of suffering for Christ's sake are inseparable.

At the end of that message, we held hands around the sanctuary and declared the words from this passage, "By the grace of God, I will live as a citizen of heaven, worthy of Jesus, standing firm in one spirit, of one conviction, striving side by side for the sake of the Gospel, not being frightened, receiving the gracious gifts of believing and suffering, engaged in the conflict. So help me God!"

In chapter two Paul exhorts us to *² complete his (my) joy by being of the same mind, having the same love, being in full accord and of one mind. ³ Do nothing from rivalry or conceit, but in humility count others more significant than yourselves.* 2:2-3 (ESV) He was asking them to have the mind of Christ. It is a call to humility. (1Peter 5:6) The contention in the church would end if they would count others more significant than themselves. That is a miracle of grace. The true church of Jesus will have diversity in non-essentials, unity in essentials, and in all things love.

Pride is so subtle and destructive. (Proverbs 16:18) We are so quick to think, "But I *do* know better and am more mature!" Paul is telling us that if you are mature, go down low. Be humble. Listen. Learn. Look for the gift in others. Don't demand to be heard, rather demand that your flesh listen to and respect others out of the love of Christ.

He followed this plea for humility with one of the most important hymns in the New Testament. It was the example of Jesus' suffering and the reward for obedience to the Father. It was a demonstration of the verse, God exalts the humble. (Luke 14:11) Jesus emptied Himself and became a servant, completely surrendered to the will of His Father, obedient even to death on a cross. That is why God highly exalted Him and gave Him a name that is above every other, Lord. That is the name of God, the Tetragrammaton (YHWH), the eternal God of Israel. (John 17:11) He shares the name of the Father which means He shares the attributes of God. That is why every knee will bow and every tongue confess that He is Lord to the glory of God the Father. (Isaiah 45:22-23)

He follows that hymn with an exhortation for us to do the same. *12 Therefore, my beloved, as you have always obeyed, so now, not only as in my presence but much more in my absence, work out your own salvation with fear and trembling, 13 for it is God who works in you, both to will and to work for his good pleasure.* 2:12-13 (ESV) Obey! What God has revealed and worked into your spirit, work out into your everyday life. Live in humility! Live in love. Prefer one another. Be of one mind.

It is an impossible goal for us, but God is working in you to will to do it, and to work for His good pleasure. This is as tough as suffering for His sake. When no one understands, when you smile and know you know better, but in obedience you silently submit, God smiles with you. Winning can be losing. (Deuteronomy 12:8) Insisting on your way or on conveying your mind may be the worst thing for others and you. Do you really believe God exalts the humble?

It was at this point in the series that I confessed I didn't expect what I should expect from you. I should expect that you will go over the last message and apply it daily. I should expect you will preview the next portion of Scripture and come with questions and expectation. I'd love to see you come to the Sunday morning Bible study having read the cross-references, ready to share. I expect that now because I know God is working in you. I know you've seen how applicable these passages have been right when God ordains them to meet a need in your life.

Several of you have asked why I always preach to you personally. That just means you are open to what the Spirit is saying to you today. (Revelation 2:29) Let's be diligent to let the passage each week be a part of our lives. Have you taken up this challenge?

We talked about Timothy and Epaphrodites' great examples. Epaphrodites risked his life to get the gift to Paul, and Timothy was said to have a genuine interest in the Philippians like no one else. (2:20) What an example of genuinely living with God's heart beating in your own.

In chapter 3 we read of Paul's great religious heritage and training, yet he gave it all up. *7 But whatever gain I had, I counted as loss for the sake of Christ. 8 Indeed, I count everything as loss because of the surpassing worth of knowing Christ Jesus my Lord. For his sake I have suffered the loss of all things and count them as rubbish, in order that I may gain Christ.* 3:7-8 (ESV) These verses are perhaps some of the most clear on the contrast between religion and relationship. Paul had religion. He compared it to excrement. This is when we learned the meaning of *skubala*. Whatever gets in the way of your relationship with Jesus, you need to consider as *skubala*. Paul said that he gave up everything to gain Christ. It's not just knowing Him, it's gaining Him like a bride gains a husband. It's finding Mr. Right, your Prince Charming, your everything. Sorry men. I know it's hard to relate. That's one reason the church has more women than men. That's the best illustration and Paul said so in Ephesians 5:32.

Men, if you are having a hard time with that concept, try thinking of the perfect Father, the one who always has time for you. He not only finds your strengths and teaches you how to apply them. He is at every game cheering for you. He corrects your failures only to encourage you to be all you can be. He is the perfect example. He tells you He loves you and that you make Him proud. He loves your Mom (the church) and treats her like a princess. He's a man's man! (Psalm 24:8) You feel sorry for the other guys that they don't have a Father like you! Can anything come between you and your awesome Dad? Anything that does is *skubala*. Does that help?

Now watch the humility with which Paul follows that great thought. *12 Not that I have already obtained this or am already perfect, but I press on to make it my own, because Christ Jesus has made me his own. 13 Brothers, I do not consider that I have made it my own. But one thing I do: forgetting what lies behind and straining forward to what lies ahead, 14 I press on toward the goal for the prize of the upward call of God in Christ Jesus.* 3:12-14 (ESV) Paul wanted to wrap both arms around this heart cry of gaining Christ. He strained forward like a runner to break the finish line tape. He had one motto that was behind every action. Forget about the past! Strain forward to the upward call of God in Christ. That's all that mattered. We were challenged to do the same, to be 100% in this life for all that Christ has done for and in us. We're headed to heaven. (Hebrews 12:23)

20 But our citizenship is in heaven, and from it we await a Savior, the Lord Jesus Christ, 21 who will transform our lowly body to be like his glorious body, by the power that enables him even to subject all things to himself. 3:20-21 (ESV) We're going home. We have the same dilemma the Apostle had. Going home is much better than hanging out here, but we have work to do. But when that day comes, the old caterpillars that we are will be transformed into the amazing butterflies of God's design and we will ever be with the Lord. (1Corinthians 15:51-52)

I challenged you to memorize 4:4-8. How many of you made the effort or are still working on it? *4 Rejoice in the Lord always; again I will say, Rejoice. 5 Let your reasonableness be known to everyone. The Lord is at hand; 6 do not be anxious about anything, but in everything by prayer and supplication with thanksgiving let your requests be made known to God. 7 And the peace of God, which surpasses all understanding, will guard your* *hearts and your minds in Christ Jesus. ^{8} Finally, brothers, whatever is true, whatever is honorable, whatever is just, whatever is pure, whatever is lovely, whatever is commendable, if there is any excellence, if there is anything worthy of praise, think about these things.* 4:4-8 (ESV)

What an excellent guide for daily living. If we will set these boundaries on our thought life, we'll find the Christian life to be much easier. Give your burdens to the Lord. Let His peace permeate your heart and mind. Think on the good things, the things Paul has shared in this letter like our relationship with Christ and one another, the reward for humility, the transformation of our nature and one day of our body as well. Think about your situations from God's heavenly perspective and give thanks!

Then we come to those last two well-known Scriptures that we found to be defined by their context. *^{13} I can do all things through him who strengthens me.* 4:13 (ESV) We discovered that "all things" relates to our circumstances in life, whether in poverty or riches, we can be content in Christ. He is the One that fills the void in our heart. Material things will never fill a spiritual void. The secret of contentment is being filled with Christ Jesus.

Finally, *^{19} And my God will supply every need of yours according to his riches in glory in Christ Jesus.* 4:19 (ESV) If you are generous to partner in others' ministries, the Lord will see your great need for Jesus is met in you. You will know Him more deeply. Your necessities will be provided, the basic necessities of food and clothing for the body, and the great necessity of Jesus for the soul. What a letter! What promises! What practical guidance! May the Lord work these truths deep into our spirits. Amen!

I would encourage you to go over the key verses from Philippians and share the effect (or the effect you'd like to see) on your life.

Colossians

Loving Saints Colossians 1:1-8

As we refocus the goal and calling of this body of believers, the elders felt led to this particular book to help us. Though we do not have the same heresies arising that the Colossians encountered, Paul's exhortation of the fundamental truth of the Gospel is certainly a great help in clarifying the essentials of our life in Christ.

The letter to the Colossians came under fire by critics because it so clearly points to the deity of Christ. (Colossians 1:15-16) They rightly point out that the proclamation by the early church of the divinity of Christ took years to really settle in. It was a huge spiritual step for Jewish believers in Jesus as Messiah. It is one thing to say that Jesus opened the way to God for all, (1Corinthians 1:2) and still another to say that He is God.

Has God given you a goal for this year? My personal goal for this year is to work on a book that shows the many clear links between Jesus of the New Testament and YHWH (the eternal God) of the Old. Accepting that Jesus is God is the major hurtle to becoming a Christian. It is the one thing that makes Christianity unique. Neither Buddha, nor Mohammed, nor Krishna claimed to be the only God and creator of all things. Only Jesus claimed to be the exact representation of God by saying such things as, "I and my Father are one" (John 10:30; 20:28), and "If you have seen me you have seen the Father" (John 14:9). But these were recorded by the Apostle John in the last gospel, which was written decades after Jesus died. I have no doubt they are authentic. I am just saying there are no such clear statements in the earlier gospels. The closest we have is the declaration of Paul in one of the earliest letters, perhaps even written before the gospels, who declared that Jesus is the One through whom all things came. (1Corinthians 8:6)

I think the reason behind the lack of clear expressions of Jesus' divinity was not that the Apostles did not believe in it, but rather that it was so controversial and difficult to comprehend. Before the destruction of the Temple, they avoided turning away potential converts and unnecessary persecution from the Jewish community (the main source of early persecution – Acts 8:1) by not overtly declaring that belief. When Paul wrote this letter to the Colossians and John wrote his gospel and Revelation, the recipients were in Asia Minor. Jews were a smaller part of the Christian community, but the understanding of the divinity of Christ had already developed as a part of the Christian faith.

The divinity of Jesus has always been the stumbling block, because if Jesus is God, He has every right to tell us truth and expect obedience. If He says it's better to chop off your right hand than to enter into hell with both hands (Matthew 5:30), then sin is a serious issue with serious consequences. If He says the greatest command is to love God with your all (Matthew 22:37), then that is what God expects of us and that is how we should live. If he says loving our neighbor is like loving God, we better allow His love to fill us with a loving heart of service. (Hebrews 6:10)

Paul wrote the letter while in prison, probably from Caesarea or Rome. He wrote it around the same time as the letter to the Ephesians and the little personal letter of Philemon. He wrote to the small town of Colossae in the Lycus Valley, a town that was fading into insignificance because of the nearby and much larger and more important twin cities of Hieropolis and Laodicea.

Apparently, Epaphras had been discipled by Paul in Ephesus and gone through the Lycus Valley starting new churches. Epaphras had brought news to Paul of some false teachings that were seducing the believers in Colossae. The letter is a rebuttal of those teachings and encouragement to realize all that believers have in Christ.

He begins the letter in his usual greeting format (Ephesians 1:1-2). He first states his authority in writing such a letter. Colossians 1:1 (ESV*) *1 Paul, an apostle of Christ Jesus by the will of God, and Timothy our brother,* Paul is his Greek name. It means small. His Hebrew name is Saul after the first king of Israel from the same tribe of Benjamin. His office is that of an apostle, that is to say, he is an official ambassador of God, or a representative of God. (2Corinthians 5:20) But it is not by his own will that he holds the title. In fact, he was knocked from his horse while on the way to persecute Christians when he received the appointment. (Acts 22:14; 26:14) It is the will of God that he became the apostle that he is. That is why he has the authority to address the teachings they are hearing. That is why we study his letters today. He held the same title as the disciples of Jesus, apostle.

Paul includes Timothy as a co-author. Timothy is Paul's young protégé, and yet he is given credit as co-authoring the letter. Paul recognized that every born again believer has something to say because of the Spirit of God within us. (Romans 1:11-12) And yet, there is still authority and God appointed offices within the church. Timothy was an elder. (1Timothy 1:3)

2 To the saints and faithful brothers in Christ at Colossae: Grace to you and peace from God our Father. Saints and faithful brothers refer to the same people. We can be uncomfortable with the term saints, but all believers in Jesus are sanctified by what Jesus did for us on the cross. (Hebrews 10:10) To deny that we are made holy is to deny Jesus took our sins, past, present and future. We certainly don't act holy at times, and that is what makes us uncomfortable with the term. When we use the term only for super-spiritual people, we are implying that it is works that make us right before God. Look at the person next to you and tell them they are a saint. It means separated for God's service. You were separated to serve the living God when you accepted Jesus' death in your place as the payment for your sins. (1Thessalonians 1:9)

Paul called them faithful brothers. As we will see, they were not so faithful to the doctrine that was delivered to them. Believers are called faithful because we are credited with the faithfulness of Jesus. (2Corinthians 5:21) "Brothers" is literally siblings. Paul saw the believers there as family even though he had not met them. Believers in Jesus are a family of saints.

To be "in Christ" does not mean He is the object of our faith, though He is that. The phrase refers to our sphere of life. We are no longer "of the world" in the sense that it is our identity. (John 15:19) We have a new identity in Christ. We are citizens of heaven. (Philippians 3:20) There are only two kinds of people, those in the world and those in Christ. Slabs of stone in the catacombs of Rome that covered the bones of the dead believers were inscribed with the words "In Christ". And because they were in Christ, the other inscription read, "In peace." To be a part of the mystical body of Christ is to be in the shalom of God.

Then Paul greets them with a familiar phrase, "Grace and peace from God our Father". It is in a sense a prayer that the God whom by grace they came to know as Father would continue to pour out His grace and peace on their lives. All believers are recipients of grace. (Ephesians 2:8) It is by grace we are saved. We all have the peace that comes from knowing our sins are forgiven and we are right with God. Paul desires that grace and peace to continue to flow from God into the lives of these believers and to all those to whom he wrote. As believers, we should desire to see the grace and peace of God be poured out upon every believer, even those who may have offended us. Grace is necessary for our sanctification.

Paul continues with his prayer for them. Greek letters often started out with a prayer, and that is common in Paul's letters. *3 We always thank God, the Father of our Lord Jesus Christ, when we pray for you, 4 since we heard of your faith in Christ Jesus and of the love that you have for all the saints, 5abecause of the hope laid up for you in heaven.* He always prayed a prayer of thanks first. He was thankful for their testimony of faith and love for all the saints. An attitude of gratitude permeates the letters of Paul. His gratitude was a fruit of the Spirit in his life. He had allowed God's love for mankind into his heart. (Philippians 4:1)

The Colossians' faith and love were evidences that they were family, genuine believers, holy, faithful brothers. Faith is evidenced by the fruit of the Spirit, love. (Galatians 5:6)

The love believers share is not based upon similar interests or status, or blood relations, or even agreeing on every detail of worship, but rather on the commonality we have in devoting our hearts to the same Savior. We share the same experience of forgiveness of sins and the same love of the One that paid the price. Because of that, we are willing to forgive one another and refuse to let offenses or weaknesses override our eternal relationship as the family of God. (Ephesians 4:32) This deep bond of our heart's priority is willing to look forward to a time (the hope laid up for us in heaven) when the work in us will be brought to perfection and the little annoyances and disagreements will be no more. The "my way or the highway" attitude can only prevail when we put the real passion of our heart second to temporary personal preferences. Situations will come and go, but we are a family forever!

If Paul was in Phoenix (about the same distance as Ephesus from Colossae) would he hear about our faith in Christ and love for all the saints?

It is not that we should be concerned with what others think of us, but is there evidence of life in our church? I think we might be known for things we do. That is a kind of evidence of our faith. But I don't think the Colossian believers were known for any special program. It was their faith that was manifest in fruit in their individual lives. Their love for their fellow saints was so evident that the word got around. I think we have lots of room for growth in this area. I look forward to the day when people as far away as Phoenix will hear about our faith and love for all the saints. Those are the key attributes of genuine believers, faith, hope, and love. (1Corinthians 13:13)

Of this you have heard before in the word of the truth, the gospel, *6 which has come to you, as indeed in the whole world it is bearing fruit and growing—as it also does among you, since the day you heard it and understood the grace of God in truth,* This faith, this love for the brothers, and this hope laid up for us in heaven is the fruit of the gospel. That's the good news. You've seen those three together before and indeed Paul has put them together several times in his letters. (1Thessalonians 5:8) "Faith inspires service, love energizes it, hope perpetuates it."

Is the gospel bearing the fruit of faith, hope, and love in your life? That is evidence of your salvation. And it should be growing. We should be increasing in faith, hope and love. Paul is saying that it is having that effect in people wherever it is proclaimed and the grace of God is understood in truth. (2Corinthians 5:19)

It is not special programs or idea driven efforts of anyone, but rather the simple proclamation of the truth of Jesus, of His grace and love, and of the hope available to those who place their faith in Him. The lives transformed by the grace of God into living examples of the fruit of the Spirit make others hungry to hear just what it was that changed their lives. In any culture and any time, the account of Jesus and His work and promises change lives and give hope. This is the universality of the Gospel. (1John 2:2)

Paul was using the language of Genesis 1:28, the first command of God to Adam. He was to fill the face of the world with fruit. That meant physically of course, but as Adam was yet unfallen, and created in the image of God, God meant to fill the face of the world with those in God's image, that is filling the world with His glory. Adam failed. The second Adam is Jesus (1Corinthians 15:45), who is the Word, and whose body now takes the Word to the ends of the earth, bearing fruit (subduing sin) and bringing God glory. Paul was saying the first command of God is being fulfilled through the Gospel.

7 just as you learned it from Epaphras our beloved fellow servant. He is a faithful minister of Christ on your behalf It was one evangelist, Epaphras, who faithfully declared the grace of God to the Colossians. It is amazing what one person empowered by the Holy Spirit can do. When you share the good news of how Jesus changed your life, you never know how far God can take that word. When we look at a seed, we have no idea how many times it will be reproduced, as Jesus taught, 30, 60, or 100 times. (Mark 4:8)

Epaphras was a fellow bondslave of Jesus. Paul was calling him an equal, a man fully surrendered to service to Jesus and one who carried out that service faithfully. He had relayed to Paul their love in the Spirit. It sounds as if Epaphras had shared about the messenger from whom he heard the Gospel, Paul. In response, the Colossians loved Paul as well, for he was their spiritual grandfather. The word is the power that changes lives, but when the word is proclaimed by someone who not only feels its power but lives in utter surrender to it, the word comes with conviction.

I used to watch speakers to try to understand why some were more effective than others. I saw what I later read eloquently described as "logos, pathos, and ethos". Powerful witness comes from the Word (logos), delivered by someone who feels its power and genuinely cares about the hearers (pathos), and whose life has been changed by the Word (ethos). What I was witnessing is the ethos portion – the life lived in Christ. They had that love for their brothers. That is the power of our personal witness. We need all three, but it is ethos that causes the hearer to take notice. There is no power to invite others to fall in love with our Savior if we do not possess that love.

8 and has made known to us your love in the Spirit. It is not certain that Spirit should be capitalized. (2:5) Epaphras had come to encourage Paul in prison that these spiritual grandchildren he had never met loved him. What an encouragement it must have been for the Apostle to hear that his fruit was bearing fruit! It was worth it. The imprisonment and hardships of being an apostle of Jesus resulted in lives finding faith, hope, and love in Jesus.

Before the Apostle got to the admonitions the church needed, he encouraged them with the fact that they were loving saints. If we are to be a church of Jesus Christ we must be known for the same. We must find the love of God for one another that puts self last and overlooks differences, because we share the main thing, a love of our Savior.

How do we get that love? How do we give up our selfish use of our time and begin to be those who serve one another in love? We let the love of Christ fill our hearts to overflowing.

In the early church, the wonder of what Jesus had done out of love so overwhelmed new believers, that they dropped their social status, came out of acceptable ways of the world around them, and humbly served one another. It didn't matter if they were master or slave, as long as they loved the same Lord, they loved each other.

This is what attracted the world. It was so strange, that society made up rumors to explain it. The real explanation was the transformation of the heart. Servant could be an elder to his master. Master could call his slave his brother. High society people ate with the lowliest, even serving them. The only way we can be like that is to have the same awe of a Savior that

94

accepted us while we were yet sinners. The ground is level for all at the foot of the cross.

There were personality differences and conflicts then as there are now, but there was commitment to one another then that we seem to have lost today. Do you know how committed Jesus is to you? He has that same commitment to every believer. If He has that kind of loving, enduring, commitment to us, and is living in our hearts, will we not have the same commitment to one another, whether they leave this fellowship or disagree with our doctrine, or even say hurtful things about us?

Without a first love of Jesus, we will not love our brothers. That is where the love begins. If we lack love for one another, we must love Jesus more. (1John 3:14) We love Jesus more when we meet Him in His word, in prayer, and in our daily circumstances. Our relationship with Him will translate into love for one another. It is the inevitable outcome of a genuine love for God.

Questions
1 Which books of the New Testament clearly tell us that Jesus is God?
2 Why would the earliest writers hesitate to state it so clearly?
3 What are the implications of Jesus being God?
4 Why does Paul include Timothy as a co-author?
5 Are you a saint? Why?
6 What qualities does Paul see in the Colossians?
7 Why are they essential for us?
8 How do these qualities work together?
9 What is the term Paul used for Epaphras? Application?
10 What ingredients make a powerful witness?
11 How is love for God evidenced? John 13:34; 1John 4:21

Paul's Prayer Colossians 1:9-14

Last week we introduced you to this letter to the Colossians. Paul had to address some of the false teaching that was threatening to undermine the pure teaching of the Gospel and the grace we find in Jesus. But first, he praised them for the powerful impact of their testimony. (Colossians 1:3-4) He reminded them that they had put their faith in the grace of God that resulted in their love for all the saints. Their faith was evidenced by their love, just as Jesus had predicted. (John 13:35) That is how the world knows if we are really Jesus' disciples. The Colossians were true disciples. The other evidence of their faith was that they were growing spiritually and bearing fruit. I assume that Paul meant all the fruits of the Spirit that he described in his letter to the Galatians. (Galatians 5:22-23)

Next, he wrote out a prayer that he prayed regularly for them. This is one of a number of prayers we find in the epistles of Paul. Each one is rich with insights that we should adopt as our own. (Ephesians 1:16-19; 3:14-19) As we go through the prayer today, remember that in the background is the threat of false teaching, of depending on works, and on needing something in addition to the grace we receive from Jesus.

9 And so, from the day we heard, we have not ceased to pray for you, asking that you may be filled with the knowledge of his will in all spiritual wisdom and understanding, From the day Paul heard from Epaphras about the church in Colossae, he and Timothy began to pray for them and continued to pray for them. That should be our habit whenever we hear of a new believer or new church established. The enemy doesn't attack his own. He goes after those who have switched sides hoping to discourage them or distort their understanding enough to make them ineffective. (Genesis 4:7) This church was bearing fruit and growing. That is where the enemy attacks. We counter attack, not by attacking individuals, but with truth and prayer. (Ephesians 6:17-18) Paul's prayer will show us the things we need to ask in prayer. The battle is won on our knees.

First, we need to be filled with the knowledge of God's will in all spiritual wisdom and understanding. (Philippians 1:9) What is God's will in general? It is the Word of God. (Psalm 1:1-2) But just the words on the page are not enough. We need spiritual wisdom and understanding to apply them. We can memorize a passage, and we should, but without the spiritual wisdom and spiritual understanding, we can apply the words in an unspiritual way. Just because a passage says to love one another, does not mean that you let sin slide or soft peddle serious issues. Love must be applied with spiritual wisdom and understanding or you simply enable others to continue to sin. (John 16:8-11) You've probably seen the Word used without spiritual wisdom and understanding. The Word of God must be applied with wisdom and understanding for it to be in the will of God. (Proverbs 26:4-5)

This is often one of the ways churches are sidetracked today as they were when the letter was written. Apparently someone was taking portions of Old Testament Law and saying the Colossians had to keep those laws to reach through heavenly realms to please God. You can support almost any idea with Scripture and you don't necessarily need to take it out of its immediate context. But the crux of the matter is whether or not it is applied with spiritual wisdom and understanding. (Ephesians 1:17) And so Paul and Timothy regularly prayed that the Colossians won't be duped by the misuse of Scripture but would be filled with the knowledge of God's will with all spiritual wisdom and understanding.

The world has its own knowledge that is equally seductive. (1Timothy 6:20) We need to filter what we hear through God's full knowledge so that we know what to reject and what has any value. In addition to your own time in God's word, listen carefully when God's word is faithfully preached. The Word equips us with the full knowledge we need.

We are going to be praying that prayer a lot this year. I know some are averse to any routines, but notice here that Paul writes that they don't stop praying this. Since the day they heard about the church, they continued to pray the same thing because that is what is needed. It isn't a ritual; it's a spiritual need. We need to be filled with the knowledge of God's will in all spiritual wisdom and understanding. Why?

10 so as to walk in a manner worthy of the Lord, fully pleasing to him, bearing fruit in every good work and increasing in the knowledge of God. Jesus is the worthy One. (Revelation 5:12) He deserves us to let Him have His way in us. He deserves us to live daily in a way that fully pleases Him. That should be the passion of everyone that is redeemed. After all He has done for us, we should desire to please Jesus in everything we do. This is why we need to know His will in all spiritual wisdom and understanding. Then we know how to please Him. We often do what we think is right from our perspective and yet displease the Lord because we lack the knowledge of God's will in all wisdom and understanding. (Proverbs 14:12)

When we have that insight and do live in a way that pleases God, then we bear fruit in every good work and increase in the knowledge of God. Wow! I want that testimony. Don't you want to bear fruit in every good work and increase in the knowledge of God? Then you need to know God's will – in all spiritual wisdom and understanding – so that you can live a life that is worthy of Jesus! I hope this is giving you a desire to cry out to God this same prayer, not only for yourself but for the whole congregation. You have to get into the Word, and not just the letter of the Scriptures, but to let the Spirit of God give you the wisdom and understanding to see the application to your life and the situations you face. (John 14:26) You have to be willing to let the Word have the final say, not your preferences. This is how we grow in the knowledge of God.

Now we come to the part of the prayer that I'm using for a benediction. *11 May you be strengthened with all power, according to his glorious might, for all endurance and patience with joy,* The first request is to know God's will to live in a way that pleases God and bears fruit. Next is to continually be growing stronger, but not just with the natural strength. Paul isn't praying they all be Samson. He is praying for increasing spiritual strength in the face of these tempting doctrines that were seducing the church. He prays they would be strengthened with ALL the power of God's glory! (a more literal translation) That is an audacious prayer.

The world is constantly coming against us. Our flesh would readily rise up and take back over our life. The enemy of our soul is a powerful supernatural being that is waiting to devour us. (1Peter 5:8) Our pride is ready to rise up and cause factions. (2Corinthians 12:20) No wonder we need to be strengthened with the power of God's glory! Have we been praying this way? If the Colossians needed this, we certainly do as well! (Matthew 26:41) We need people in the prayer room on Sunday. We are going to have another 24 hour prayer day in the end of February. We want to have the church open again during the week for people to pray. We need to be strengthened! But here is what we need to be strengthened for...

*for all endurance and patience...*These two words in their original Greek say so much more than our English translation. Endurance is the Greek word *hupomone*. It means to work through to the end any situation we face. It is to bear with a situation turning it into glory. It is being eventually triumphant in the circumstances we face. (James 5:7-11) In other words, it is knowing that in the power of God's glory you can see the circumstance through to a victorious end. It isn't just getting through something by gritting your teeth and hanging on until you have your way. (Romans 8:37)

The verse ends with these virtues expressed with joy. It is knowing that in the end you will be victorious no matter how long it takes because you have the power of God's glory! I like that word! It isn't a fun word, but it is a reassuring word to those who want to live in a way that is pleasing to Jesus.

Patience is the word *makrothumia* . It is to not allow people to drive you to bitterness or despair or even irritation. Never letting people alter your love. Love conquers all. (1Corinthians 13:8) It doesn't lose hope that the person might eventually come to their senses. (2Peter 3:9) Our fortitude and patience will be indestructible if it is according to the power of God's glory. Remember that glory is expressed in a consuming fire that devours selfishness and pride. (Deuteronomy 4:24) It is only when our endurance and patience is empowered with the very power of God's glory that we can joyfully bring glory to God in the painful circumstances and relationships of life. Here's how we might express it today: "Make me, O Lord, victorious over every circumstance; make me patient with every person; and withal give me the joy which no circumstance and no man will ever take from me." Barclay's Daily Study Bible (NT). How's that for a prayer!

I need to apply this verse on a daily basis. You probably do too. I know how to hang on by my fingernails and grit my teeth and bear it, but I need to experience being filled with power of God's glory to see trials joyfully through to a victorious end. Would you please pray this prayer for me, and for the whole congregation? I will pray it for you.

12 giving thanks to the Father, who has qualified you to share in the inheritance of the saints in light. So as we go through these circumstances and relationships in the power of God's glory, with joy, we are to do so with thanksgiving. Our attitude is a byproduct of our level of trust in God. If I believe in the power of God's glory, to consume my selfishness and empower me to patiently endure to a glorious end, then I can be thankful. (Ephesians 5:20) The reason Paul gives for the basis of our thanks is that God has qualified us to share in the inheritance of the saints in light. Jesus' sacrifice for our sin debt qualifies us to share in all the promises of God to His children, now.

Chrysostom explained it this way. It was as if someone gave someone the position of king, and yet, because he was not qualified to hold the title, he makes a fool of himself. Jesus not only gives us a title but also makes us fit to bear the title. He equips us to shine in this life. (1Peter 2:9) If God doesn't qualify us, we'd be miserable being among the saints for eternity.

We have a share, or portion, with the saints. The language looks back to the families of each tribe of Israel getting a portion of land, but applies it spiritually. (Joshua 14:2-3) We each have our portion in heaven but also our portion of ministry presently. How is God calling you to help? Pray about that. Look at the things you enjoy doing. See what needs touch your heart. Next week we'll be giving you an opportunity to sign up to meet some of those needs if you are not doing so already.

The next verse elaborates on qualifying us, the reason for our thanksgiving. *13 He has delivered us from the domain of darkness and transferred us to the kingdom of his beloved Son, 14 in whom we have redemption, the forgiveness of sins.* The best manuscripts do not have "through his blood" (KJV) added to the end, though that is certainly a reality. We were a part of Satan's domain. Our understanding was darkened. We lived for self and self alone, finding pleasure in destruction and reveling in dragging others along with us. That is the domain of darkness. There was absolutely no way we would have ever broken free from it had God not transferred us to the kingdom of the Son He loves. He reached down into our filthy condition and lifted us out. He took us from darkness to light, slavery to freedom, condemnation to forgiveness, pride to humility, and from sin to holiness.

The Jewish reader would have thought of the deliverance from Egypt as a type of what God did spiritually for us in Jesus. (Exodus 15:13) We were enslaved, hopeless, despairing but God did what we could never do on our own. He brought us out with a great deliverance. Today we sometimes think of slavery to genetics or upbringing. We say we have addictive personalities or are predisposed to certain weaknesses or had a dysfunctional family. It may be true, but Jesus is our Deliverer from all things that would keep us from living in the will of God.

The grace of God shined through the darkness and enabled our hearts to see the truth, and then empowered us. But that was not enough. Our debt had to be paid. God is never unjust. A judge that would simply forgive some heinous crime is not good or gracious; he's evil. The penalty for sin had to be paid for God to remain righteous and good and for us to value His goodness. So God stepped down into time and space and took the penalty for us, redeeming us from the slavery we were under, forgiving us of our sins. He then empowered us to live a new life. (Galatians 2:20)

The power of His glory is ours for the asking, so that we can joyfully endure the circumstances of life to the glory of God. We can refuse to give up on a difficult relationship and see God glorified in the end. We can discern His will with all spiritual wisdom and understanding. These are the victories waiting to be given to those who draw near to God through Jesus. (Hebrews 7:25)

Even when given God's glorious grace we must be willing to apply it. I hear people say they just can't forgive. Sorry, that's not Scriptural and therefore untrue. (Matthew 6:14) You can't, but God can enable you to forgive and endure patiently. I just had someone tell me it wouldn't do any good to obey a Scripture. That is a lack of faith in God's word!

Will you take up this prayer with me for this year and put it by your bed or on your mirror and pray it from your heart? Please pray it for this congregation. Pray it for those who have wounded you. Pray it for the church of the Verde Valley. Let's close today by praying it.

Lord Jesus, we come to you knowing we are in need of your divine power. Help us to not stop praying that we may be filled with the knowledge of Your will with all spiritual wisdom and understanding, so that we can live in a way that is worthy of You and pleasing to You, bearing fruit in every good work and increasing in the knowledge of You. May we be strengthened with all power according to Your glorious might, with all endurance and patience with joy, giving thanks to You for qualifying us to share in the inheritance of the saints in light. Amen!

I suggest that you copy this prayer. Meditate on it. Pray it often. Watch God answer! Praise God!

Questions
1 What did Paul and Timothy do when they heard of the church of Colossae? Why?
2 Why do we need to pray this prayer?
3 How do we know the will of God?
4 Why do we want to know the will of God?
5 How do we bear fruit in every good work and increase in the knowledge of God?
6 What was the source of their strength?
7 What are we strengthened for?
8 How does our trust in God affect our attitude?
9 How were we qualified to share in the inheritance of the saints in light?
10 What must we do with the power we receive?
11 Will you pray this prayer throughout this year?

Majestic Jesus Colossians 1:15-17

In the introduction of the letter to the Colossians, we saw the importance of the fruit of love in a church. It will be a focus for this church for the coming year. Many of you are already doing a wonderful job of expressing it by caring for one another. Most of us need to increasingly die to our selfish use of time and let Jesus serve others through us. (Galatians 6:10) We need to dwell in His presence through His word so that the love of Jesus overflows from our lives into the lives of one another.

We also saw this wonderful prayer that we will be praying for our families and for one another throughout the year. We're praying to be filled with the knowledge of God's will, and to be strengthened with the power of His glory to be patiently victorious in circumstances and relationships. Victory is God being glorified! And through it all we pray to be joyful and grateful. We are joyful and grateful because we've been transferred from the kingdom of darkness into the kingdom of light. We share in the inheritance of the saints.

What a fantastic introduction and prayer! But now Paul continues the opening of the letter with a crescendo! He is going to clearly tell us of the glory of Jesus. Before Jesus was crucified, Jesus asked the Father to glorify Him with the glory He had with the Father before the world existed. (John 17:5) John the Beloved had a clear understanding that Jesus had ever been with God (John 1:1) and was one with God. (John 10:30) The more you examine the language and the Gospels' inferences to Old Testament passages, the more you come to the conclusion that the Trinity concept is the only answer to the mystery. There are three, but they are one. (See my book Divine Messiah)

Let's begin Paul's description from verse 15. *15 He is the image of the invisible God,...* Paul is echoing the very words of Jesus in John 14:9, "Whoever has seen me has seen the Father." We need some background to understand how radical a declaration this was for the Apostle Paul. He had helped to stone Stephen for just saying Jesus had authority over the Temple and the Law (in other words for saying Jesus is the long awaited Messiah who would deliver from the hedge of the Law). (Acts 22:20; Genesis 38:29) Now, Paul is declaring for himself that Jesus is not only Messiah, but the very image of God Almighty!

How is it possible that Paul came to such a radical shift in his beliefs? He was educated under the leading rabbi of the day. (Acts 22:3) He was considered to be one of the up and coming young scholars. We know from the three reports of his conversion that it was on the road to Damascus that he was confronted by a vision of Jesus, blinded for a time, and commissioned to be an Apostle. (Acts 22:10) But I suspect there was something that led up to that fateful day. Long after his conversion, he wrote a letter to a church warning them not to believe any vision of an angel from heaven that preached anything other than what they had been taught. (Galatians 1:8) Why would he write that if his conversion was solely based on a vision of Jesus?

Let me speculate for just a moment based on what we know of Paul. He knew the Old Testament Scriptures better than most of today's Bible professors. He probably had much of the Old Testament committed to memory. As he persecuted the church, he would hear the stories of the one they worshiped, Jesus. He heard Stephen remind him that the tabernacle was only shadow and not the substance, and that the prophets predicted the coming of the Righteous One. (Acts 7:49, 52 The Righteous One of the Old Testament is God (Proverbs 21:12; Isaiah 24:16). Isaiah called God the Righteous One, but he also called the Suffering Servant the Righteous One (Isaiah 53:11). There were probably a dozen other passages that stirred in Paul's spirit as doubts about the path he was on troubled his mind. The shining face of the martyrs just reinforced those doubts. When Jesus appeared to Paul and Paul responded, "Who are you Lord?"(Acts 22:8), I think he knew full well who Jesus was. Paul's own standard was that the Word held more importance than any vision. (1Corinthians 4:6)

Then, over the following years in Arabia and Damascus, he must have studied all the passages that had been nagging him to see how they had come to pass in Jesus. (Galatians 1:17-18) Time after time, the Word declared something unique to YHWH that was seen in the life of Jesus.

Let me give you just a couple of examples. Joel 2:32 declared that those who call on the name of YHWH are saved, but Paul saw the followers of Jesus declare that those who call on the name of Jesus were transformed. (Acts 9:14, 21) He knew it was YHWH that sanctifies His people (Exodus 31:13) and yet he could see lives were sanctified by Jesus (Acts 26:18). He knew it was YHWH that walks on the waves of the sea (Job 9:8) but he heard from the disciples that Jesus walked on the waves of Galilee (Matthew 14:25). Over and over again the Scriptures spoke of things that were true of YHWH alone and yet he saw that Jesus had done those very things. There was only one conclusion. Jesus is the image of the invisible God!

The Greek word that Paul used for image (eikon) meant a representation of something, like a picture, so in that loose sense you could say Paul only meant Jesus represented God. However, he clarifies that he means more than that in the following verses. If an image was exact enough, it could mean the manifestation of the thing, which is the way Paul is using it here.

Old Testament literature declares Wisdom as being eternally with God. (Proverbs 2:6) The inter-testament book of Wisdom (7:26) declares wisdom as the image of God. Philo called the Word, logos, the image of God. So Paul's use of the word was something both Jews and Greeks could acknowledge as eternally present with God and yet one with God.

The average Jewish reader may not have thought that deeply, but they would certainly have thought back to Genesis chapter one, where man was made in the image of God. (Genesis 1:27) Paul seems to be saying that Adam was meant to be like Jesus. He failed to achieve the destiny God intended for him because of sin, and so God had to become man to show us what Adam was meant to be. The righteous life of Jesus was what God intended for mankind. Jesus is not only the perfect image of God, but the image of what God intended for man. Even more, He is the image of what God will yet achieve in those who call on Him as Lord. (1John 3:2) When we see Him we will be like Him for we shall see Him as He is. The image distorted by sin will be restored.

Even for the Greeks that had no Bible knowledge, the word eikon had a rich meaning. When a contract was drawn up, there was a description of the two parties involved so there would be no mistake. Distinguishing characteristics of each person were mentioned. In that sense of the word eikon, Jesus has the distinguishing characteristics of God. What makes God unique is seen in Jesus.

Paul goes on to say in verse 19 that all the fullness of God is seen in Jesus. It's not just the main characteristics, it's everything about Jesus. If you want to understand God, to visualize God, look at Jesus. In answer to the Gnostic suggestions that Jesus was simply a man with higher wisdom than other men, Paul was declaring Jesus to be wisdom Himself, the very image of God.

Understanding this truth means that we must interpret the manifestations of God in the Old Testament as pre-incarnate appearances of Jesus. He is the person of the Trinity that appears to man. The Father and the Spirit are unseen. (For more on this see Jesus Concealed in the Old Testament) Interpreting the Old Testament in this manner means that Jesus is just continuing the work He always had, revealing the Father in a way that man can relate. From walking with man in the Garden (Genesis 3:8), to warning of the judgment on Sodom (Genesis 18:1), to wrestling with Jacob (Genesis 32:24), to giving plans for battle to Joshua (Joshua 5:13), to dying on a cross because of love for the world, the One that appeared was the eikon of the invisible God. The entire book is about Jesus!

Next, Paul pointed to Jesus' relationship to creation. *He is the firstborn of all creation.* That does not mean that He was the first thing created as the Jehovah's Witness believe. The context shows that interpretation to be incorrect. Firstborn is a position or rank of importance within a family. The firstborn was the main heir. It was used as a title of honor. God called the nation of Israel His firstborn son. (Exodus 4:22) That does not mean Israel was the first people of God chronologically but positionally.

Jews used it as a Messianic title, pointing to Psalm 89:27, 27 And I will make him the firstborn, the highest of the kings of the earth. This has nothing to do with time, but rather of importance. Paul is saying that in all of creation Jesus holds the highest position.

In fact, Paul may have had that verse in mind when he wrote this. It may have been one of those verses Paul wrestled with while in Arabia. In the previous verse of that Psalm it predicted the Messiah would cry out to God, "You are my Father." "Father" was one of Jesus' most common expressions when praying to God, a term that was highly uncommon in that day.

Paul goes on to say that not only is Jesus the very image of God, the Supreme Being over creation, but He is in fact the Creator of all things. *16 For by him all things were created, in heaven and on earth, visible and invisible, whether thrones or dominions or rulers or authorities—all things were created through him and for him.* The false teachers presented a hierarchy of intermediary angels between man and God, beings which must be appeased by our actions before we could reach God. Those false teachers would put Jesus in amongst these as another intermediary. Paul bypasses all that and declares that Jesus is the Creator of all things visible and invisible. (1Corinthians 8:6) If there are angel hierarchies He is not among them, He is over them as Creator. They were created to serve Him!

He created everything out of nothing. God spoke and it was. (Genesis 1:3) Jesus is that Word, one with God. (John 1:14) Think of it. We are still discovering new life forms at the bottom of the ocean floor that are unlike anything we have seen, forms that do not require oxygen but thrive on other chemicals. We are still cataloging the creatures of the sea. 800,000 insect species have been identified and new ones are still being discovered. There is the fascinating microbiological world and the grand cosmos with black holes and supernovas of which we know so little. He made it all.

Think of how He designed a blueprint, DNA, which He could reorder so as to come up with the amazing variety we see in the earth. But He made more. He made an unseen world of angelic beings as well. We know almost nothing of that!

I understand the verse to say that Jesus planned every authority and every ruler that would exist in every realm. He planned it all and is carrying it out in spite of the will of man. He is the final authority for all things were created through Him and for Him. (Revelation 4:11)

Instead of beginning the letter to the Colossians by demeaning the false teachers, Paul began by declaring Jesus, Jesus in His glory, Jesus in His rightful title. He was following the very command of Jesus, "If I be lifted up, I will draw all men to me." (John 12:32) Of course Jesus was speaking of the cross, but the same effect happens when we just tell people of how wonderful is the Lord we serve. When people get a glimpse of the real Jesus, nothing else comes close.

I'm so glad He is the image of God. That tells me God is most patient and understanding, for Jesus was. (John 8:11) It tells me that God hates the abuse of power and the corruption of power for personal gain, for Jesus did. (John 2:15-16) It tells me God does not esteem people because of their position in life or their wealth, for Jesus did not. (Mark 10:21) It tells me God loves us more than we can imagine, for Jesus, the image of God, went to the cross for you and me.

And He is firstborn, King of kings and Lord of lords. (Revelation 19:16) Satan doesn't stand a chance. His days are numbered, and so are the days of all those who refuse to bow to the loving goodness of God. Nothing can stand against Jesus for all things were created for Him. Even the wrath of man will praise Him! All rebellion will one day cease. This is the glorious Jesus we need to share with others.

17 And he is before all things, and in him all things hold together. He is preeminent. If for a moment Jesus ceased to be, all things would cease to be. Everything is held together by Him, electrons in their orbits and planets, moons and galaxies in theirs. Incomprehensible, but He does it all! Jesus! What a name!

Let me close with a parallel passage, probably by a different author, but one that said the very same things we just read in these short three verses. Hebrews 1:1-3 (NIV) 1 In the past God spoke to our forefathers through the prophets at many times and in various ways, 2 but in these last days he has spoken to us by his Son, whom he appointed heir of all things, and through whom he made the universe. 3 The Son is the radiance of God's glory and the exact representation of his being, sustaining all things by his powerful word. After he had provided purification for sins, he sat down at the right hand of the Majesty in heaven.

This is Jesus! He is our glorious Savior. He is the radiance of God's glory. He's the exact representation of His being. He holds all things together by His powerful word. I hope you've asked Him to be your Savior, God, and King, because there is no other name under heaven by which we must be saved. (Acts 4:12)

Questions
1 Have you been praying the prayer?
2 Did Jesus ever say what Paul claimed in verse 15?
3 Why is this a radical thing for Paul to say?
4 How would Paul come to such a conclusion? Give example passages.
5 What did eikon mean to the Greek?
6 How was it used on documents?
7 What would it say to the Jews?
8 What are the implications to the Old Testament?
9 What does "firstborn" mean? Psalm 89:27
10 Why do things exist?
11 What do we know of God when we look at Jesus?
12 Compare the passage with Hebrews 1:1-3

The Beginning Colossians 1:18-20

Last week we saw Jesus, the image of the invisible God. We saw that He is the Creator and sustainer of all things and that all things were created for Him. In our passage today we move from the first creation to the new creation. It's going to get a bit mystical and maybe out of our comfort zone, but we are going to try to follow Paul into these realms.

Jesus is not only the creator and sustainer of the first creation, but He is also *18 ... the head of the body, the church. He is the beginning, the firstborn from the dead, that in everything he might be preeminent.* Let's look at each of these three descriptions of Christ in the new creation. He is the head of the body. Though Paul has referred to the church being like a body in some of his previous letters (Romans 12:5; 1Corinthians 12:12), this is the first time he refers to Jesus as the head. (Ephesians 1:22) From the head comes direction to the members of the body and the will that determines what the body will do. Paul probably had more in mind as we will see in 2:19. The head is the life giving source and in the mind of that age, the source of growth. The pituitary gland within the head does in fact regulate growth.

In the next chapter, the leader of the false doctrine is said to have lost connection from the head (Jesus) and therefore had not grown along with the rest of the body of believers.

The next declaration is that Jesus is the beginning. To understand the depth of this word (arche) "beginning", we need to see its use in

Scripture. The book of Genesis is the book of beginnings. The Greek version uses the same word Paul is using here. The Gospels of Mark and John both start using this word in their opening line just as in the book of Genesis. (Mark 1:1; John 1:1; Genesis 1:1) Jesus is a new beginning. He is head over the old creation, but He is also head of the new creation, the new beginning. That is why in the book of Revelation He declares that He makes all things new. (Revelation 21:5) All things are yet to be made new. We do have the beginning however, Jesus! There is also the new creation of the church, the bride of Christ.

God's purpose has been to reverse the effects of the fall (Genesis 3:16-19), but there is something more. God was not surprised by the fall. For the full purposes of God to come to fruition, God had to enter creation and take upon Himself our nature. We were meant to be more than a "living soul". (Genesis 2:7) The destiny that God planned for man was that we might receive His "life-giving Spirit". (1Corinthians 15:45) When a soul receives the redemptive work of Christ, they become a part of the new creation that Jesus began in the resurrection. That is why the third description of Jesus is "firstborn from among the dead".

When Jesus was raised, it was not like any previous resurrection in which the person aged and eventually died. He was raised in a transformed body that was the beginning of the new creation that cannot die. (Romans 6:9) Each new believer is spiritually transformed within to be a part of the new creation. That is why Jesus told Martha and Mary that the one who believes in Him will never die. (John 11:25-26) The body may perish, but we have become a part of the new creation that is eternal life; thus the saying, "even though he die yet shall he live!" We are in Christ. But as the passage goes on to indicate, this is just the beginning.

We live in world where the old creation and the new exist side by side. The day will come when creation will be redeemed, but in the end the old things will pass away and all things will be made new. That day is already here for believers spiritually. (2Corinthians 5:17)

He is the firstborn from the dead, the beginning, the head of the church. Jesus is Creator and the One who began all things is bringing about the new creation. That is why He is preeminent in all things. He is not one of a number of ascended masters or intermediaries, He is all in all.

Heresies always attempt to describe Jesus as something less than He is, the preeminent One, the Creator of both the old and new creation. The false teaching that was being offered to the Colossians was trying to make Jesus something far less than what He is, and Paul was saying He is so much more than even the Colossian believers understood Him to be. I would dare to say He is so much more than we in this life will ever comprehend Him to be! How magnificent is Jesus to you?

In case the reader couldn't understand what Paul had written to this point, if they didn't understand to what extent Jesus was the image of God, Paul clarified it further. *19 For in him all the fullness of God was pleased to dwell,*

The combination of the verbs pleased and dwell are only found in one other place in Scripture, Psalm 67:17 LXX. It is not the same in our Bibles, but it was the version of the Old Testament often referred to by the New Testament authors. A direct translation would be as follows: "God was pleased to dwell in it. The Lord will dwell forever in the holy place." The New Testament authors saw Jesus as the new tabernacle, the place where God resides with man, the place where we go to meet with God, and the place where sin is atoned.

All the fullness of God was pleased to be at home in the sanctified holy place of Jesus. "Fullness" was a favorite term of Gnostics. Paul was saying that Jesus didn't just have fullness of wisdom or secret knowledge but that ALL the fullness of God was pleased to live in Him. (Hebrews 1:3) And He invites us to be in Him! (John 15:4) That is so much more than what the false teachers were offering.

Paul was clarifying the choice that was before the Colossians. They were offered a so-called secret knowledge, or they could continue to be in the One in whom all the fullness of God was pleased to dwell. Once the choice is clarified, we shouldn't have a problem deciding. It is the same for us. Everything the world has to offer, whether relationships, pleasure or possessions pales when we compare it to what is offered to us in Christ! We need to make a real comparison. We need to see the temporal nature of everything of the old creation. (1John 2:18) We also need to see Christ in His glory, the wonder of His character, and the love and grace He offers. Both cannot be first in our life.

The old creation is to be enjoyed in the boundaries of God's will, but it is the new creation that should by far be the joy of our heart and reason for living. He must be preeminent in our desires. (Deuteronomy 6:5) There is no fullness in life outside of Christ. The old always leave you wanting more. Only Christ can fully satisfy our longings for all the fullness of God is at home in Him.

You've often heard me say that Jesus is our example in everything. How does that relate to this incredible fact that all the fullness of God is pleased to be at home in Him? Everything of God finds a place in Jesus. All God's justice, righteousness, holiness, grace, mercy and every other attribute finds itself without resistance in Jesus.

Are the attributes of God at home in you? If we are in Christ, a part of that new creation, they certainly should be at home in us. We are not perfected. We are still a work in progress, but grace should be at home while unforgiveness should be seen as a thief sneaking into our home to rob us. Love should be at home in our heart while apathy should be like a mangy mutt that wandered in unwelcomed. That's the assurance that you are a part of the new creation in Jesus.

20 God was pleased ...through him to reconcile to himself all things, whether on earth or in heaven, making peace by the blood of his cross. The old fallen creation will be reconciled to God. The word for "all" in the Greek is neuter, meaning this is referring to physical objects not living souls. The fallen state of the universe will be undone and we will experience it as it was originally created, at least for a time. (Matthew 24:35)

Universalists would like to read into this passage that all people and angels will be reconciled to God. That ignores the rest of Scripture. (John 3:36) Certainly God will reconcile all people that will accept what Jesus has done. The blood of the cross reconciles all who will have that change of mind and heart that the Bible calls repentance, but it will also have an effect on all of creation that is presently groaning to be delivered from its bondage to decay. (Romans 8:21-22) Jesus' blood shed on the cross defeated death and hell and gave Him a right to take back the Lordship over creation that was lost when man fell. The right was restored to man, the God man, Jesus. (Revelation 1:18)

The verse tells us that this is how God was pleased to make peace. The universe has been at war. You don't have to take it by faith, just look at the newspaper or turn on the news. It is one non-stop reporting of the war that is taking place. It is a spiritual war that is manifest in the physical creation. (Ephesians 6:12) It is a war that started when Satan decided he wanted God's throne. His pride prevailed in his thinking and then was manifest in his actions as he drew a third of the angels to follow him in his rebellion. (Revelation 12:4) He was able to seduce man into joining that rebellion as well with the same temptation to which he succumbed. "You shall be as gods!" (Genesis 3:5) The war has raged on ever since.

God worked through the rebellion to help man understand that God is loving and good and to resist Him is evil and death. He provided the victory through the blood of the cross. God used the Old Testament system of sacrifice to give us an idea of what was taking place. Substitution is the basis. There is a foundation for it in the first chapters of Genesis when God provided an animal skin as a covering for Adam and Eve. (Genesis 3:21) The covering of glory that they lost when they sinned exposed them. They tried to cover themselves with leaves but still knew they were exposed. Then the Lord provided a covering. Some animal died to provide a covering. In that picture, we have the outline of what God would one day do for mankind in providing a covering (atonement) for the sins of mankind, peace through the blood of the cross.

The author or Hebrews puts it like this: *8b At present, we do not yet see everything in subjection to him. 9 But we see him who for a little while was made lower than the angels, namely Jesus, crowned with glory and honor because of the suffering of death, so that by the grace of God he might taste death for everyone.* Hebrews 2:8b-9 (ESV) The old creation is not yet in subjection to Jesus, though He has certainly claimed the right to subject it and will do so at the time of His choosing. (1Corinthians 15:25) But being in wonderful subjection to Him can begin right now in all who will receive Him tasting death for you. That means your life is no longer your own. You become a servant of the living God and that is why we call Him Lord.

This is why it is so difficult for people to make the choice to surrender to Jesus as Lord. They still fall for the lie that we can be our own god. They don't realize that they are remaining as a part of the old creation which is fallen and under a curse. They don't realize the benefits of being a part of the new creation and knowing Jesus as Lord and Savior, the beginning, the head of the church, the firstborn from among the dead. Firstborn from among the dead means those in Him are guaranteed to follow Him in physical resurrection for we are a part of that new creation. (1Corinthians 15:52)

The verses we have gone over these past two Sundays (15-20) are believed by some to be an ancient hymn of praise to the glory of Jesus. We can't be sure, but it is a beautiful expression of His majesty and preeminence over the original creation and the new creation of which He is the beginning. If there is one thing I would like you to take from this, it is that what we have in Jesus is incomparable to anything, anything! (Romans 8:32) And in Him we have all things eternal!

As we continue to pray for the full knowledge of His will with all spiritual wisdom and understanding, I believe we are going to see that God's will is for us to know Jesus, to know Him in a deeper and richer and more surrendered way than we have known Him to this point. The more you see of Him the more you will love Him. The more you love Him the more you will love those He loves. In serving others you will see that you are serving Him. (Matthew 25:40)

These few verses are rich with theology that we have only scratched the surface, but the point is this, Jesus is the Supreme One. He is the head of the church. The elders are his undershepherds but He is the head. Good ideas have no place. We need the head to give us direction. Our will has no place. The head must share with the body His will. We must learn to wait upon Him and not go off on our own, at our own whim or at the leading of any individual or program that presents itself as the answer. That is why the elders pray together to discern what the head is saying to the body. Jesus must be the preeminent One in the church.

He must be the preeminent One in each of our daily lives, in how we spend our time, in how we order our thoughts, and in each of our families. He must be preeminent in our work and leisure. Jesus must be first and foremost in our worship, in our music, in our missions, in our service. Most of all He must be the preeminent love of our life, and He will be if we will see Him as He is, the image of the invisible God, the Creator and sustainer of all things, the firstborn of creation and the firstborn from among the dead, the head of the church, the beginning. His blood has reconciled us to God, and for that we owe Him everything!

Are you a work of His new creation? Are the attributes of God at home in you? If not, you can be transformed today by accepting the reconciliation that the blood of the cross made possible for you. Just come to Him and let Him to be your loving Lord and Savior. Let go of any area of resistance and let His nature be at home in you.

Questions

1 What are the implications of Jesus being the head of the body?
2 What is the connection with "beginning" in Genesis and Mark and John?
3 What could be more than reversing the fall?
4 How is Jesus' resurrection different from all others?
5 What was the choice the Colossians had to make? And ours?
6 Are the attributes of God at home in us?
7 What are the "all things" reconciled to God through the cross?
8 What was the earliest picture of atonement?
9 Why do people have such a hard time receiving Christ as Savior?
10 What is one way to serve Jesus?
11 Is Jesus the preeminent One in your life?

Reconciliation Colossians 1:21-23

I keep thinking I'll be able to take a larger section of text, but there is just too much in every few verses to rush through. Though we have hit some of these topics before, our congregation has changed over the years and we can't rush through some of these essential topics.

The church at Colossae was full of new believers. Epaphras had led them to a saving knowledge of Jesus. It appears from the letter that one in the congregation had decided that Jesus was just fine, but thought Epaphras didn't have the whole story. This individual knew a lot about Judaism and an up and coming idea that would become known as Gnosticism. He combined all three and tried to influence the new Christians at Colossae to follow his teachings.

Some individuals find their self-worth in being the one that others follow. (3John 9) Paul will address that individual's self-delusion later in the letter. (Colossians 2:18) But Paul begins by reminding them how they became a body of believers in the first place. Understanding the basics of who Jesus is and what He did for them was the strongest defense against false doctrine. It is the same everywhere and in every age. It is much more difficult to distort the teaching of the Apostles when you understand what Jesus did for us. That is the foundation. The building may lean this way or that, but if the foundation is correct, all the rest can be properly repaired. (1Corinthians 3:11)

Paul reminded them how much their lives had changed. *21 And you, who once were alienated and hostile in mind, doing evil deeds*, They had been alienated from God. That is, they had no relationship with the one true God. Most of the people in that church had probably worshiped the gods of their city, guild, and family. When they would go to a town meeting they would throw some incense on an altar and bow to the city god. When they went to work they would offer some incense on the altar of the god of their particular trade, praying for success. In their homes, their hearth was the center of worship and they would have a particular god for their family.

All these Greek or Roman gods were thought to be capricious and uncaring. You just had to keep them happy by honoring them or there would be some kind of natural disaster or illness that would strike. They had no concept of any of these gods caring about them, and a loving god was almost unheard of. They paid their obligatory offerings just to keep them from getting angry. In an area prone to earthquakes and without the understanding of germs and viruses, the evidence of the gods' displeasure seemed to appear on a regular basis. That caused people to wonder just what they had done that angered the gods.

That is what the Apostle called alienation from the true God. Today we have a similar mindset. Those without knowledge of the love of God and the gospel of Jesus often think God is angry with them and caused some kind of disaster in their life. Sometimes they will respond with anger toward God. They ask, "What did I do to deserve this?" Like the Greeks in Colossae, they thought they were paying sufficient reverence to keep an angry god off their back. That too is alienation from God, as the prophet wrote, "All our righteousness is as filthy rags!" (Isaiah 64:6-7)

Does anyone really believe some incense on an altar would be enough honor for the creator and sustainer of our life? Is it right to think of God as demanding our little acts of ritual worship or He'll whack us? That is alienation from God because it is thinking of God in a way that is contrary to His good and holy nature. Everyone is alienated from God before they meet God in Jesus because of sin but also because they have so many misconceptions in regards to who He is and what He expects.

We don't like the indictment and tend to think we are better than most. The sad story of the Titanic lifeboats tells us this alienation assessment is an absolutely accurate description of the heart of fallen man. Of the eighteen life boats that entered the water, most were a little over half full, only one went back to answer the cries of the 1600 people swimming in the frigid water. That boat went back one hour after Titanic sank, when the cries had dwindled to just thirteen voices. This is the selfish nature alienated from God.

We were all hostile in our minds. That is because we have a fallen nature that we inherited from Adam. (1Corinthians 15:22) We all come into life falling for the lie in the Garden that you can be your own god. (Genesis 3:5) You can call your own shots and go your own way and do a good deed now and then to keep God off your back. That is the position of an adversary. It's as if God was the playground bully you have to give your lunch money to or you get beat up.

Many of the cults that I have looked into began with a believer who became angry with God because of a painful incident in their life. They decided to reshape God into an image they could handle, one that put them at the pinnacle of a new revelation that everyone else could follow while allowing them to indulge their carnal nature. That is the by-product of hostility of the mind. (Jeremiah 5:21-25)

I have to ask you, because it is all too common, are you angry with God? Is there something painful in your past that you blame on God? Never mind that we live in a fallen world, and people have freewill; God could have stopped it, right? And so a root of bitterness has developed in our heart. (Hebrews 12:15) That bitterness will keep you from your loving heavenly Father. He's ready to welcome you back. (Luke 15:20) The hostility in our mind is because we have distorted who He really is, a God who loves us with a greater love than we can comprehend.

The hostility toward God exhibits itself in hostility to our fellow man. Just as love for God is expressed in love for our fellow man, so our hostility toward God translates into hostility toward others. When you see someone who is angry with others and speaks evil of others, you can be sure their relationship with God is hostile as well. (1John 2:10-11)

It goes without saying that if we are alienated from God and hostile in our minds, we will do evil deeds. It is the natural outcome of being our own god. Selfishness will express itself in all kinds of evil deeds: Theft – I deserve it; slander – I'm right and they are bad people; inappropriate sexual behavior – it's all about my pleasure; lies – whatever I need to say to promote my image; and on and on. In some way or another, this is the life of every person before repentance, which is a change of mind. (Romans 1:28-31) We'd like to think we are more altruistic, until we imagine ourselves in one of those Titanic lifeboats.

Repentance is going from alienation and hostility toward God to a loving relationship with God. It's a mind shift. It is forsaking your old way of viewing God, and seeing Him as He truly is, holy, righteous, loving, merciful and, perhaps most importantly, worthy of our love. How is it possible for a just God to overlook our past rebellion and welcome us into a relationship with His holy being?

22 he has now reconciled in his body of flesh by his death, in order to present you holy and blameless and above reproach before him, Paul is reminding the Colossians what Jesus did for them. He gave Himself as a substitute to take the punishment they deserved. By becoming man and living a sinless life, He could die in the place of sinners. The just penalty for sin is death. Jesus volunteered to pay it for the Colossians, and for you and me. That is how we could be reconciled to a loving but just and holy God. (1Corinthian 6:11)

With our sin debt cancelled, Jesus can present us holy and blameless and above reproach before God. The past alienation and hostility of our minds are no more in the sight of God. Unlike the Greek gods that just wanted a little deference; the true God demands holiness. His demand comes not out of a capricious demand but out of His own perfect nature. Because He is good, He must judge all that is evil. (Psalm 97:10)

The language also points to presenting an unblemished sacrifice to God. Paul may be pointing to presenting us as living sacrifices holy, blameless, and acceptable to God. (Romans 12:1)

When we accept this loving act of reconciliation that God offers to everyone in Jesus, we find that we become a part of the new creation we talked about last week. (2Corinthians 5:17) Our hearts have new desires and the old loses its appeal. Instead of alienation there is relationship with our

112

loving and holy God. Instead of hostility there is love and a desire to please Him in the way that we live. Our minds no longer interpret events from our selfish perspective but from a faith in our sovereign God. That is why our actions change. Instead of evil deeds of selfishness, we serve God in unselfish obedience. That is the transformation that takes place in the one that is born again.

Jesus presents us to God, holy, blameless and above reproach... *23 if indeed you continue in the faith, stable and steadfast, not shifting from the hope of the gospel that you heard, which has been proclaimed in all creation under heaven, and of which I, Paul, became a minister.* There is the big IF that we see throughout the New Testament. (John 15:10; Hebrews 3:6) There is a lot of controversy over the "ifs" in relationship to salvation. Honest and fruitful theologians have come down on both sides of the issue. Can you lose your salvation? Can you give back the gift? Does it matter what you do after you are saved? Are you eternally secure?

The passage clearly says that you will be presented blameless *"if indeed you continue in the faith"*. The implication is obvious. You won't be presented blameless if you do not continue in the faith. How are we to reconcile this with other passages of Scripture? Must we come down on one side or the other? Whenever I see what appears to be a contradiction in Scripture, I know there must be something I do not understand.

Allow me to go at this from a slightly different approach. What if there was no "if"? Can we be reconciled to God, made holy in His sight, and then live as we please? Would it not be a temptation to the believer to revert to the old life and, in the words of Hebrews 10, trample on the son of God, treat as unholy the blood of the covenant, and insult the Spirit of grace? (Hebrews 10:29) Before you get up and walk out and say, "Oh no! Pastor Paul is an Armenian!", hear me out. There's an "if" in this passage and many others. (2Peter 1:9-10) It's the Word of God. We ignore it to our own peril.

Now let us look at the other Scriptures that the Calvinists would quote in response. Jesus said that the one that believes in Him has eternal life. (John 6:47) It's not eternal if you can lose it! He said no man can pluck the believer from His hand. (John 10:28) He said that when we believe we have passed from death to life. (John 5:24) How could you possibly nullify the work of Jesus in a heart? Does He not promise to finish the work He began in us? (Philippians 1:6)

What if we did not have these assurances? Every time we stumbled we would be wondering if we had lost our salvation. Every Sunday we would be at the altar hoping God would somehow take us back. (Hebrews 6:4-6) Would we not be saying that the blood of Jesus had failed to cover all our sins? Would we not be saying that Jesus' work on the cross was insufficient to save us?

And so you see the quandary. There must somehow be both, both are in Scripture if we will just read it as written and not twist the text; and yet they seem like a contradiction. First let me say that I do not believe they are a contradiction. I do believe an honest interpretation makes it sound like they are.

The most balanced approach I've ever heard came from a professor and pastor. He said, "If you are worried about losing your salvation, if you think somehow you are too weak or Satan is too cunning, then you better be a Calvinist!" Do you see what he was saying? Trust your great Shepherd. Don't fear. Yes, you may be weak, but He is strong. Yes, Jesus loves you, and He will finish the work he began in you!

But, he went on to add, "If you think that since you are secure in Christ, you can go out and live in a way that will please your flesh, ignoring God and selfishly indulging in every pleasure you might desire, because after all, you have a ticket to heaven, then you better believe you can lose your salvation!"

Well, that is good practical advice, but I'm not sure it is faithful to the authors' intent when they wrote these passages we are considering. One other solution comes in the suggestion from the Calvinist perspective, that if the person lives the life of the unredeemed, they never were redeemed. I'm not sure that is faithful to the text either.

Can we leave it as a mystery? The Trinity is a mystery to me. I can define it and illustrate it but I can't really comprehend it. Are we eternally secure or must we persevere in our faith? Yes! The Bible declares both are true. Rather than taking sides, can we take the practical approach of the professor? Can we leave it as a mystery and say we better persevere if we are genuine followers of Jesus? Let's move beyond the "if" and look at the rest of the verse.

23 if indeed you continue in the faith, stable and steadfast, not shifting from the hope of the gospel that you heard, which has been proclaimed in all creation under heaven, and of which I, Paul, became a minister. We're exhorted to continue in the faith, and to remain stable and steadfast, to continue to cling to the hope of the good news that we first heard.

Does that describe your life in the faith? It should! If we are waffling around, tossed like a ship in storm, we are looking at two different sources. (James 1:6) We cannot serve two masters. (Matthew 6:24) God expects us to be all out committed to Him, because He is to us. If He didn't withhold His Son, is there any good thing He would withhold from us? (Romans 8:32) So why would we be anything less than stable and steadfast?

Paul ends the verse by saying that this gospel has been proclaimed in all creation, or we could translate it "to every creature". He may have been referring to Mark 16:15, Jesus' Great Commission to take the news of what He has done for us to the world.

Paul says he became minister of this gospel. Minister is a really nice term for the Greek word that most commonly meant one who runs errands or waits on tables. Paul says he is so sold out to his conviction that he lives his life as an errand boy running here and there to spread this good news.

114

That is why he is writing the Colossians. The good news was getting corrupted and complicated by someone who wanted to be a leader. The good news was simple. Jesus paid their debt and made them holy before God. Don't let go of that. Cling to the hope if offers. Don't waiver. Let it transform your life. Let it change the way you think. Remember how far you've come… and keep going forward!

Our response to the wonder of being reconciled to God should be a life that is dedicated to the One who paid our debt. In gratitude for being made holy and blameless and above reproach before God, we should live a life that is holy, blameless, and above reproach by cooperating with the Holy Spirit within us. Every day should be a walk with God no longer in alienation, but in loving relationship. I hope that is a description of the transformation that has taken place in your life since you were reconciled to God.

Questions
1 What's the best defense against the false teaching?
2 Describe being alienated and hostile in mind.
3 What are the results of that condition?
4 How were we reconciled?
5 What is the result?
6 What's the big IF?
7 What are some verses that seem to indicate we can't lose salvation?
8 What are some that sound like we can?
9 What was the professor's suggestion?
10 What does minister mean? Are you one?

The Hope of Glory Colossians 1:24-29

We've had a fantastic introduction to Jesus. Paul's beginning defense of the Gospel and counterargument to the false teachers was a declaration of the greatness of Christ and what He had done for the believers. When we see Jesus as He truly is, everything else pales in comparison. The glitter of the false teacher's secret wisdom faded into insignificance when compared to the brilliant glory of Jesus.

Paul moved into what Jesus has done for them and the calling on his personal life as an Apostle to the Gentiles. *24 Now I rejoice in my sufferings for your sake, and in my flesh I am filling up what is lacking in Christ's afflictions for the sake of his body, that is, the church*, This is a difficult passage to understand when we just look at it on the surface, but understanding Paul's theology it makes perfect sense.

I remember clearly that one of the first missionaries I met in Japan asked me if I understood this verse. He was going through a difficult time and wondered if this verse somehow related to his life. I can't remember my response, but I don't think I really understood the passage at that time.

First, we should not overlook that Paul considered suffering for the church a reason to rejoice. (Matthew 5:11-12) He was not in prison for doing anything directly with the Colossian church, so how could he see his suffering as being "for their sake"? It appears that he is speaking of his role as the Apostle to the Gentiles. (Galatians 2:8) It was indirectly because he was winning people like Epaphras who did start the church of the Colossians.

The increasing growth of the Christian church caused the Jews in Roman cities to complain to the authorities that Christianity was not Judaism and was therefore illegal. The only worship allowed other than the Greek and Roman gods and Emperor worship was Judaism. If the Christian church was deemed to be a break from Judaism, it faced the persecution of Rome. Jealous Jewish leaders who saw their worshipers leave the synagogue to follow Jesus as Messiah had the recourse of complaining to Roman public officials. (Acts 18:12-13) This is why Paul was imprisoned, jealousy over converts. (Acts 13:45) He was converting Jews, Romans, and Greeks to a faith that was quickly becoming unacceptable to Rome.

It was Paul's proclamation of the good news of Jesus that brought people to the faith and strengthened the fledgling churches. He is suffering for the body of Christ, the church's sake. But how can he say he is filling up what is lacking in Christ's afflictions?

First, let's look at what he is not saying. He is not saying that somehow he had to suffer as a co-redeemer, as if his suffering somehow added to what Jesus did on the cross. We know that is not the case because he has written that it was through faith alone in the Son of God that we have redemption, the forgiveness of sins. (Romans 3:21-25) Let's look carefully at the context and at Paul's teaching and we'll see what he is saying.

In verse 28, Paul gives us the goal of his suffering and labor, to present everyone mature in Christ. As a member of the body of Christ, he is suffering to mature the believers. Christ suffered to redeem us, saving our souls, making us right with God. As a part of the body of Christ, Paul was suffering for his efforts to mature the believers in this life. (2Corinthians 1:5-7)

One is salvation of our soul, a work accomplished through the suffering of Jesus and shedding of His blood. The other is our sanctification, maturing, which is salvation from this evil world. (Galatians 1:4) That's a work that is partly accomplished through the suffering of fellow believers who face the persecution of the world to build up the body of Christ. Of course, it is Christ in Paul accomplishing this task.

Paul remembers that when Jesus met him, He was told that when he persecuted the body he was persecuting Jesus. (Acts 9:4) Now he is a part of that body that is being persecuted by others for the sake of building up what he once tried to tear down. His participation with Christ results in Christ's suffering for the sake of believers to overflow into his life.

Let me state it a bit differently to clarify. Jesus died for your sins, to make you right with God. Nothing can add to that work on the cross and His blood shed for you. (Titus 3:5-7) The body of Christ, your fellow believers, allow themselves to suffer to help fellow believers mature and live a sanctified life in the knowledge of God. Those who are called to teach and preach the word could ignore the call and save themselves a lot of heartache and in many places of the world avoid persecution and even death. But in accepting the call, they know they will participate in the sufferings of Christ, not to add to what Christ did for their salvation, but that others might hear the Gospel and mature in the knowledge of God. Jesus died to save us from judgment, but the results of that salvation should be a righteous life. In that sense the pastor/teacher/elder participates in the sufferings of Christ as they are persecuted for teaching the Scriptures. Whatever is loss in their life for the sake of the Gospel, financial, relational, or physical, is filling up the suffering of Christ to see the body mature in Christ.

Here is how the Message translation states the verse. 25 *When I became a servant in this church, I experienced this suffering as a sheer gift, God's way of helping me serve you, laying out the whole truth.* Colossians 1:25 MSG The translator dropped the "sufferings of Christ" phrase but got at the substance of what Paul was conveying.

That missionary in Japan had seen a drop in support and was wondering if the hardship his family was enduring was somehow related to this. I think it does. I think Mac and Jory leaving behind the blessings of the culture they were born in and going to a primitive place for a year to grow in Christ and disciple a few individuals toward maturity was filling up what is lacking in Christ's afflictions for the sake of his body, that is, the church.

All the missionaries we sponsor and many of you in your daily lives do the same. We put our own comfort and convenience second to serving the body of Christ and seeing them mature. And Paul says he isn't discouraged about that loss, but rather rejoices! Why? Because He is serving a Master that he loves dearly. (Philippians 3:8-10) He knows he'll reap an eternal reward. (2Corinthians 4:17) He realizes he is doing something of eternal value, participating with Jesus in turning people from darkness to light. Paul has an eternal perspective. He'd rather be in prison chained to a soldier and writing letters to a despised church than sitting as a respected and wealthy leader of the Sanhedrin. He has an eternal perspective! What's your perspective?

He writes that he is suffering for the sake of the church, *25 of which I became a minister according to the stewardship from God that was given to me for you, to make the word of God fully known,* We have some nice sounding theological terms, minister and stewardship, but in Greek they are much more humble, something more like an errand boy of who was given a treasure to manage for his master. (Ephesians 3:2) You see, that is why he is suffering. He's carrying out his duty as an errand boy by investing this treasure in service to his Master. The treasure is the Word of God, and his investment is to make it known to others so that it can produce fruit in their lives as well. This is expressed as making the Word of God fully known.

There is a famine today for the Word. (Amos 8:11) There are Bibles everywhere, but Bible illiteracy is probably higher than it has ever been in our country. This nation once spoke in Biblical terms and analogies. We commonly used expressions like "thorn in the flesh" or "divine Providence" or "Jacob's ladder", etc. If you do that today, most people won't know what you're talking about. Some that still use Bible terms distort them from their context and no one knows the difference because they never read or thought about the context. People come out of many seminaries today so confused about what the Bible teaches and what is truth that they give up on entering the ministry, and in some cases it is better that they did.

God is calling more people out of secular jobs, people who have been in the Word all their life and have the good sense to use commentaries by people who believe the Word as their study material. Now more than ever the Word of God needs to be made fully known. Many clear Bible doctrines are ignored or explained away and few people seem to care.

Just this week I read of the battle over whether or not the Old Testament was Messianic that has gone on since the 1700s. Jesus said it is! Isn't that the proof? If the foundations are destroyed, what can the righteous do? (Psalm 11:3)

We need people who fully know the Word of God and will speak up when it is distorted, when people need to hear what the Word teaches regardless whether they like it or not. If we are shunned or suffer because we proclaim the Word, let us do as the Apostle Paul and rejoice! Amen? Just be sure you fully know the Word you are proclaiming and proclaim it in love. (2Corinthians 4:2)

Paul had a specific treasure within the Word that he was to share. He calls it *26 the mystery hidden for ages and generations but now revealed to his saints.* This is the light that went on (pardon the pun) on the road to Damascus. (Acts 9:3) As a studious Jew, he knew about a coming Messiah. He knew the prophecies, but within the Scriptures he'd gone over a million times was a mystery. He writes that this mystery was now unveiled to the holy people, the ones God had called. That was a term he had applied to the Colossians at the beginning of the letter, but here, I believe it is applied to the Apostles. The next verse spells it out.

27 To them God chose to make known how great among the Gentiles are the riches of the glory of this mystery, which is Christ in you, the hope of glory. The book of Acts tells the story of how the elders and Apostles in Jerusalem came to understand that the Gentiles were being filled with the Holy Spirit. (Acts 11:18) Jesus' outreach to Gentiles toward the end of His ministry should have been a clue, but they needed to see for themselves that this good news was for all people, just as the prophets had predicted. (Isaiah 11:10) When they realized the Gentiles were filled with the Holy Spirit just as they were, the teachings of Jesus took on an even greater significance. This new covenant that Jesus ushered in was for all who would believe by faith. (Jeremiah 33:31-33) It was the manifestation of the Spirit in the form of spiritual gifts in that first century that convinced them

118

that God was offering entrance into the new covenant to all, irrespective of nationality or status. (Acts 11:15-17) It was just by faith through grace for all who would believe. If the Holy Spirit was in them, they had been sanctified as well and had the same hope and calling on their lives. It was quite a revelation.

"The hope of glory" means the abiding presence of Christ in us. If He lives within us, has taken up residence in us (John 14:23), if we are a part of that new creation we talked about a few weeks ago, then we know we will be with Him in glory. (Colossians 3:4) We can rest assured that when He returns on the clouds in great glory, we will be with Him. We know because of the change in our heart. Our desires have been transformed. We have a love for His Word. We want to know Him! The Holy Spirit vetoes our decisions at times and makes us uncomfortable when we are out of His will. At other times He nudges us in the right direction and affirms our decision and gives us the words to say. Christ in you is the hope of glory! It assures you that you are a part of the new creation.

28 Him we proclaim, warning everyone and teaching everyone with all wisdom, that we may present everyone mature in Christ. I purchased a book on preaching recently with the title, Him We Proclaim, taken from this verse. The theme of the book is the theme of this verse. Preaching should proclaim Jesus, as He is the theme of the entire Bible. If we preach from any Scripture and don't somehow return to Jesus, we've missed the main thing. He is the One that made the new covenant in His own blood that makes Jew and Gentile one in Him. (Ephesians 2:14-17) We can't share the Gospel without sharing about Jesus.

Paul got a jab in at the Gnostic vernacular when he said they warn everyone with all wisdom. Gnostics thought they had a corner on wisdom, deeper wisdom, or secret wisdom. For them, it was just for the few elites that rose to the top of their ranks. Paul is saying those who proclaim Jesus do so with ALL wisdom.

A quick look back at the chapter shows the conviction that Paul had in the fullness of Christ. Already he has used the word ALL (from the root *pas* in Greek) to describe wisdom, pleasing God, good works, power, endurance, things Jesus created, things Jesus sustains, things His blood reconciles, creation effected by the Gospel, and now to the wisdom proclaimed in the Gospel. Paul is emphasizing that Jesus isn't missing anything that they can attain from the false teachers. We have everything in Jesus! He is our all in all!

Jesus is all we need to attain spiritual maturity. This is Paul's goal, the focus of his ministry. It is not only to make converts, but as Jesus taught, to make disciples. (Matthew 28:19-20) That is why he hasn't stopped praying for them. He doesn't want them simply to make a declaration, but to be rooted and grounded in the faith, able to share with others as well, and to endure. Jesus called it fruit that remains. (Philippians 1:9-11, John 15:16)

Jesus' parable of the sower is so instructive here. Paul wanted to make sure the seed was not snatched away, and that the roots grow deep, and that the thorns not choke them from fruitfulness. (Matthew 15:4-8) Jesus wants a bride pure and spotless. (Ephesians 5:27) This harkens back to verse 22. We are made pure and spotless by the blood of Jesus, but the goal of the servant is to help the babe in Christ to mature to live outwardly what Jesus has made of him inwardly. In other words, to help them apply the Scriptures to their life so that their relationship with Jesus and their holiness of life might reach its richest state before He returns or calls them home. Maturity is what guards us from false teaching. It keeps us from those "ifs" we talked about last week.

29 For this I toil, struggling with all his energy that he powerfully works within me. This was what Paul labored at with dynamic energy of the resurrection power of Jesus that was working in Paul. (2Corinthians 4:10) That's why he was writing the letter. That's why it's so rich and we're taking it so slow. Paul gave it all he had, but all he had was supernaturally empowered! If it would help the Colossians mature, it will certainly help us mature!

Are you giving all you've got and letting the resurrection power of Jesus work in you as you encourage other believers, share with seekers, or use your gifts for God's glory? No wonder Paul could say, "Follow me, as I follow Christ." (2Corinthians 11:1) The power is there, but we need to give it all we've got WITH all the Spirit's energy. Cooperation is necessary. He won't take us where we refuse to go.

The goal of Paul is the goal of your elders and all mature believers. In proclaiming Christ, in making His Word fully known, we want to see every individual in our fellowship mature. We want to know that if you move on from here you will remain steadfast and stable in the Lord. We want to know that whatever doctrines confront you, you know Christ in you is the hope of glory! And if you understand what Paul is saying in this chapter, that ALL that we need is in Jesus, then that is sure to be true of you.

Mature believer, it is our duty to share in the sufferings of Christ to see the body mature. Young believer, feast on God's Word so that you may be equipped to share in that suffering. New believer, find someone that can encourage your faith and direct you in your life in Christ. Unbeliever, without Christ, there is no hope in eternity. Jesus' arms are open to you, inviting you to come home. You are here for a reason. It's to love God and enjoy Him forever!

Questions
1 Why could Paul say he was suffering for their sake?
2 How could he fill up the sufferings of Christ?
3 Can we participate in the sufferings of Christ? How?
4 And what should be our reaction to suffering and sacrifice?
5 What is a minister? A steward?
6 Are you one? In what way?
7 Who are "those who God chose"?
8 What is "the hope of glory"?

9 What was Paul's goal?
10 What are the "all"s in this chapter?
11 What is the point of all the "all"s?
12 What energy works in us?

The Healthy Church Colossians 2:1-5

The Apostle Paul began his letter to the Colossians by clarifying the choice that was before them. They could choose a path of pride that the false teacher offered, or remain in the abundance of what they had in Christ.

Paul used the words "fullness, mystery, wisdom, and knowledge" and applied them to Jesus which by contrast showed the false teacher's use of the words to be a lie. By speaking of the glory of Jesus, Paul was showing how vain the false teacher's ideas really were. Those ideas fell far short of what we have in Jesus.

Paul ended the last chapter describing his God given mission. (1:28) He was the apostle to the Gentiles, the revealer of the mystery of how God had made Jew and Gentile one by faith in Christ Jesus. (Ephesians 2:13-16) The life of Christ in the believer was the mystery that had been hidden for ages. (1:27) Looking back through the pages of Scripture, it became clear that the rules and ceremony of the Law were to prepare us for the coming of the Messiah, the fulfillment of the Law. (Matthew 5:17) The emphasis of Paul's message is that access to God is through the work of Jesus, not obedience to the Law. (Ephesians 2:8-9) Our obedience to the spirit of the law is a result of the life of Christ in us. If the life of Christ is in us, we have a sure hope of being in glory with Jesus.

Chapter two continues with Paul's mission in relationship to the Colossian church. He continues, *1 For I want you to know how great a struggle I have for you and for those at Laodicea and for all who have not seen me face to face,* Paul wanted them to know that they were on his heart. Though they had never met him, he was their spiritual grandfather. He knew how precarious this new church was, how vulnerable they were to false teaching. He also knew how important these locations were to the future spread of the Gospel. So not only for their sake but also for all those who would hear the good news through them, he entered into a great contest. That is a literal translation. We get our word "agony" from the Greek word that is used here for contest or struggle.

There are a number of ideas as to what the struggle was in regards to. It was for the church in Laodicea and Colossae. My opinion is that this is the struggle he referred to earlier and in the following verse, the prayer that they be filled with the knowledge of God's will and empowered to face their circumstances and relationships with the power of God's glory. Specifically, he was praying that they not succumb to the false teaching, but instead increase in the true knowledge of God. (1:25; 4:12)

This kind of laboring in prayer is something we usually think of as the work of specially called people like prayer warriors or intercessors.

Certainly, some people have a gift of really entering into prayer. In chapter 4 verse 2, Paul will encourage the whole church to continue steadfastly in prayer and to be watchful in it. He's inviting all believers to enter into serious times of prayer, to join in the struggle for the advancement of the kingdom of God. We have the opportunity to practice this every day.

The next verse tells us the specifics of the prayer to attain that end. *2 that their hearts may be encouraged, being knit together in love, to reach all the riches of full assurance of understanding and the knowledge of God's mystery, which is Christ,* We can add this to our prayer that we took up several weeks ago. Every church needs to have divine encouragement of the heart. It is easy to become discouraged, with our own failures, with people who leave the fellowship, with the conflicts that arise in the church because of differences. Is there any one of us that have not been discouraged at one time or another because the church is made up of fallible humans who are not yet perfected?

How many people do you know that no longer attend a church because they became discouraged over the way people act or decisions that were made? And so rather than face the pain and endure until God is glorified, they withdraw from fellowship. They decide to ignore the command to not forsake the assembling of ourselves together. (Hebrews 10:25) Perhaps the Lord will use you to encourage them back into fellowship.

You can see why Paul prayed that their hearts be encouraged. Amen? Shall we add this to our prayer, that God encourage our hearts? I think every believer needs this prayer! (1Thessalonians 5:11)

He goes on to pray that their hearts be knit together in love. One thing that can keep us from being discouraged and forsaking worshiping together is to be knit together in love. That is what we are endeavoring to do through Ida's Dinner 6. We need to get to know and love one another. When our hearts become knit together in love, we will endure little differences and offenses and work through them until God is glorified. That is the word we learned in chapter one verse eleven, *makrothumia.* (Colossians 1:11) Understanding the fullness of the Greek terms helps us to see how these prayers of Paul all fit together.

That word reminds me of the martyr of Cali, Columbia, Julio Ruibal. He quit attending a pastors' gathering because someone offended him. The Lord convicted him with the phrase, "Refuse to be offended." He went back to the meeting and repented, seeking forgiveness from the group. Out of that humility and obedience came revival to the entire city. It so affected the drug trafficking that the drug lords had Julio assassinated, but it was too late. His message and example had transformed the city. He learned the depths of *makrothumia*, of hearts being knit together in love and patience that overlooks faults.

This encouragement and knitting of the hearts was to reach all the riches of full assurance of understanding and the knowledge of God's mystery, The false teacher offered mysteries, secret wisdom, and a way to please God through works, but it was a lie. Paul is saying the path to the greatest mystery, and true wisdom, and really pleasing God is found in Christ through being encouraged and knit together in love and the unity of salvation.

It isn't found through keeping men's rules or secret wisdom. To reach the riches of full assurance we must continue in fellowship, allowing God to encourage our hearts, knitting them together in love. It's life in the body of Christ! "The one mark which distinguishes a true Church is love for God and for the brethren. When love dies, the Church dies." (Barclay commentary on Col 2:3) When we go Lone Ranger, we fail to reach the riches that are ours in Christ. If the church is the body of Christ, how are we supposed to know the fullness of Christ without being with His body? (Acts 20:7)

It's in the endurance through trials that we really grow together, whether friends, couples, or a church body. The trials are inevitable and they either make us stronger and more united or we give up on obedience to God and go our own way not realizing the easy way is the way of great loss.

...God's mystery, which is Christ, 3 in whom are hidden all the treasures of wisdom and knowledge. The end of verse two is usually watered down in most translations. The Greek literally reads, "the mystery, the God Christ!" But that so clearly says Jesus is God that it must not be the intended meaning, right? Why not? I think it means what was written in the earliest manuscripts! I wish man would quit trying to make it fit their theories and just read it as is! That's when we get fed and grow spiritually. The Bible is meant to transform our thinking. Our thinking isn't supposed to transform the Bible! (Colossians 3:10)

The hidden treasures of wisdom and knowledge are not for an elite few but available to all who will come to Christ. (1Corinthians 2:10; Isaiah 45:3) Through the ages the spiritual seeker wondered how they could be made right with God. The Jew wondered at Abraham being justified by faith (Genesis 15:6), and at David counting himself blessed for having his sins covered (Psalm 32:1). They knew sin was serious and required blood, but they also knew God was not satisfied with the blood of bulls and goats that were offered in sacrifice. (Hebrews 10:4) The mystery all came together in Jesus who was the Lamb of God who would die in our place. (John 1:29) That was the mystery, the plan of God from the beginning.

There are three Greek words for wisdom in verses two and three. In verse 3 we are to be encouraged and united in love and understanding. Understanding is described as critical knowledge, in other words discerning what to do in a given situation. We understood the mystery, the plan of salvation which is one of our main uniting factors. That leads us to discover in Christ the other two words, wisdom and knowledge. Wisdom is to confirm and commend the truth with wise and intelligent argument. Knowledge is the instinctive power to grasp the truth when we hear it. Put these together and you have a church that discerns the will of God intellectually and then finds in Christ spiritual wisdom and then understands how to respond. This is what we have in Christ, every kind of wisdom that we need for a life that honors God. (1:9-10)

Paul is really confronting the false teacher's doctrine head on. He is contradicting him in the strongest possible way. The false teacher offered the treasures to a select few. What kind of a God would that represent? It would be an unloving and bigoted god at best. But Jesus' arms are open to all who will come to Him. (Matthew 11:28-30) He freely gives them those treasures, the ability to discern the will of God intellectually and spiritually, and understanding how to proceed. That represents the God that loves the world. (Proverbs 2:3-6)

4 I say this in order that no one may delude you with plausible arguments. Paul was so clear about what was needed to help them deal with the slick talkers. We can't out argue people into faith, but we can point them to the God Christ! It is a personal encounter with Him and the forgiveness of sin that no argument can ever overcome. We know what happened in our heart. We find a deeper wisdom in Him. We know our desires have changed.

The words "persuasive arguments" in this verse were used for lawyers whose gift of rhetoric allowed the guilty to go free. Know Christ and let Him strengthen you, be filled with the wisdom that is hidden in Him, and you won't be deluded.

5 For though I am absent in body, yet I am with you in spirit, rejoicing to see your good order and the firmness of your faith in Christ. Paul was not present in some esoteric sense. He means it just the same way we would mean it today. "I am with you in spirit." It means my heart is there. (1Corinthians 5:3)

He next told them what it was about their fellowship that caused him to rejoice, their good order and firmness in their faith in Christ. These were two military terms. Good order is (taxis) an ordered military arrangement. (1Corinthians 14:40) Those who despise structure need to consider the term and its defense against false teaching. Though there is equality in the church, there is also order, structure, and authority. Each person has a role without which there is a weakness.

Firm in the faith (*stereoma*) is the term for an immovable phalanx. They were trained to take a position and hold it with each man holding a square meter of ground, side by side. (1Peter 5:9) These military terms are applicable to the spiritual battle they were facing. Each person had a role and is aided by all the others. Any loss is a costly one. Paul wanted them to see themselves as spiritual soldiers of the kingdom of God under attack from a spiritual force.

I believe the Spirit wants us to see how important each of us are in encouraging others and aiding one another spiritually with prayer, fortitude, and loving concern.

In these verses we have the description of a healthy church. First, there are those who pray for the church. We need the power of prayer to withstand the spiritual attacks all churches face on a regular basis. Some of you have taken up that call to pray for the service each Sunday in the prayer room. If you feel led to participate in that, see Lara Snider who is coordinating that effort. We will have 24 hours of prayer a week from Tuesday. We are all praying the prayer from chapter one and can add some of these points from the passage today to that prayer. Prayer is the unseen power behind all we do!

We need to be encouraged. The author of Hebrews suggested that we encourage one another more and more. (Hebrews 10:25) We need to pray that all our hearts be encouraged in our faith. Look for opportunities to encourage fellow believers. Write a note or an email. Give a phone call and offer a prayer for them to have a day of walking with Jesus in victory.

We need to focus on being knit together in love. Some worry about the church being too inward focused. In our world, the tendency is to be isolated and self -absorbed. If we don't love one another, how can that love overflow to the community? (Romans 12:10) People should be drawn from the world into the family of God because of the love the church enjoys. This is our focus this year, to be knit together in love for one another that others might know we are truly Jesus' disciples. (John 13:35)

As we encourage one another and knit our hearts in love, we access the treasures of wisdom and knowledge that are in Christ. That is, the ability to discern the will of God intellectually and spiritually and to understand how to proceed in a way that will glorify God.

Finally, we need to see that we are in a spiritual war and continue to maintain order within the church. We need to hold our position, side by side understanding that our spiritual success or failure affects those around us. We need one another! A healthy church isn't a perfect church, for there are no perfect churches. A healthy church is a church that refuses to be offended, that loves and prays for one another, and plumbs the riches of the wisdom in Christ. Ministry will naturally flow from that kind of church.

We are a family and like the family in Colossae, our success or failure will affect not just us, but those in the future who would hear the Gospel because of the faithfulness of this church. It's about bringing glory to Jesus, our Savior and King and living a life that is worthy of Him, not to earn heaven but in response for all He has done for us!

Questions
1 What was Paul's struggle?
2 Who should heed Colossians 4:1?
3 What are we adding to our prayer?
4 What is the testimony of Julio Ruibal?
5 What is the result of being knit together in love?
6 What are the three kinds of knowledge?
7 How does verse 2 end?
8 How can we prepare for slick arguments?
9 What two military terms did Paul apply to the Colossian church?
Application?
10 What are the ingredients of a healthy church?

Alive In Christ Colossians 2:6-15

In the previous passage we heard the Apostle's instruction and commendation relating to the health of the organism we call the church. The church is all the individual members united in love, encouraging one another, certain in our knowledge of Christ, plumbing the depths of the riches of His wisdom, and moving forward in an orderly and tight battle formation against the darkness of this evil world.

He continues, in our passage today, to encourage the Colossians with exhortation, warnings, and doctrine that no doubt came out of his wrestling in prayer for them. *6 Therefore, as you received Christ Jesus the Lord, so walk in him,* Ephaphras had shared the good news of Jesus with them and they had accepted Jesus as the Lord of their life. Paul is reminding them that since they had received Him as Master of their life, then they should walk, or we could say "live", in Him. (1Thessalonians 4:1) Wait for His instruction each morning. Ask for His leading throughout the day. Sing to Him. Worship Him. Lift up prayers to Him. He is the best master anyone could ever hope to know. He's a master that cares about His servants and loves them so much that He wants to live in them.

This is one of several one line commands that can guide your life and be indicator of your spiritual health. If you received Christ Jesus as the Lord of your life, are you living in Him at this moment? (1John 2:6) Are you constantly aware of His presence?

At church this morning, this verse asks us if our mind is on the Word that is being proclaimed, or is it wondering off to something else. (Hebrews 4:2) At work, living in Jesus might challenge us in our response to an angry customer. At home, He may ask if we are treating our spouse as Christ would treat them. That is walking in Him. If He is Lord, then we obey His instruction. If we are not obeying, we need to ask ourselves if we ever really received Him as Lord of our life. Living moment by moment in His presence is victorious Christian living, and that is true success.

This also tells us that walking in Christ as Lord is not automatic. Paul had to remind them to live in the Spirit. The next verse goes on to describe in more general terms what that means. *7 rooted and built up in him and established in the faith, just as you were taught, abounding in thanksgiving.* He is encouraging them to stay rooted in Christ, to have their foundation upon Him. That is what Epaphras taught them.

Roots not only secure the tree but draw up nourishment from the ground. It is a perfect analogy for Paul had told them previously that the depths of wisdom and knowledge were in Christ. (Ephesians 3:17) If they are to grow in wisdom and understanding, they need to draw upon Christ Jesus. Surely Epaphras taught them what he was taught from Paul, the Apostles doctrine of the life and teachings of Jesus. Paul will elaborate on that in the next few verses. (Acts 2:42)

"Built up in Him" means to add to what was started. Don't stay in the infant stage. (Hebrews 5:12) Roots are for the purpose of feeding what is

above so that it may grow. We need to be moving forward in our spiritual maturity or we are moving backward. A plant grows or dies. There is no in-between.

"Built" reminds me of weight lifters. They keep adding more and more resistance to gain more and more muscle. The same is true spiritually. We have to keep stretching and not get comfortable. (Acts 20:32)

They were also to be established in Jesus. The teaching they received of Jesus is their foundation to which they are to be secured. (Ephesians 2:20) Someone was trying to get them to turn back to the shadows in the Old Testament instead of the substance that was in Christ. The foundation is Jesus. The laws were a blueprint. We'll have more on that next week.

Essentially, he is saying to stay faithful to what they received and become more and more certain of it. Remember your first love while growing in conviction of the truth. (Revelation 2:4) Jesus is the power that changed their lives and ours as well. When we get away from that foundation, if we fail to sink our roots in deep, the next wind of doctrine that blows will turn us in a different direction. (Hebrews 13:9)

This is the second time in two chapters that Paul has exhorted them to be thankful (1:12), and before the short letter is over he'll remind them in each remaining chapter. (3:15; 4:2) When we see all that God has done for us in Christ, all that He offers us, all that He has planned for us, thanksgiving is the only right response. (Ephesians 5:20) If we are not abounding in thanksgiving, we are taking for granted the incredible generosity of our holy God. We have forgotten our former condition and what we actually deserve.

The believer that is not abounding in thanksgiving has either not seen what has been done for him or her, or has allowed the world to dominate their thinking. If they haven't seen, then they need to get into God's Word and realize the wonder of salvation. If the world is dominating our thinking, we need to take our thoughts captive. (2Corinthians 10:5)

There are believers that only speak of their difficulties. They say they are redeemed by the blood of Jesus, that they trust Him for their salvation, that they are bound for heaven, but the dominate topic is their ills, or their troubles, or their conditions. You surely have met people like that, and you may realize you fit into that description to one degree or another. We all do at some time. What's wrong with that picture?

There are times when we allow the temporary things of life to capture our soul. We think about them constantly. We speak of them every chance we get, when what we should do is capture them and take them to Jesus and leave them with Him. (1Peter 5:7) The more we meditate on all that we have in Jesus and the more we are in the Word, the more we see His gracious hand in our lives and thank Him for all His goodness. (Joshua 1:8) I can't start a prayer without thanking Him first. He's so good that He defines goodness. Are you abounding in thankfulness?

8 See to it that no one takes you captive by philosophy and empty deceit, according to human tradition, according to the elemental spirits of the world, and not according to Christ. The language here is of someone being taken as a slave. There were all kinds of philosophies in both the Jewish and Greek world. "Empty deceit" is saying that their lies have nothing substantial to offer you. Human tradition is what Jesus sometimes referred to, all the extra-Biblical rules that had sprung up in Judaism through the traditions of men. (Matthew 15:3) Paul says these are also according to elemental spirits of the world.

After further study, I have discovered that Paul is not so likely to be referring to the ABCs of Gnosticism but rather evil spirits or what is called doctrines of devils in 1 Timothy 4:1. Though early ideas of Gnosticism were around at that time, the usage of the Greek word in circulation then referred to demon angels. (See *stoicheia* in the Testament of Solomon)

Why can we ignore all the other philosophies according to man's traditions or any other teaching that is not according to Christ? *9 For in him the whole fullness of deity dwells bodily,* Every spiritual teaching that is outside of Christ either was made up by men or demons. Every truth is found in Jesus for in Him the fullness of deity dwells in a human body! Yes, I know that is intolerant. Years ago we had people leave the church that had attended for years because I said Buddhism and Islam and Hinduism are not equal to Christianity. If you really think that all religions are equal, I challenge you to go to the countries where those religions are dominant and see the dark side that doesn't show up in text books. (Matthew 7:20) Read of the sexual activities and lust of their gods. Watch the worship of snakes. Watch the neglect of helping the suffering "because it is their karma". Or in Islam see the abuse of women. Read of how Mohammed rose to power. Then tell me they are all the same. The historical evils of Christianity are because they disobeyed the teachings of Jesus. The evils I mention in the other major religions are because they are consistent with their religion. That's not politically correct, but it is honest.

In Christ, all of God took on a bodily form. (John 1:14) When we see Jesus, we see God. His reactions were God's reactions. His words were the very words of God. There was nothing of God that was not in Jesus. (Colossians 1:19) As we have seen several times previously, by this time in Paul's presentation of the Gospel, he declares unequivocally that Jesus is one with God. He is the Tabernacle that houses Shekina. You don't need to go anywhere else to get anything else! It's all in Christ!

10 and you have been filled in him, who is the head of all rule and authority. You are filled in Jesus! (Ephesians 3:19) You don't need anything else. (Philippians 4:19) He is the head of power. He has the final say. He has all wisdom. What more do you need? If He doesn't fill you up, nothing will! That God shaped hole in your heart is so big that He is the only One that can fill it. You have been filled in Him!

Like the Colossians, we need to be reminded that this is the case. Not because we've found Jesus lacking, but because we take our eyes off

His all sufficiency. The world is constantly enticing us. Every commercial says, "This is what you need to be happy, to really feel fulfilled." When we take our eyes off of Christ, when we stop walking in Him, experiencing His presence moment by moment, the world is right there to tell you that satisfaction can be found in something else. We must continually experience the fullness we have in Jesus or we will be distracted.

11 In him also you were circumcised with a circumcision made without hands, by putting off the body of the flesh, by the circumcision of Christ, Even in the Old Testament times they understood that circumcision was a picture of the circumcised heart. (Deuteronomy 10:16) It was a cutting away of the world and being separated from it. Made without hands is meant to be a contrast to the phrase, "made with hands" which always referred to idols in the Old Testament. (Psalm 115:4) Paul is implying that religious ritual had become idolatry. Relying on methodology rather than God is idolatry!

Putting off the body of the flesh was to put away the desires of the old nature, the things we once put between us and God. That was what was supposed to happen in our hearts. (Romans 2:29) The sages believed that this is what the Messiah would do for us when He came, and they were right. (Deuteronomy 30:6)

Paul continues with the description of how Christ circumcised our hearts. *12 having been buried with him in baptism, in which you were also raised with him through faith in the powerful working of God, who raised him from the dead.* This is the verse which we have on our baptismal. Baptism was a declaration that a person had been associated with Christ in His death and raised with Jesus to newness of life. That death is the putting off the body of the flesh. It doesn't mean that we deny all desires as in Buddhism, but rather that Christ is now our great desire and all others are subservient to Him as Lord. He gives us all things richly to enjoy, (1 Timothy 6:17) but in moderation and in their proper time and place. It is the Adamic fallen nature that is put off as dead.

Our new life is the result of being raised with Him through faith in the God who raised Jesus. If you are having trouble realizing you are a new creation, it comes back to having faith that the God who raised Jesus can, by the same power, transform your life. (Ephesians 1:19-20) Do you believe He can? Then you act on it and live it out by faith.

Every time the old nature would rise up, we continue to count it dead by faith. Remember faith isn't always something you see, but it is something you can always act on! We fail to walk in victory because we quit seeing who we are in Christ. We lose heart because we don't appreciate our position in Christ.

13 And you, who were dead in your trespasses and the uncircumcision of your flesh, God made alive together with him, Before we believed by faith, our spirit was dead. We acted out of our soulish nature, our desires and thoughts that were of the nature of fallen Adam. Our actions and our desires showed that our spirit was dead. The spirit is a part of our being created for God to inhabit, but without life there, we can only sin. But then we believed and accepted the work of Christ on our behalf on the cross. When He died, we died to our old self with Him. (Galatians 2:20)

...having forgiven us all our trespasses, 14 by canceling the record of debt that stood against us with its legal demands. This he set aside, nailing it to the cross. Every sin of which we were guilty and for which a just and holy God should punish us was put upon Christ. His death was the payment we deserved. The record of our sins and the debt we owed was legally cancelled. Upon that debt was written, "It is finished!", or we could translate it accurately, "Paid in Full!" (John 19:30) Your bill for every evil thought, every selfish desire, every intentional and unintentional evil act from your young age to your death is nailed to the cross on the body of Jesus. (2Corinthians 5:21) Jesus paid it all!

But that isn't the end. He rose victorious over death. In doing so, *15 He disarmed the rulers and authorities and put them to open shame, by triumphing over them in him.* God won the battle with the evil powers that opposed Him and mankind. God triumphed over them all in Jesus. He shamed them by showing them that sacrificial love was more powerful than all the selfish evil they could muster. Hallelujah! What a Savior!

Paul prayed in the opening chapter of Ephesians that we might know *19... his incomparably great power for us who believe. That power is like the working of his mighty strength, 20 which he exerted in Christ when he raised him from the dead and seated him at his right hand in the heavenly realms, 21 far above all rule and authority, power and dominion, and every title that can be given, not only in the present age but also in the one to come. 22 And God placed all things under his feet and appointed him to be head over everything for the church, 23 which is his body, the fullness of him who fills everything in every way.* Ephesians 1:19-23 (NIV)

Are your sins cancelled, nailed on the cross? Are you living in Jesus? Is He your Master? Are you raised with Him in baptism? Are you filled? Are you, by faith, living in resurrection life? If not, why not?

Questions
1 What does it meant to "walk in Jesus"?
2 What does it mean for Him to be Lord?
3 What are the implications of verse 7?
4 What does thankfulness or lack thereof indicate?
5 What things does Paul say will enslave us?
6 Where can we find everything of God that we need?
7 How are we filled in Jesus?
8 How were our hearts circumcised? What does it mean?
9 What happens to a believer's sin debt?
10 What happened to the evil powers that would feed us empty deceit?

The Mystery – Shadow and Substance
Colossians 2:16-17; Acts 9:19-22
(Inspired from The Messianic Hope by M. Rydelnik)

When the rabbi Saul became a Christian, he went through a dramatic shift in his understanding of the Scriptures. He had spent his life devoted to the Judaism that he was taught in the traditions of his elders. He was a most anticipated young Jewish leader, (Acts 22:3) and was one of the most zealous Jews you could expect to meet. He was so zealous, that he saw the Christian movement as a perversion of Judaism. (1Timothy 1:13) He thought it was his God given duty to stamp out the movement. It was on his way to Damascus that he had a supernatural experience and was converted to the very faith he was on his way to persecute. (Acts 9:15)

Following his dramatic conversion, he escaped the persecution of his fellow Jews by going over the wall of the city in a basket tied to ropes. (Acts 9:25) He then spent three years in Arabia. (Galatians 1:17-18) We don't know exactly what he was doing there, but I would imagine it was revisiting the Scriptures to understand how he could have been so wrong. (Acts 9:22) He thought his whole life was being faithful to the Scriptures, but after the encounter with Christ he knew he must have missed their whole intent. I've been there, but for me it was three months in a deserted village in the mountains of Japan. I had the advantage of having Paul's writings to help me.

The Book of Acts and the letters of Paul give us the details of a busy ministry evangelizing new areas and establishing and caring for churches, but of the time in Arabia we have no record. After that time, he visited the Apostles in Jerusalem. There, he could hear firsthand what they had seen and heard during their time with Jesus. But Paul was only with them a very short time. I think it was those three years of going back over the Scriptures with born-again eyes that cemented his understanding of Christ. Paul now had the key to interpreting the Scriptures. (Acts 9:20) Jesus is the Messiah, the Christ.

In our Colossian passage today, he refers to this change in his perception of the Scriptures as the mystery and as shadow and substance. The Jews of Jesus' day were longing for a Messiah that they saw as the fulfillment of numerous prophecies. They believed he would usher in the kingdom of God by defeating the enemies of Israel and helping his own people, Israel, to understand the Law as it was meant to be understood. Some of the sages of Israel even saw messiah as breaking down "the hedge of the Law" so that they could be led by the heart of God. (Ezekiel 11:19-20)

They saw the Scriptures as clearly culminating in this messiah figure. It was their hope. Jewish women prayed that they might give birth to the one. Numerous men claimed to be the messiah and rallied the zealots and discontents to them only to be mercilessly crushed by Rome. You could say there was a messianic fever in Israel in the first century. Even if their hope for a military leader was misguided, was the hope of a messiah really something the Scriptures predicted?

Many scholars today say that they were reading into the Scriptures something that never was meant by the authors. Others, including myself, have held the position that the author was writing about the immediate future and did not realize his wording was inspired by God to also apply to the Messiah (*sensus plenior*). The most conservative view is that the authors knew it was about the Messiah, but that sometimes there were also events that followed the prophecy that foreshadowed the Messiah.

Jesus seemed to hold the last view. He spoke to the two on the road to Emmaus explaining from the Law, the Psalms, and the prophets that the Christ must suffer before entering into His glory. (Luke 24:25-27) Whenever we read the word Christ, we can substitute the word Messiah. The meaning is the same, the anointed one. He explained to the disciples in the locked upper room all that was written about Him in the Law, the Psalms and the Prophets. (Luke 24:44) That should be good enough for us. He spoke as the One who came down from heaven. (John 6:33) If we say we are Christians, then shouldn't we accept the teachings of Christ? In spite of this, many evangelical seminaries today teach the second view, and some even teach the first.

However, I think if we understand what transformed Paul's thinking, what this mystery was that he declares was revealed to the saints, then we must take the side of the last view point. That is that the authors of Scripture wrote about a coming Messiah that was their future hope. One of the great evidences of this is in the way the Jews assembled the Scriptures. To the Jews, the Scriptures are in three books or sections. The first and most sacred is the Torah, the books of Moses. Genesis, Numbers, and Deuteronomy all have a narrative, a poem, and an epilogue. The narrative is the bulk of each book. The poems all mention "the last days". (Genesis 49:1; Numbers 24:14; Deuteronomy 31:29) They point to a culmination to which history is headed. This Torah covers creation to the death of Moses.

The second section is the *Nevi'im*. We would say the prophets. It covers Joshua to exile. The third is the Ketuvim, also called the Writings. It covers the exile to the restoration. The acronym for these three sections is the *TaNaK*. That is how the Jews refer to their Bible, that we call the Old Testament. Christians accept this as sacred Scripture just as the Jews accept it today and in the days of Jesus.

The fascinating thing is how the books were assembled. Each section ends with a messianic forecast, and the following section begins with encouragement to meditate on the Scriptures. The end of the Torah is Deuteronomy 34. Verses 9 through 10 are clearly looking forward to a Messiah. Joshua is introduced, but it is made clear that he is not the one that is like Moses, the One predicted in Deuteronomy 18:15.

The next section begins by encouraging Joshua to be a person of faith in the Word, and to meditate in it day and night. (Joshua 1:7-8) He is not the One, but he is to be faithful to look to the Scriptures and model them until Messiah comes.

The connection between the Prophets and the Writings is the same. The last verses of the Prophets (Malachi 4:4-5) speak of Elijah who will prepare the way for the coming of the Messiah. Then the Writings begin with Psalm one in which the wise man meditates in the Scriptures. (Psalm 1:2-3) This was not a mere coincidence, but the intention of those (of whom we do not have any historical account) that put the books in order to point to how we should live until Messiah comes.

In addition to this structure, we should also see that each book that was chosen as inspired (canon) has some portion which clearly has a messianic hope. In fact, one famous rabbi, Rabbi Johannan, declared "Every prophet prophesied only of the days of the Messiah." That is basically the same as Jesus' declaration.

But are we just reading into passages that for which we long? Students of Scripture call it isogesis instead of exegesis, in other words read into it instead of understanding it. Or were the writers really seeing the same thing as those who assembled the sections of the Bible? Let's look at a key passage in each of the three sections and see. We could spend a morning on each one, but you can do the research on your own if you want to go deeper.

The first is the beginning of Messianic expectation in Genesis 3:15. *15 I will put enmity between you and the woman, and between your offspring and her offspring; he shall bruise your head, and you shall bruise his heel."* Seminaries today are teaching everything from "this is intended to describe man's hatred of snakes" to "this teaches of man's constant battle with evil", but rarely is it taught today as clearly pointing to Jesus. The theme of "the seed" clearly runs throughout the entire Old Testament. This one verse establishes the plot of the whole *Tanak*. Consider that God is giving Adam and Eve hope in the midst of their sentencing, just as He will later do in the sentencing of Cain (Genesis 4:15) and the judgment of the flood (Genesis 6:18).

How can we be sure this is about a coming messiah? First, this is not just any snake; He talks! And this is not Narnia! It is not an allegory but intended to be read as history. All creation was declared good, even snakes, but this creature is animated by evil. Note too, that it is not the serpent's seed but the serpent himself that will have his head crushed, and that would require more than a normal lifetime. The first readers would have read it as a divinely empowered deliverer defeating this evil power, but being killed in the process.

Ancient Jewish interpreters read it as a messianic passage. It wasn't until they began to defend Judaism against Christian claims that the interpretation was altered. (Especially Rashi 1040-1105)

A careful look at the Hebrew also shows that it is a singular verb form and pronoun that describe the seed. There is one particular offspring in view in Genesis 3:15. A particular descendent (seed) of Eve will crush the tempter's head. (Galatians 3:16) If you were with us in the study through

133

Genesis, you saw the trail of the two seeds that started in the very next chapter.

The verb "strike" is used for both beings, the offspring and the tempter. The bite of the snake is deadly. Both die in the conflict. There is a part of the mystery. It was a victory achieved THROUGH death. (Hebrews 2:14-15)

Next we'll look at a passage from the Prophets, Isaiah 7:14. 14 *Therefore the Lord himself will give you a sign. Behold, the virgin shall conceive and bear a son, and shall call his name Immanuel.* It has come under intense debate during our lifetime, mostly because of the use of the Hebrew word *almah* for virgin.

I remember as a High School student a man told me about how Christianity distorted the history of the Bible. He pointed to this passage and then showed me how it was fulfilled a few chapters later, and then how the New Testament lied about what it meant.

A closer examination shows that there are two prophecies. At the time of the passage, King Ahaz was threatened from the northern tribes that had joined with Syria and threatened to replace Ahaz with the son of Tabeel. Would the lineage of David end? That would mean an end of the Messianic lineage. (2 Samuel 7:16) Isaiah predicted in 7:13-15 that the Davidic reign would continue. In 7:16-25 he addressed the short-term situation.

Once again, we must ask if we are reading into the text something we'd like to see? In verse 13, Isaiah addresses the house of David. When addressing Ahaz alone, the verbs are singular. In verses 4,5 and 11 they have switched to plural commands. In verse 13, "listen" is plural. The English word "you" comes from the plural Hebrew pronoun. God is addressing the whole house of David and the sign is for them, not just the king. They have tried God's patience by being ungodly kings, but would God not bring to pass the promise of the seed coming from the house of David? What was the miraculous sign? A woman becoming pregnant is a miracle of sorts, but nothing which would assure the house of David that God would keep a promise.

There are arguments as to the meaning of the word translated into virgin. Without getting into all the arguments, let me just say there are strong arguments on both sides. But how would it be a miraculous sign if it was simply a young woman? In every other usage of the word in the Bible, it is either used of a virgin or in a neutral sense. Literally it reads, "Look! The virgin is pregnant!" It's as if he saw a vision of wonder. And the name of the child is to be "God with us". Isaiah 9 goes on to speak of the one that will reign on David's throne, even the area of messiah's ministry. 9:6 gives us other divine titles, such as Mighty God and Everlasting Father, for this One that will be born to the virgin. In addition, Micah 5:2-5a alludes to this passage (especially verse 5 in the variant readings) as referring to the coming Messiah born in the town of David, Bethlehem.

In 7:16 the text returns to the singular "you" (the king) and God addresses the boy that the king was instructed to bring with him (7:3). The fulfillment of the short term prediction would help the people have faith in the long term prediction. We are not twisting Isaiah's words; rather we are correctly interpreting them.

The final text is from the third section, the Writings, and is the one Jesus cited, Psalm 110. 1 *The LORD says to my Lord: "Sit at my right hand, until I make your enemies your footstool."* There are few that will deny this as being messianic. Those who make a vain attempt to say it was written from David to Solomon on his coronation must also call it a false prediction or flowery exaggeration. Instead it speaks the same words as the second Psalm and Daniel 7:13. Even the Jews that Jesus addressed could not understand the mystery how the Messiah could both be YHWH and the Son of David. (Mark 12:37)

Before Rabbi Saul left Damascus, he was declaring that Jesus is the Messiah, the Son of God! Then he went into the desert of Arabia, like Moses before him to look again at Messiah in the *Tanak*. Wonder with him how it is that this "seed" of Eve can crush the power of evil but dies? Why must this One to come to be born of a virgin? How can He be called God? How could this One be a king and a priest and reign in the midst of His enemies? Mysteries! And yet as Saul studied in solitude and put the life of Jesus alongside these prophecies He began to understand that all of Scripture was pointing to Jesus. The Law was our guardian to bring us to Messiah. (Galatians 3:24) The Law condemns us. How can we have life? The answer is the mystery kept hidden for ages but now revealed to the saints, Jesus is Messiah. (Acts 26:22-23)

All these pictures throughout the Old Testament: light, the gate to Eden, the tree of life, the ark, the tabernacle, the rock that followed them, living water, manna, the Captain of the Hosts, the angel of the Lord, Joseph the savior, King David, kinsman redeemer, and on and on, are just shadows to lead us to the substance. They are shadows from which we can learn, because in them we see Jesus. The Law was guidance to help us live until the One that would fulfill the Law should come and be the living Spirit of the law in our hearts. (Matthew 5:17; Jeremiah 31:33)

The greatest mystery of all was how man could be made right with God. How can the Lord be our righteousness? (Jeremiah 23:6) The greatest answer ever given was Jesus, God's answer to our separation. He would sanctify us through His death and come and live in us. (John 14:23) Christ in us, the hope of glory! The mystery was revealed to Paul and the saints (Colossians 1:26) and they were so overwhelmed by the profoundness of it that they invested the rest of their lives declaring it. Hope for every person had come in Jesus. God would make us His tabernacle and be our righteousness if we will come to Jesus and accept that He paid the debt we owed.

We don't have to look at shadows and wonder. We don't have to ponder how the pieces of the messianic promises would come together. The mystery has been revealed. The Scriptures are for the purpose of leading us to Jesus!

Questions
1 What did Paul do after his conversion?
2 What are the three main views regarding messianic passages?
3 Which view did Jesus have?
4 How do we know Jews saw the Scriptures as messianic?
5 What are the three sections of Scripture and how are they joined?
6 Why is Genesis 3:15 about more than fear of snakes?
7 What is the significance of the word "strike"?
8 How is Isaiah 7 prediction divided? How do we know that?
9 What it Jesus' question regarding Psalm 110?
10 What is the mystery that was revealed to Saul of Tarsus and the saints?

Freedom in Christ   Colossians 2:16-23

Last Sunday, we delved into the mystery of Christ. We saw that the shadow of the Old Testament pointed to a reality, the Messiah, Jesus Christ. It was a revelation that completely changed the way the Apostle Paul interpreted the Scriptures. It was in no way a diminishing of the importance or inspiration of the Scriptures, but rather gave them a new filter to understand where it was pointing. (Acts 26:22-23) It was not that they did not see it pointing to the Messiah, but rather that with the life of Christ, they could now see it with more clarity. They could correct their misinterpretations. Now a first and second coming of Messiah clarified what seemed to be conflicting predictions. (Zechariah 9:9-10)

But some wanted to stay with the shadow and pictures instead of moving to the reality. *16 Therefore let no one pass judgment on you in questions of food and drink, or with regard to a festival or a new moon or a Sabbath. 17 These are a shadow of the things to come, but the substance belongs to Christ.* All the regulations for worship and religious purity kept the nation of Israel distinct from the world around them. The dietary laws had a great deal to do with health. The religious festivals brought national unity and pointed forward in picture form to what God was going to do in the future. Now that the reality had come, the unity of the kingdom of God is no longer in what we eat (Romans 14:17) but the One of whom we partake, Jesus, the bread of life. It is not in our worship styles or rituals, but in the One we worship. (Ephesians 2:14-15) The shadows of the Law are cast by the body of Christ. Now that we have come to Him, we can still learn from the Law and how it points to Him. Whether we observe a ritual or not, our focus is the reality. The demands of the Law were met in Him. The Law said we are sinners, but Jesus said He came to give His life a ransom for us. (Matthew 20:28) In Him we have forgiveness of sins and become a part of the new creation. (2Corinthians 5:17)

The false teacher was telling the Christians in Colossae that they were inferior spiritually because they did not do God's will. You'll hear that today by those who put ritual and rules above a relationship. They will judge you because you are not doing what they are doing as if uniformity with their preferred actions earned you some favor with God. But never fear; they will pray for you, you poor, weak, immature believer. The works road to righteousness or sanctification will always compare their life with yours and count themselves more spiritual because they do certain things. They are quick to judge you as inferior. (Mark 7:5) That is the extreme of legalism. Spiritual maturity is living in Christ and being led by His Spirit.

18 Let no one disqualify you, insisting on asceticism and worship of angels, going on in detail about visions, puffed up without reason by his sensuous mind, The last verse encouraged the Colossian Christians not to feel condemned by the legalist's prideful judgments. Now he warns them to not be judged by the super-spiritual experiences of the false teacher's delusions. By depriving themselves of physical necessities, they induced hallucinations that they thought to be spiritual experiences. In these states of physical deprivation, they allowed their minds to imagine they were communing with God. They then let the so-called vision interpret the Scriptures on what they thought was a higher plane.

Paul is warning them to not give in to the desire to elevate oneself above others through works of self-deprivation like fasting or self-torture or any denial of the physical body's needs. It is common for the world to praise such actions that appear spiritual. Fasting is a spiritual discipline, but we must ask if it the leading of the Holy Spirit or is it a routine? Is it something you tell others about for respect? That is why Jesus suggested we not let others know if we are fasting. (Matthew 6:17-18) Then it remains only about your relationship with God.

Prayer is absolutely a part of our spiritual walk with our Savior, but if we deprive our body of sleep, night after night, we better be sure it is the leading of the Spirit and not spiritual pride or works. Let's face it! Our old nature wants to be a religious giant, but it hates being a humble servant submitted to Jesus. We have an ungodly appetite for ecstatic states of esoteric experiences. (Luke 23:8) That hunger opens us up to deception. We interpret it a sign that we are special. Some of God's servants had such experiences but when it is from God, the result is humility, not pride. Whatever our experience, the objective truth of Scripture must be the filter through which we interpret it. (Isaiah 8:20) Christ rather than experiences determines spiritual reality.

We have had a number of these systems come through our town. One insisted the way to real spiritual breakthrough was for us all to stay up all night in prayer. Another insisted that we pray by pleading the blood of Jesus over everything. Another was sure that the power of Masonic Lodge had to be broken before Sedona would change. Another even directly contradicted our passage today by declaring that Jewish Feast Days are special times when the heavens are open for God's power to come down. And all of them judged the faithful believers here to be unspiritual if they didn't jump on board. And yes they had visions and special revelation that showed them something no one else had seen. Some things never change.

That's because we are still dealing with life in Jesus or life in the flesh. It's the same throughout history and around the world. It is heartbreaking to see the body of Christ in in our town fall for it decade after decade after decade. And the fruit of it is always a fracturing of the body of Christ. (Titus 3:10) If we don't learn from the past, we will continue to repeat the same mistakes.

Paul goes on to describe the real problem with the false teacher. *19 and not holding fast to the Head, from whom the whole body, nourished and knit together through its joints and ligaments, grows with a growth that is from God.* The false teacher had lost connection with the Head, Jesus. He thought he had a direct connection. Instead of submitting to Jesus, he thought his special spirituality had made him the new avenue for truth. Everyone else was just too immature to see what he had seen, and now he and he alone must lead them into the full truth. To that, Paul reminds them that all the fullness of God is in Jesus! (Colossians 2:9)

By declaring the false teacher had lost connection with the Head, Paul was pointing out that even if he claims to be a Christian, his teaching showed him to be severed from the body. The Head nourishes the body and directs its growth. It's the personal relationship with Jesus that knits us together and causes us to function as a body. If we are growing and maturing, it should be together as a body, not separately from the rest. (1Corinthians 12:7) A body grows at the same rate or it becomes deformed. The false teacher deceived himself into thinking he had surpassed everyone else and become their superior in all spiritual knowledge. Paul is saying he's an amputee. If he's growing, it's not a godly growth but ungodly.

When we all focus on Christ, we are knit together in love and grow together in Him. (Colossians 2:2) He is our nourishment, and He is the Word. We grow in a godly way which is love, true humility, and service to one another.

20 If with Christ you died to the elemental spirits of the world, why, as if you were still alive in the world, do you submit to regulations— 21 "Do not handle, Do not taste, Do not touch" 22 (referring to things that all perish as they are used)—according to human precepts and teachings? Paul reminds them that they died with Christ. Since that is true, why would they go back to the old worldly ways? Why would they subject themselves to the demonic suggestion of works? Why would they think that keeping the shadow laws would somehow earn them God's favor when they have the reality in Jesus?

In verse 21 he appears to be quoting the false teacher. "You shouldn't use certain things or touch certain things. You shouldn't eat certain foods." All these are perishable things that are temporal. Jesus addressed the issue when He said, *17"Don't you see that whatever enters the mouth goes into the stomach and then out of the body? 18But the things that come out of the mouth come from the heart, and these make a man 'unclean.' 19For out of the heart come evil thoughts, murder, adultery, sexual immorality, theft, false testimony, slander.* Matthew 15:17-19 (ESV)

138

Preoccupation with the world and its ways sidetracks us from the eternal issues of life. One extreme is luxury, living for bodily comfort and satisfaction. The other is to measure our spiritual growth by worldly references. Do I consider myself a spiritual giant because of the things I do or don't do? Do I measure myself by the distance I've put between me and my old life? The only real measure of growth is Jesus. Am I in Him? Is He Lord of my life? Do I act out of love for Him or the pride of being a spiritual leader?

All the do's and don'ts of religions are about appearance. Jesus' life transforms the heart. *23 These have indeed an appearance of wisdom in promoting self-made religion and asceticism and severity to the body, but they are of no value in stopping the indulgence of the flesh.* It looks like they are really spiritually dedicated. Consider some of the Buddhist or Hindu monks. They look very spiritual. But spirituality is not measured in denial of physical needs. (Hebrews 13:9) You can actually feed the flesh nature while starving the fleshly body. Spirituality is measured by our relationship with Jesus, both the Head and the body. True growth in one affects growth in the other. Spirituality is not measured by your good works, no matter if they are good things, Biblical things, or church things. (1John 2:6)

All the good deeds and religious actions in the world can't change the heart. You can lash yourself with chains, fast for 40 days, refuse to watch TV or movies, pray through the night, and worship from dawn to dusk on every special feast day, new moon and Sabbath, witness to everyone you meet, while your heart remains unchanged. (Galatians 5:25-26) A relationship with Jesus is the only thing that changes the heart. A love relationship with Jesus is the only way to really change your desires.

The message of Scripture is that of the restoration of the relationship of man with God. It is not about ritual or modified behavior. Eve ate the fruit because she wanted to be exalted in position and knowledge. (Genesis 3:6) She put her desire before her relationship with God. God doesn't just want a people that will be obedient to do's and don'ts. He wants a bride for the Son that will act based on a relationship of love. Out of relationship comes the works that God prepared in advance for us to do. (Ephesians 2:10)

Don't let me tell you what you are supposed to do. That is God's calling on your life and it comes out of your relationship with Him. What He calls you to do will be Spirit empowered and will bear fruit that remains. (John 15:16) It will be a part of the growth of the body.

Last week I had the blessing of sharing the chapel session with the Indian Bible Mission in Flagstaff. I had no time to really prepare, so I shared with them the tabernacle message that we shared when the model of the tabernacle was erected here. I thought it would be a good teaching for them and inspiring, but I wasn't really expecting the Holy Spirit to grab hold of my heart and remind me again that it's all about restoring what was lost in the fall. God wants to walk with us again. But what we inherited from Adam is so evil, so self-centered, that it took the cross to restore such an enormous breach, not so we would obey, but so that we would truly love again.

These religious things that come along, legalism and hyper-spiritual experiences are all about "me". They don't really bring us closer to Jesus; they just boost my ego, my pride in my spiritual condition. My head knowledge may have increased, but the gap is still there. The only way back is through the brazen altar of the cross where the Lamb of God spilled His blood to pay for my sins. (Ephesians 2:17-18) Then I can see in the Laver my true condition and wash in the water of the Word. (Ephesians 5:26) I can enter into the tabernacle and feast on the Bread of Life and be illuminated by His Spirit and join in His prayers. But He wants me to come all the way in to His awesome presence. (Psalm 16:11)

There, in the Holy of Holies, I am not puffed up in pride, but broken by His the gracious love that comes from His awesome holiness. I am humbled by the vision of how far I have to go, undone, unraveled. (Isaiah 6:5) I have no desire to boast about the experience, for it is devastating, but wonderful. I just want to share of how gracious He can be to anyone who will come to the cross. I don't want to share that out of duty, but because it overflows from my heart.

The dietary rituals and feast days were to bring Israel together in the Temple to worship God. Jesus is the Temple, and all believers are the Temple of the living God. (1Corinthians 6:19) Jesus' sacrifice brings us in unity and qualifies us to come into God's presence to worship Him. We share the joy and freedom that come in knowing we are accepted in Jesus. Spiritual freedom is being free from do's and don'ts and joyfully acting only out of loving cooperation with the Holy Spirit.

Now, when someone comes along and judges you because you don't do this or that, don't let them get away with it! Tell them the Lord is your righteousness. (Jeremiah 23:6) And if they try to tell you that you need to have a certain spiritual experience, tell them you had the greatest spiritual experience, your sins were nailed to the cross of Jesus. And when Satan tries to get you under condemnation that you aren't doing this or that, first check your relationship with Jesus. If you are loving Him and living in Him, waiting on His Spirit, then tell Satan to get behind you! You died with Christ!

The new you is right with God because you are clothed in the righteousness of Christ. You are growing with His body, and He is transforming your heart. That is true spirituality that you were created to possess. That is true freedom in Christ!

Questions
1 What was the function of the Law?
2 How can we describe spiritual maturity?
3 What was "spiritual" to the false teachers?
4 What is "spiritual" to our old nature?
5 What is the result of being connected with the Head?

140

6 Why is our death with Christ a death to the Law?
7 How do "do's and don'ts" sidetrack us?
8 How do our desires change?
9 What is the message of Scripture?
10 What is spiritual freedom?

Raised In Christ! Colossians 3:1-4

Our passage for today is based on Paul's theology of baptism, which he first mentioned in 2:12. *12 having been buried with him in baptism, in which you were also raised with him through faith in the powerful working of God, who raised him from the dead.* In the parallel letter of Ephesians, which was written around the same time as Colossians, Paul stated that the incredible power that raised Christ from the dead was working in us. (Ephesians 1:19-23) Since he didn't elaborate, he must have known that the Colossians understood the concept. Before we go further, let us make sure that we do.

Modern American Christian lifestyles differ little from the average person who makes no claim to have faith in Christ. Apparently, most people who call themselves Christians don't understand that a believer in Jesus dies with Jesus on the cross and is raised with Christ to a new life. It must be a concept that we have lost or intentionally ignore. So just what does it mean?

In chapter two, Paul compared it to the first covenant rite of circumcision. (2:11) That represented a cutting away of our old Adam nature, a separation from it, to be a people separated for God, a nation of priests. (Exodus 19:5-6) The old nature was defined in the Garden of Eden as living by what looks enjoyable, what is pleasurable to do, and what will exalt us over others. (Genesis 3:6; 1John 2:16) The Apostle John calls it the lust of the eyes, the lust of the flesh and the pride of life. When we come to Christ and seek forgiveness, we nail that worldliness to the cross with Jesus and it dies with Him. (2:14)

Too many people come to Jesus with a desire to have the promise of heaven but no desire to die to their worldly nature. They want forgiveness but don't want to make any changes. This is the main reason so many will baulk at accepting the salvation of Jesus. They know that repentance should mean a change in the way we live. If I love my wife, and say I am sorry for not acting like it, and then go on living as I please, is my repentance genuine? Your actions prove your words are sincere or not. If you repent of your selfish indulgence in the world, then there should be a radical change in your life. This is what Paul calls dying with Jesus. (Romans 6:8)

The change is just as evident in what is new as it is in what is no longer. Just because there is generosity and self-sacrifice does not necessarily mean you are a new creation. The new life is resurrection life, Holy Spirit empowered life! If you truly die with Jesus, then you will be raised with Jesus to newness of life. There is an entire shift in desires. They were once selfishly indulgent, but now they become God centered desires.

You want to do the things that please Him because that is what pleases you. (Psalm 37:4)

In addition to a desire shift, there is a power shift. All the pleasure and pride seeking came at the efforts of our own cunning and ability. The power to walk in a way that pleases God, led by His Spirit, is empowered by His Spirit. It is not that we don't make an effort, but that our effort is supernaturally empowered. (Philippians 2:13) We cooperate with a much greater power and our meager efforts get carried along in the current of His will. It's a bit like rowing downstream.

So Paul begins with the supposition that this is what has happened already in the life of the Colossian believers. They died and were raised with Christ. Then he points to what should be the result of that death and resurrection. *1 If then you have been raised with Christ, seek the things that are above, where Christ is, seated at the right hand of God. Seek the things that are above in contrast to what you once sought. Set your heart on those things.* (NIV) Again, in the parallel letter of Ephesians, Paul clarifies a bit more the things that are below. He tells us that we all gratified the cravings of our sinful nature and followed its desires and thoughts. We were by nature objects of wrath. But because we were loved so much, God raised us up with Christ and seated us in the heavenly realms in Christ Jesus. (Ephesians 2:3-7)

The things that are above are privileges we have in Christ. We have His love! We have a destiny and a calling. We have the promise of heaven and heavenly rewards for our labor. We have the entire family of God that will be perfected and can look forward to uninterrupted fellowship with them. We have fellowship with God!

I went through a time of discouragement awhile back. I got my eyes on the world instead of on Christ. I started counting problems and discouragements instead of counting blessings. A pastor friend of mine calls it "thumb sucking". What a great phrase! Are you "thumb sucking" this week? Aren't we too big to suck our thumbs? So I pulled my thumb out of my mouth (figuratively) and started realizing I was raised with Christ! And what do you know, the place I was in Scripture that morning reminded me, *22 But you have come to Mount Zion and to the city of the living God, the heavenly Jerusalem, and to innumerable angels in festal gathering, 23 and to the assembly of the firstborn who are enrolled in heaven, and to God, the judge of all, and to the spirits of the righteous made perfect, 24 and to Jesus, the mediator of a new covenant, and to the sprinkled blood that speaks a better word than the blood of Abel.* Hebrews 12:22-24 (ESV) Wow! All that is ours!

That's seeking the things that are above! Loving our Savior for all He has done for us and seeking His will in every situation is a result. That even includes how I respond to adversity and disappointment.

If Eve was seeking the things that were above when the Tempter came, what a different history we would have had. If you and I sought the things that were above, what a difference our lives would have been and can be in the future!

As I watched the pictures in Japan of the tsunami carrying off homes, cars, fields and greenhouses as if they were toys on the beach, I realized that it related to our passage that I was working on. Some of those people will be devastated because their hearts were set on all the things that were swept away. Others will go on with little change in their daily exuberance for life because their hearts are set on things above. What a difference! (2Corinthians 4:18)

Paul says those things above are where Christ is seated at the right hand of God. He's making one of the most common references in the new covenant, that of Psalm 110. We touched on that briefly two weeks ago. The first verse says,1 The LORD says to my Lord: "Sit at my right hand, until I make your enemies your footstool." Psalm 110:1 (ESV) King David calls someone his Lord. YHWH (the eternal God) says to David's Lord to sit at His right hand. That is a place of authority and power. The position and authority are secured, but the final submission of the world ("your enemies") is yet to come. The next verse tells us the Lord will rule in the midst of His enemies. It was how the early church came to understand what seemed to be a contradiction in the prophecies of Messiah. He reigns but not yet over all. That part of the prophecies is yet to come. Still, Jesus' victory is accomplished. He reigns in our hearts and one day soon will reign on the earth as the enemies of our Lord are put under His feet.

We are still in that time of Jesus sitting and waiting until the times are fulfilled. In the meantime, the enemies are out sowing false teaching. The spirits that were defeated by the cross are still sowing the idea of works, rules, and esoteric experiences instead of a relationship with Jesus. In Ephesians Paul calls these powers spiritual forces of evil in heavenly realms. (Ephesians 6:12) That is what we are struggling against and that was what was behind the false teacher in Colossae.

When we listen to them, we turn our eyes to the world and our pride tells us we are not doing enough. We desire to be more respected by others, so we discipline our body even more and purchase the latest class on "The Secret Teachings of Jesus" or whatever lie they are peddling at the time. All the while we have everything we need in Jesus who is willing to live in us. Turn the eyes of your heart upon Jesus!

2 Set your minds on things that are above, not on things that are on earth. It is not only our heart that must be set on things above, but our mind as well. Both verses are telling us that these are urgent actions that must be taken. We must seek heavenly things. We must be mindful of the things above. In the second verse, we are called to discipline our thought life. That thumb sucking that I spoke of earlier, is the result of focusing on earthly things and situations. The more you focus your thoughts on the world, the more depressed and discouraged you become. We must capture our thoughts and turn them toward heaven, toward all that we have in Christ and the sure outcome of our faith, if we want to continue by faith. (2Corinthians 10:5)

Jesus warned that if we take our hand off the plow and look back, we aren't fit for the kingdom of Heaven. (Luke 9:62) Our hand on the plow is laboring for our King in His field, the world. Looking back is taking our eyes off of Jesus and turning them back to the weed saturated fields of self-centeredness. (Matthew 13:7)

3 For you have died, and your life is hidden with Christ in God. Paul reminds them, and us, again that we died. We died, and yet we must continue to seek and fill our minds with the things above.

If we count ourselves dead to worldliness, separated from it for the purposes of God, then what do we do when we find ourselves focused on it again? We immediately remind our self that that is our old nature. We intentionally shift our focus back on to what is true of our new nature. We obey this imperative command of the Holy Spirit via the Apostle, and we seek what is above and fill our minds with what is above. (Philippians 4:8)

The Apostle declared that he was crucified with Christ and yet he lives. Still, it was not the old Saul that was living, rather it was Christ in Him! (Galatians 2:20) How we need that kind of believer today! We need dead men and women, dead to their old nature, but alive in Christ. Dead men don't argue. They don't demand to have their way. They don't even want to be recognized. They are hidden in Christ in God. They just quietly go about serving the Lord of the universe and affecting lives for eternity. All the recognition goes to their Savior. Hidden in Christ with their mind set on things above, they seek to yield to their Savior in all that they do.

4 When Christ who is your life appears, then you also will appear with him in glory. Why can we give up everything the world has to offer and die to self? Love is the motivation. God so loved us that He gave His only Son. (1John3:16) How can we offer anything less than complete submission? But there is more. He becomes our life. He means everything to us. We are filled in Him. (2:10)

But there is still more. There is a day coming when He will be revealed to the world. The rest of Psalm 110 will come to pass just as the first half did. The glory of Jesus that has been hidden from the eyes of all but a few will be revealed, unveiled, and faith will become sight. (Psalm 110:5-7) When that day comes, every believer who has the righteousness of God in Christ will also be revealed. (2Corinthians 5:21) All that He is in you will no longer be hidden but will be manifest. All the mockers' and critics' mouths will be stopped. (Psalm 63:11) Because you are in Jesus, you share in that revealing of glory. (Song of Songs 8:5a) He would have it no other way, for when they mocked you, they mocked Him. (Psalm 69:9) When they were critical of you, they were critical of Him, for you were dead and your life was hidden in Him.

Now, let us sum up these four verses as expressed in the Message translation:

1 So if you're serious about living this new resurrection life with Christ, act like it. Pursue the things over which Christ presides.

2 Don't shuffle along, eyes to the ground, absorbed with the things right in front of you. Look up, and be alert to what is going on around Christ—that's where the action is. See things from his perspective.

3 Your old life is dead. Your new life, which is your real life—even though invisible to spectators—is with Christ in God. He is your life.

4 When Christ (your real life, remember) shows up again on this earth, you'll show up, too—the real you, the glorious you. Meanwhile, be content with obscurity, like Christ.

Does this life of focus on Jesus and seeking Him describe your life? I remember as a teenager reading a passage of Scripture and realizing I was not remotely like the description of a believer that it outlined. Every boy there realized they weren't. We stopped and prayed silently and asked God what was missing in our life that we would fall so short of the Bible's description of a believer. I can't put into words what happened. I just know we all had a new awareness of the reality of Jesus. Our hearts were broken because we realized how much He loved us and how pathetic our response to that love really was. Maybe you need a moment like that this morning.

Are you seeking Jesus with your whole heart and mind? Or are you shuffling along, eyes to the ground, absorbed with the things right in front of you? Is your mind on things above? What are you missing? Are you responding to His love today? Is the reality of His resurrected life at work in you?

Questions

1 What is the basis of these commands?
2 Is it a reality in your life?
3 What is seeking the world?
4 What are the two fundamental differences?
5 What are "things above"?
6 What are the benefits of seeking them?
7 What's the connection with Psalm 110?
8 What is the hidden life?
9 When will it be revealed?
10 Are you content with obscurity?

Kill the Zombie! Colossians 3:5-14

Last week we looked at how important it is for us to set our heart and mind on eternal things, heavenly things, and not focus on the earthly. It is often said that some people are so heavenly minded they are no earthly good. The problem is really that most are so earthly minded they are of no eternal good. We get wrapped up in the temporal, whether the food laws or religious rituals and esoteric experiences of the false teacher, or in our culture, the priority of comfort and pleasure. Paul reminded them that they had died with Christ and been raised with Him. That's why we should fix our heart and mind on what is eternal. (Romans 8:4-6)

We noted that even though dying with Christ is a one-time act with continuing effects, we still must continue in a heart and mind cooperation with the Holy Spirit. That old nature that died with Christ would like to resurrect itself and dominate your life again. (Hebrews 10:38) It would like to remove Jesus from the throne in your heart and rule your life once more. It would like you to return to the old desires and thoughts that you once thought were the way to satisfaction. (John 8:34)

The old nature is like the mythical zombie. It's dead, but it can crawl out of the grave and ruin your life. (Romans 5:12) So every time that zombie climbs out of the grave we need to do what our text instructs, *5 Put to death therefore what is earthly in you: sexual immorality, impurity, passion, evil desire, and covetousness, which is idolatry.* You died with Christ, yet, you must continue to put to death what is earthly in you. This is another of the imperative commands of this chapter. The language here means you must do it and keep doing it. That is our experience, isn't it?

A few weeks ago, when in the second chapter, we talked about how important it is to know that the work is done by Jesus. We don't have to do or not do something to earn God's favor. (Galatians 3:11) We are accepted in Christ. That is absolutely true as far as salvation is concerned. Then we are to live in Christ and in His resurrection power. It's important that we don't think we can then just relax and go back to our old life style. That would mean we are only fooling ourselves about our salvation. To be raised with Christ means we are a new creation. (2Corinthians 5:17) It doesn't mean the old zombie won't make a desperate attempt to retake the throne of your heart. (Psalm 85:8)

What Paul is describing in verse 5 is not only what happens when we are saved, but what continues to happen. Christianity is the one belief system that truly matches the reality we face every day. We live in a fallen world of sinful man. We can have a heart transplant, but we must continue to suppress the old nature and recognize it for what it is. That is why Paul went on to describe the actions that come from the old nature, sexual immorality, impurity, passion, evil desire, and covetousness, which is idolatry.

We could look into the meaning of each of those words, but all we have to do is look at our old nature and you can understand the definition of them. It's all about pleasing self with disregard for others. Paul gives a slightly longer list in Galatians 5:19-21 (ESV) *19 Now the works of the flesh are evident: sexual immorality, impurity, sensuality, 20 idolatry, sorcery, enmity, strife, jealousy, fits of anger, rivalries, dissensions, divisions, 21a envy, drunkenness, orgies, and things like these.* If these describe our life, we never became a new creation, or we let the old zombie back on the throne of our heart. If you received Christ and the zombie is back on the throne of our heart, you will be miserable. How do I know? I've experienced it. Your joy will disappear. The peace of God will leave your life until you repent and go back to putting the old nature to death. (Psalm 119:165)

This is why the Apostle Paul described his life as dying every day. (1Corinthians 15:31) There are things the old nature would tempt us to do until the day we die, but like Paul, we die daily. We continue to see that old nature stays off the throne of our heart and that Christ remains there instructing us with His word and directing our thoughts to things that are above.

I once thought that if I grew enough in Christ that I would no longer be tempted and wouldn't have to fight these battles so frequently. There is some truth to that, but we will only be free of this internal strife of the old and new nature when we see our Savior face to face. (1John 3:2) Meanwhile, kill the zombie! God empowers you to continue to do so. Recognize that lust and greed are lying about what they can deliver and that real fulfillment is knowing Jesus. (Galatians 5:16)

In this passage and in Ephesians, Paul calls covetousness idolatry. (Ephesians 5:5) He is referring to the second and tenth commandment. (Exodus 20:3-5,17) The old nature wants what someone else has been blessed with. We can even make the gifts of God things that we idolize. To covet is to complain that God should have given you the gift He gave someone else. That turns into idolatry. It's thinking that the thing or ability would satisfy your heart. God alone satisfies the heart of the believer!

Any time you start to think something else will satisfy, you become an idolater. Then you have to recognize it and continue to put it to death. Paul is giving them these descriptions because the heart is deceitful. (Jeremiah 17:9) We can justify in our mind that doing something is not really the old nature. So Paul spells it out clearly so that we don't delude ourselves or be deluded by some false teacher. False doctrine will always end up in either self-righteousness or sexual indulgence or both.

6 On account of these the wrath of God is coming. Here is a reminder for those who would compromise. If you think those things aren't so bad, remember, this is the reason for Noah's flood. (Genesis 6:11) This is the reason behind the destruction of Sodom. (Genesis 19:5) This is the reason for the vials of wrath that will be poured out on the earth. (Revelation 9:20-21) God is just. He will execute justice! It will not be restrained by uncertainty. These things mock God's goodness and hurt others and must be judged. Justice is one of the attributes of God we should highly value. (Genesis 18:25) In this world, injustice abounds. But we can know that the day is coming when the books will balance. If we are in Christ, we have nothing to fear. If you are not in Christ you'd better run to Him, the only way to escape certain judgment. (John 5:24)

7 In these you too once walked, when you were living in them. It's not that Christians are any better than anyone else. We did all the same things in mind if not in body as well. It was our life. We simply took the opportunity to be forgiven that was offered us in Christ. That is why we should now be different. He saved us from the wrath to come. Out of love and appreciation we should yield to Him reigning within our hearts. But now that we are raised with Christ our lives should be dramatically different.

8 But now you must put them all away: anger, wrath, malice, slander, and obscene talk from your mouth. Are you hanging on to anger over something that was done to you? That isn't consistent with new life in Jesus. (James 1:19-20) Maybe that is where your joy has gone. Sometimes we even get angry with God for things He allows in our lives. That will certainly steal your joy and peace. Do you slander others? It doesn't matter if it is true or not. If you are speaking evil of others, remember it is not consistent with the life of Christ in you. That does not mean we do not condemn what is evil, but when it becomes personal, it becomes ungodly. (1John 4:20)

Recently within the movement called the emerging church, some of its leaders began using foul language on a regular basis and justifying it. This passage says that is inconsistent with our new life. It may be popular, but it is still ungodly. Some say it makes us fit in better so we don't look too holy. The Apostle says, "Get rid of it!" (Genesis 35:2)

It's interesting to hear people's language change when they find out I'm a pastor. Sometimes they will even apologize. The world is convicted about their language while some of the church is trying to talk us out of that conviction. God help us. We are supposed to be different! Don't confuse "holier than thou" with holy.

9 Do not lie to one another, seeing that you have put off the old self with its practices Deception must go with the old self and all its practices. The zombie lies to impress or gain an advantage. There is no need to do that in Christ! Our value is in Jesus and His love for us. Our advantage is that we are His chosen ones, God's children. Now we can finally be honest and not hide under masks of deception. (Ephesians 4:25)

Paul uses a couple of terms that were used for undressing and dressing. We take off the old self like a set of dirty work overalls. Then we put on the new man. *10 and have put on the new self, which is being renewed in knowledge after the image of its creator.* The new wardrobe is in fact Christ Jesus. (Romans 13:14) He is what people are to see in the way we go about our work, in our responses, in our concern, and in the way we live our lives each day. We are supposed live the "What Would Jesus Do" motto continually.

And we are to be renewed in knowledge. The Amplified Version puts it like this, [ever in the process of being] renewed and remolded into [fuller and more perfect knowledge upon] knowledge… The way we think and see the world is continually being transformed as we study God's Word and live in Christ Jesus. (Romans 12:2) We gain true knowledge. We get God's eternal perspective. We continue to grow and grow. If you think you've arrived, it just shows you've got a long way to go. The more we see, the more we realize how much more there is to see. (Ephesians 1:17)

11 Here there is not Greek and Jew, circumcised and uncircumcised, barbarian, Scythian, slave, free; but Christ is all, and in all. In Christ, our background does not matter. Our status in society or our income level is not a factor. For the believer, it is all about Jesus. If He's in you, you're my brother or sister. We have the same great fixation, Jesus!

We read of what the old self looks like, and we know the new self looks like Jesus, but Paul gets a little more specific about what we put on when our wardrobe is Jesus. He gets into the individual articles of our dress. *12 Put on then, as God's chosen ones, holy and beloved, compassionate hearts, kindness, humility, meekness, and patience, 13 bearing with one another and, if one has a complaint against another, forgiving each other; as the Lord has forgiven you, so you also must forgive.* Because we are chosen ones made holy by the blood of Jesus, loved by God, here is what we should look like. Our heart should feel with others, which is what compassionate means. That is how Jesus is with us! (Hebrews 4:15) We should be kind toward all, even our enemies. We should be humble, considering others above ourselves. Our strength should be controlled, which is what it means to be meek.

We should patiently bear with one another. This is one of the church's greatest failures. We refuse to forgive like we have been forgiven. Jesus had some pretty stern words to say about that. (Matthew 18:34-35) God puts up with so much in me and you. Can't we reflect that grace to others? We will if we put Jesus on each day and continue to kill the zombie.

That old zombie is reigning in the heart of too many Christians. Jesus died to set us free from unforgiveness, anger, slander, all sensuality and greed. Take it off! Put Jesus on! Get dressed up, fellow believer, and don't let that zombie out of his coffin! Amen? The world needs to see Jesus in you and me. They need to be freed from the bondage of their earthly nature. How can they desire that freedom if they don't see it lived out in us? (1Peter 2:12)

Questions
1 How is our old nature like a zombie?
2 In what ways does the Bible fit our true life experience?
3 Describe the zombie?
4 How often do we have to kill it?
5 Why is coveting idolatry?
6 Why is God's wrath coming?
7 What are the throw away clothes?
8 What are the new clothes?
9 Why are there no class distinctions in Christ?
10 Why is it important to keep putting them on?

Gracious Imperatives Colossians 3:15-17

We've come to three of the most helpful instructions in Scripture. Before we delve into them, I want to explain the Jewish concept of the boundaries of the Law. Our culture see rules and commands as confining, but the attitude of the Jews toward the Law of God is more like a path to blessing. They felt that they were very special people because, of all the people on earth, God had chosen to give His Law to them. The Law and its commands were seen as a revelation for a life of peace and goodness. (Psalm 119:1) To study the Scriptures and apply them to life was to put on "the yoke of the Kingdom of heaven". (Avot R. Nat. verse B ch. 26)

This should certainly be the attitude of the born again believer in Jesus. (John 15:7) These instructions within the New Covenant are a blessing. They keep us from the destructive effects of sin. They guide us to a life of peace and joy. (Psalm 119:165) They open our eyes to discern what is truly good and what is deceptively evil. We should treasure these lists of instructions Paul gave as a blessing to the churches and to us.

Last week we looked at the importance of taking off the old clothes of our sinful nature and dressing in Christ. We saw the importance of continuing to kill that zombie (the old nature) so that we can be the person we truly are now. The final instruction was to put on love over all the other godly virtues, because love is what keeps all the other virtues in their place.

Without skipping a beat Paul continues with the word "and". We should not forget that these instructions flow together. Put on love over all *15 And let the peace of Christ rule in your hearts, to which indeed you were called in one body. And be thankful.* Like many of the previous commands, these are expressed in an imperative present active tense. We must now and always allow the peace of Christ to govern our heart.

What is the peace of Christ? It is the third fruit of the Spirit. (Galatians 5:22) It is the peace that the Son has of knowing that the Father is good and sovereign over all things. It is the peace that knows that all things work together for good to those who love God and are called according to His purposes. (Romans 8:28) It is the peace that can say when faced with unspeakable torment, "Not my will but yours be done." (Luke 22:42) We can sense it deep within. We know when it is not present and when it is. And though we do not rely on feelings within our soul, this peace is a sense that goes deeper, to the very condition of our spirit.

We first experience the peace of Christ when we ask Him to be our Savior and forgive us of our sin. (Psalm 20:5) Surely you have heard of people expressing it as a load being lifted. Then, when we compromise in our walk with the Lord, there is the sense that it is not present or is disturbed. It is uncomfortable for the believer who has become used to having the peace of Christ. (Psalm 51:12) The mature believer becomes very sensitive to when this peace is present and when it is disturbed. When it is disturbed, they immediately go to prayer to find out why. I realize I haven't given you a very specific definition, but the believer will know exactly what I am talking about.

The command is to let the peace of Christ rule our heart. The word "rule" can also be translated "govern" or "arbitrate". It is the word that is also used for an umpire of a sport. The peace of Christ is to be the umpire in your heart. He says what is fair or what is against the rules. That peace arbitrates between two opposing desires. Which one is of that old nature and which is of the new? The peace of Christ can make that call for you. The peace of Christ can govern your heart.

That peace will not allow unforgiveness. He'll call it, "Out!" every time. It will not allow lust to comfortably occupy your thoughts. He'll call it out of bounds. I appreciate most of all that even when there is no clear instruction from the Word, the peace of Christ will arbitrate what is right. You aren't left to guess which path is the will of God and which is a road that is not His will. The peace of Christ will call it for you. Our part is to allow or let it govern our heart. It's our choice. We can ignore it to our peril, or heed it for our good. (Isaiah 30:21) Like all the commands from the Lord, we can partake of the blessing or not. Have you learned to let the peace of Christ rule your heart for your good?

to which indeed you were called in one body. When we became a child of God we were called to peace. We all have a unique calling and we all have a corporate calling. The body of the local church was called to walk in the peace of Christ. Every dispute, every conflict, every bitter experience is because we do not walk in the peace of Christ as one body of believers. (Galatians 5:20) When the peace of Christ rules in our hearts individually, then we have that peace corporately.

And be thankful. I believe this is the third reminder in this letter that the believer is to be thankful. (2:7; 1:12) We have so much! We have fullness in Christ. We have the peace of Christ within our spirit. When the Spirit says, "Out of bounds!", we should be thankful that we can walk away from that desire and thank God we did not go down a path of destruction. If we could see the destruction from which the peace of Christ has spared us, we would be so very thankful! If you want to get a glimpse of it, just look at what it cost you when you went against the peace of Christ in your past. I could tell you story after story of heartache and loss in my own life because I ignored the peace of Christ. I think I'm finally getting it. By the grace of God may we all understand that the peace of Christ is a good arbitrator and be thankful for it. Amen?

16 Let the word of Christ dwell in you richly, teaching and admonishing one another in all wisdom, singing psalms and hymns and spiritual songs, with thankfulness in your hearts to God. We come to the next instruction, allowing the Word of Christ to be dwelling in us richly. The Jews understood this concept. The children of Galilee all made an attempt to memorize the entire Torah. The people sang the Psalms. They talked about the prophecies. The words of Scripture were their life. ("...two students who walk together without discussing the Torah deserve to be burned." Sotah 49a) The highest calling a Jew could have was to be a student and teacher of the Scriptures.

The Apostle is using the imagery of the Temple. As He has said in other passages, we are to be the dwelling of the living God, the Temple. (Ephesians 2:22) The Spirit of God is to reside in us. Here he expresses it as the Word of Christ. The words of Jesus are the very heart of God. He said nothing but what He had heard from the Father. (John 12:49) The logos of Messiah is to make His home in us – richly! It is not only the words of Jesus, but any portion of Scripture, for He is the word (logos) of God made flesh. (John 1:14)

That means not only to memorize the Scriptures, but to meditate on them. (Joshua 1:8) They are to be our companions, our instructors. This is one area where we have really failed. It's no wonder the church is so anemic! The average Christian might be able to quote four or five verses. They rarely if ever meditate on them, and would never consider bringing them up in a conversation. But that is exactly what we are commanded to do. Paul probably drew this instruction from the Shema, Israel's daily prayer. *6 And these words that I command you today shall be on your heart. 7 You shall teach them diligently to your children, and shall talk of them when you sit in your house, and when you walk by the way, and when you lie down, and when you rise. 8 You shall bind them as a sign on your hand, and they shall be as frontlets between your eyes. 9 You shall write them on the doorposts of your house and on your gates.* Deuteronomy 6:6-9 (ESV)

The Gentiles of the Colossian church needed to develop a passion for the word like their Jewish brothers. By calling it the Word of Christ, Paul was emphasizing that the words of Jesus should obviously be a part of our treasure that we commit to memory and talk about. (John 15:7) This is a privilege and a blessing. The old nature abhors it because this is one way to make sure the zombie (old nature) stays in his grave! (Psalm 119:11) Satan is so cunning and subtle. He wants us to believe that memorizing the word is tedious and useless. I don't know anyone that hasn't heard the lie, "memorizing is not your gift." Or how about this one, "You don't need the letter, just the Spirit." If that is so, why was Jesus always talking about Scripture? Most of His messages were exegetical sermons explaining a Scripture passage. Of course, you can misuse Scripture, but that is not an excuse to neglect the living powerful word of God! (Hebrews 4:12)

I could harp on this for the rest of the year, and some will see the blessing in taking the time and effort to memorize the Scriptures and some of will never do it. That is their loss.

I know a drug user that came to Christ and had a great desire to memorize but was just unable. He would work all week on one simple verse. Finally he got desperate in prayer and asked God to heal his mind so he could store up the word of Christ. God healed his drug fried brain, and that day he memorized almost entire chapter. If you want it bad enough, God will help you. It's His will, and where He guides, He provides. (Philippians 4:19)

When the Word is in you, when the Scriptures fill your mind and heart, then you can teach and admonish one another with all wisdom. Paul was reminding the Colossians that the false teacher's wisdom was not based on the eternal Word of God. True wisdom is found in the Word. (Psalm 19:7) A preacher once said that you can tell a person has carried a full bucket by their wet feet. Get full of the word and it overflows in wise counsel. It spilis over from a full heart and mind to bless the lives of others. The author of Hebrews shamed his readers by telling them that by this time they should have been teachers. (Hebrews 5:12) They should have had a full bucket by now. Most believers today stay in the spiritual child stage all their physical life. They don't become the teachers they could have been because they don't let the Word dwell in them richly.

And when your mind is full of the Word, when you are meditating on it, you find yourself singing psalms and hymns and spiritual songs, with thankfulness in your hearts to God. That's the bucket overflowing. Our cup runs over when walk with Jesus in the Word. (Psalm 23:5)

Music is like the peace of Christ. It can reside in a place that is deeper than the soul. I've led worship at care homes where many of the residents have lost touch with the world around them. They'll hold the hymnal upside-down, but they know every word of every verse of a hymn. They can't tell you their own child's name. How is that possible? Music goes deeper than the mind and those words of praise are captured deep in the spirit. I'd like to hear some humanist's explanation for that! We are spiritual beings with a human body, not human beings with a spirit. (2Peter 1:13-14) We are going to praise God for all eternity, as that is what we are designed to do. You don't have to, but praise is that expression of a spirit overflowing with God.

I see in this verse instruction for blended worship. Now, I know I'm on controversial ground, but consider this, by the time Paul wrote this letter, most of the psalms they sang were 400 to 1000 years old! The spiritual songs that erupted from the spirit of the worshiper were brand new. They sang both! I wonder if they had the same conflict over music then? But if either or both are sung with thankfulness in the heart, and sung to God, I think we won't be so concerned about the style. Songs are meant to be an expression of thankfulness of the heart. This is the fourth command to be thankful!

17 And whatever you do, in word or deed, do everything in the name of the Lord Jesus, giving thanks to God the Father through him. Our final gracious imperative in this passage today is speaking and acting in the name of the Lord Jesus. Police are to act in the name of the law. In other words, their words and actions are to represent the authority under which they serve. We are to speak and act under the authority of our Lord, Jesus. Our words should be what He would say. (1Peter 4:11) Our actions should be how He would act. (1John 2:6) We don't have the same calling so we won't die for sins or establish a new covenant or save people, but we are to represent our heavenly Father in the earth. The Scriptures tell us that if we speak, we should speak as the oracles of God. They tell us that if we claim to be in Jesus, we should walk as He walked.

And now for the fifth time in this letter, and the third time in as many verses, Paul reminds us that if believers are to be anything, they are to be thankful. We give thanks to God through glorifying the name of Jesus. When we act in the fruits of the Spirit, when we put on the attributes of Christ, then God is glorified. (2Corinthians 4:11)

Are you a thankful believer? An unthankful believer is an oxymoron. Are you thankful for the gracious imperative to let the peace of

Christ rule in your heart? Then it will be your guide each day. And what about the command to let the word of Christ dwell in you richly? If you see it as a gift from God, it won't be a mere duty, but a joyful privilege. Will you speak and act under the authority of Jesus with a thankful heart? As believers, we certainly should.

These verses point us back to the beginning of the chapter. Is your heart and mind set on things above or on earthly things? (3:1-2) These instructions are the gift of God for you today. Will you receive them?

Questions
1 How did Jews feel about the commands of God?
2 Summarize the commands that preceded our passage.
3 What is the first imperative in our text?
4 How do you experience it?
5 What is the second?
6 What are the results?
7 What is the third?
8 What does "in the name" mean?
9 What do they all have in common?
10 In what way do you see these as a path to blessing?
11 What stops us from doing these?

Heavenly Living Colossians 3:18-4:1

The previous passage has addressed the fact that the believer has died with Christ and been raised with Him. Paul explained what the old life looks like, and warned that we have to keep putting it to death. (Colossians 3:5) He also gave us some gracious imperative commands, commands to set our heart and minds on things above, to let the peace of Christ rule in our hearts, to let the Word dwell in us richly, and to speak and act under the authority of Jesus (in His name). Tall orders! But they are not out of reach because we are to be clothed with Christ and access His resurrection power. (Romans 13:14) Those who make the excuse that they can't change are really saying they refuse to yield to the power of God and would rather cling to their sin. God's word is true! If there is a failure, it is in our unwillingness to cooperate with His Spirit. (Philippians 4:13)

Today we continue with instructions on how to live a godly life. It doesn't just happen. We don't just sit back and watch our life change. We must cooperate with the new life within us and continue to put the old nature to death. We have to make the effort to conform to the image of Christ, while realizing that we can only do so by His enabling power. It sounds like a contradiction. "You can't do it. You must do it." You can't do it in your own power, but God can enable you to do it if you will yield to His Spirit. (Romans 8:11)

Paul had been writing about our individual spiritual condition. In our text today he moves to our social obligations as people who live in

Christ. The basis of society is the home. If the home is sound, society will be healthy. If the home disintegrates, society does as well. That is what you see happening in our culture. It was the downfall of Rome as well as a number of other societies.

What was God's design for the home? It seems odd that God would begin with the wife's role, but the reason goes all the way back to Eden. *18 Wives, submit to your husbands, as is fitting in the Lord.* If a woman is in Christ, if she is raised with Jesus, walking in Him, it is fitting that she should submit to her husband.

Now, before you run out screaming, "Chauvinist women haters!", listen to the reasons and the godly application. After the fall from perfection in the Garden, God announced some of the consequences. (Genesis 3:14-19) One of those consequences was that the woman would have the desire to rule over her husband. She was designed to be his helper, but sin had changed the heart to go against its own design. That is a devastating effect! When we desire to do what we aren't designed to do, we end up frustrated and unfulfilled.

This is not saying that women can't have careers. It is not teaching that they should be doormats. It is not implying that they should not have any say in the decisions of the home. What it is saying is that a woman in Christ will recognize her God given design and will allow her husband to make the final decisions and trust God for the outcome.

The ideal Biblical woman is the woman of Proverbs 31. She is industrious, cares for her family, is strong, generous, invests, is wise, teaches kindness, but most of all has respect for the Lord. She is honored by her husband and children and respected by the community. Now that is a fulfilled and happy woman! Amen?

So why would the Spirit through Paul start the family instructions with the command for wives to submit to their husbands? It's because the greatest danger to the home is a wife who insists on always having her way. It crushes the spirit of the husband who longs for her respect. (Ephesians 5:33) It gives the children a distorted view of how a family is meant to operate. It is the natural tendency of fallen woman. Like all the other imperative instructions in the chapter, this is one that she must intentionally allow the Spirit of God to change in her life. She must continually put to death that desire to rule over her husband. It does not result in passivity, but rather in the influential woman of Proverbs 31.

If we just had that instruction, the burden would all fall on the woman, but it doesn't stop there. We now have the husband's role. *19 Husbands, love your wives, and do not be harsh with them.* The woman's greatest need is to feel loved. The husband is to model the love of Christ. The parallel passage in Ephesians 5 tells us that the husband is to love like Christ loved the church. (Ephesians 5:25) Jesus died for the church! That is as intense as love can get. (John 15:13)

Husbands are also affected by the fall. We are affected by seeing our value in our work. We are affected by lust. Our tendency is to use our wife   for our ends and to take her for granted. So we overwork. We look for love in the wrong places. We are selfish, ungrateful, and treat our wife with harshness. All that must be put to death, and in its place, we must allow the Spirit of God to give us genuine love, His love, for our wife.

When a woman feels secure in her husband's love, it is much easier for her to show her husband the respect he needs and submit to his leading. When a man feels respected and honored by his wife, it is much easier for him to put to death his fallen tendencies and truly love her. (Ephesians 5:21) The result is a heavenly home that is secure and sound. It won't be free of problems, but the problems are easier to deal with because of the stability in the home. The children grow up in an environment that sets the right example. They feel secure and are not worried about their parents divorcing. Society is stable and productive.

That leads us to the children. They have a role as well. *20 Children, obey your parents in everything, for this pleases the Lord.* If a child is in Christ, just like his or her parents, they should put to death the old nature that tends toward rebellion. They should obey the authority God has placed over them. The picture in the home is to be a mirror of our relationship with our heavenly Father. We place our trust in Him and are obedient. The father in the home, for better or worse, represents God to the children. Fathers have a heavy responsibility to represent Him. How we do that forms their first impressions of God, the heavenly Father. That is the reason for the next instruction.

21 Fathers, do not provoke your children, lest they become discouraged. We must encourage our children and grandchildren more than we correct them. They need loving guidance, but more than anything else they need to be encouraged in their God given abilities and gifts. Encouraging them in the right direction goes a lot further than making them feel bad about wrong choices. Love is more powerful than anger. Seeing their value in the Lord, will overcome the esteem the world gives them when they follow its ways. Watch for signs of them yielding to Christ and tell them what it means to you to see that in them. Share how you found your calling. And that is one of our greatest callings in life.

Today's music is seducing another generation toward hate and self-destruction. Rather than knock it for its style, find the same style that has godly content. Talk about the content of the destructive music and ask them if they really want to think about those things. (Philippians 4:8) For the child that is in Christ, ask them if they would be comfortable sharing those headphones with Jesus during that song. Instead of discouraging them, you are encouraging them to think about what they are doing and to make godly choices. If you aren't sure what to offer as an alternative, ask one of the young adults that are in Christ and they will probably be able to guide you to the same style with godly lyrics. I listened to some recently that had a solid Biblical perspective. It wasn't my style of music, but I was impressed!

Next, the Apostle moves to the field of labor. *22 Slaves, obey in everything those who are your earthly masters, not by way of eye-service, as people-pleasers, but with sincerity of heart, fearing the Lord.* A large percentage of the early church was slaves. We can relate this to employees. When I was in the workforce, this verse always convicted me. The boss has the right to ask you to do anything that is ethical. Unlike slaves, you have a choice to work for them or not. So if they are paying for your time, you have an obligation to give your time to them. The warning goes to the heart of the issue. You can look like you are doing what was requested, but not be doing it with a sincere heart. God sees the heart. To cheat those in authority over you is to mock the final and great authority, God.

There is a great general instruction within this command to slaves. Christians should be sincere and act from the heart. Earlier in the passage we were warned to not be deceitful. (Colossians 3:9) If we are faking our actions to impress people, we are living for the approval of man rather than God. It means we haven't found the security of knowing how valued we are in Jesus. Our life is focused around the wrong things. People-pleasing is a difficult thing to forsake. (Galatians 1:10) We all want to be valued and respected. The only way to really overcome it is to know our value is in Jesus and His love for us.

Sometimes we act differently than we feel out of respect and love for others. That is a different matter. That is putting the old nature to death. Only you and God really know the condition of your heart. If you detect that your behavior is just for the approval of man, take time with the Lord to let Him show you why you are so desirous of that. Let Him reveal how He can meet that need in your heart. There are times when this issue needs counseling to help overcome some habits or thought patterns that have been formed. Believers should always act out of sincerity and never for the sake of impressing or deceiving others.

To the slaves, Paul goes on to say, *23 Whatever you do, work heartily, as for the Lord and not for men, 24 knowing that from the Lord you will receive the inheritance as your reward. You are serving the Lord Christ.* He's reminding them that all service to those placed over us is ultimately service to the Lord. (Ephesians 6:7) That is why we should be sincere whether we are seen or not. It applies to every laborer. The Christian labors for God. (Matthew 9:37-38) This is where the Christian work ethic originated. The Christian should be the best employee. He works as unto God, not himself, not even the company. The Lord is the unseen observer of all that we do. Since we know He is just and repays for all service done for Him, we should work knowing we are investing in eternity. (Luke 14:14) Our eternal inheritance is not speculation. It can't rust or be stolen. (Matthew 6:20) It is the only sure way to invest for the future.

If every employment is about serving Christ, then shouldn't we be excited to go to work? Shouldn't we see our work as ministry? Just like the instructions for the home make the home a heavenly home, so these instructions for our mindset toward work will make our employment a blessing rather than a burden. A happy sincere employee is more likely to be promoted and trusted than the one who is constantly complaining about his work.

I wrote our Christian radio station and reminded them that work isn't meant to be a burden but an opportunity to serve God. (1Corinthians 10:31) The way they talk about Mondays and Fridays makes it sound like we have to do this drudgery that is forced on us by the curse. That is not the attitude of the New Testament! You are serving the Lord Christ! Should we speak despairingly about serving Him? I don't think so! It perpetuates a wrong attitude toward work and keeps us from the joy of service to Christ. (Psalm 100:2) It causes us to think of ministry separate from our employment.

25 For the wrongdoer will be paid back for the wrong he has done, and there is no partiality. This is in regards to the slave deceiving his master about his work. It certainly applies to all situations. God is just. The books will balance. You don't escape justice because of your status in life. Money may buy you a good lawyer, but it won't buy God. In the Roman world there were all kinds of preferential treatment according to your status or occupation. In the kingdom of God there is no such thing. The only favor you get is in Christ, and that doesn't spare you from the consequences of sin in this life.

Now for the other side of the employer – employee relationship.*1 Masters, treat your slaves justly and fairly, knowing that you also have a Master in heaven.* The Christian owner of slaves had to change his mindset. Romans treated slaves like tools, mere objects to be used up and discarded. The Christian slave owner was to be just and fair, and so too, the Christian employer. (Leviticus 19:13) Remember, we represent our Master in heaven and He expects you to treat others as He treats you. (Matthew 18:33) He is the standard for the father and the slave owner/employer.

Consider how this would have created a much more favorable environment for the servant. It would help them to work with sincerity. It would even make them feel special among slaves to be treated better than the average. If they weren't a believer, it would certainly make them think about what had made such a change in their employer. (Ephesians 6:9) That is a side issue but an important one. When the world looks at the Christian home and work place, it should draw them to the One that made the change, our Savior.

While the Bible does not condemn slavery, by giving work dignity, it undercut the premise of it. The ending of slavery was largely a Christian effort. Paul wrote Philemon that he should take back his runaway slave not as a servant but as a brother (Philemon 1:16).

The great Master is God, and we are all servants (Ephesians 6:9). Some refuse to serve and will only serve self. Others do so insincerely thinking that heartless performance is enough. But if we who believe will heed God's instructions, others will see God's good intentions for our homes and our work are for our good. When we do things out of selfishness, we make it difficult for those around us to see the goodness of God.

158

When it comes to home and work, are you clothed in Christ? Are you renewed in knowledge? Do you have the heavenly mindset? Are you demonstrating for others the goodness of God by yielding to His design? Are you passing on the design of God to your progeny?

Paul was giving these instructions to help the Colossians experience Christ in their daily life. How are they speaking to you today so that you can experience more of the goodness of God in your home and work? Do you need an attitude adjustment about the role God has for you? Do you really believe His way is the best way?

Questions
1 Go over the preceding instructions.
2 Why is the home so important?
3 Why start with the wife?
4 What is her struggle?
5 What is the ideal Biblical wife?
6 What is the man's struggle?
7 What does the ideal home look like?
8 What is at the root of employee discontentment?
9 What should the heart attitude be?
10 What is required of the employer?
11 What should a Christian business be like?
12 Why is this good for business?

Devotion to Prayer Colossians 4:2-6

Before the Apostle closes his letter to the Colossians with greetings, he has some final instructions. The first is *2 Continue steadfastly in prayer, being watchful in it with thanksgiving.* The NIV translation of those first words is "Devote yourselves to prayer". It is important to understand just how the word was used so we can get a better grasp on what Paul was asking them to do. Strong's Greek Dictionary defines the compound word used here in a number of ways. I believe they all apply. "The word means to be earnest towards, to persevere in, be constantly diligent, or to attend assiduously all the exercises, or to adhere closely, to attend (give self) continually, continue in, wait on continually."

I'll be the first to admit that I don't feel like this describes my prayer life. I pray all the time, but I rarely take hours of continual prayer. I so appreciate those who do, and I would like to do so more often. I also appreciate those who pray for my ministry of preaching. I pray throughout the day, but I usually take the time to really wait on the Lord when in a trial or sermon preparation. But I'm not your perfect example, far from it. Our example is Jesus. Let's take a brief look at His prayer life.

35 And rising very early in the morning, while it was still dark, he departed and went out to a desolate place, and there he prayed. Mark 1:35 (ESV) Jesus took time to be alone with His Father and commune with Him.

The disciples got up that morning and couldn't find Jesus. He had gone before the dawn, while it was still dark. One of the best times to pray is when the Lord wakes you in the night. It's quiet and without distractions. (Psalm 63:6; 119:148) I have nights when I wake at 2 or 3AM and can't go back to sleep. I used to just lay there and keep trying to sleep, and finally around dawn I'd go back to sleep for a few minutes. What a waste of good prayer time! Get up! Go to where you usually pray. You do have a place don't you? Open your Bible and your heart and talk with Jesus.

When there are not urgent matters on your heart, you can go through the Lord's prayer, elaborating as you go. Or you can use the acronym ACTS to help, Adoration, Confession, Thanksgiving, Supplication. You'd be surprised how quickly the time flies. When you're prayed up, you'll be pleased to see how quickly you fall back to sleep.

My favorite verse about Jesus praying is from Hebrews. We went over it recently in our Hebrews Bible study. *7 In the days of his flesh, Jesus offered up prayers and supplications, with loud cries and tears, to him who was able to save him from death, and he was heard because of his reverence.* Hebrews 5:7 (ESV) The Greek word used in the passage for "loud cries" is that involuntary sound that comes up from the depths of your being when you are overwhelmed with emotional pain. You've probably heard or personally experienced that involuntary sound of pain. Imagine the intensity of prayer that would produce this kind of an involuntary cry. I think Jesus must have prayed like that many times, though the writer is probably referring to the prayer in the Garden of Gethsemane. (Matthew 26:38-39) Jesus was heard because he reverently surrendered His will to that of the Father. That is an important ingredient in prayer, submission to God's will in our circumstances.

Prayer should be a two way communication. Though we should tune our heart to hear the still, small voice of the Lord, we also need to test everything with the Word of God. The vast majority of the time the Lord speaks to my heart, it is through a passage of Scripture. That is His voice. Whatever He speaks to your heart will be Scriptural if it is His voice.

It saddens me to hear the family of God command God to heal or to save or any number of things. There is a verse in Isaiah in which God asks if we will command Him (45:11). In the King James translation it sounds as if God is asking us to command Him. (45:11KJV) In almost all more recent translations the phrase is a question asking if we would dare to command Him! When we ask of the Father something in the name of Jesus, we are asking with Jesus' authority which means that it is His will. We pray God's will into the earth, not our own. (1John 5:14) Prayer is aligning our heart with the Father's.

The Apostle goes on to say that we should be watchful in it. This may mean that we should take care not to fall asleep. The Greek literally means to be wakeful. Paul may have been recalling the stories of the Transfiguration (Luke 9:32) and the Garden of Gethsemane (Matthew 26:40). Vigilance is implied. It's not something we do with a half-hearted effort. Prayer is something that we should give our whole heart to on a consistent basis. Prayer should be a way of life. (1Thessalonians 5:17) If Jesus is our life, we should be in constant communion with Him.

The Apostle then adds the now familiar command to be thankful. I believe this is the sixth time in this short letter he has told of the necessity to be thankful. I can't add anymore to what I have already said so I'll repeat myself. Gratitude is the heart of the genuine believer. If we are not thankful something is very wrong with our spiritual life. We are saved from judgment! We have a world-wide family that would die for us and for whom we would die. We have the opportunity to labor with our Creator and lay up eternal rewards. We have a full heart of love and peace. What more could we ask? The trials of this life can't even begin to compare to the glory that will be revealed in us! (Romans 8:18) Praise Him! Thank Him! Quit siding with the enemy of your soul by murmuring (Philippians 2:14) and get out of your selfish old nature and praise the living God for who He is! Amen?

3 At the same time, pray also for us, that God may open to us a door for the word, to declare the mystery of Christ, on account of which I am in prison— Paul goes on to add, *"While you are praying in this vigilant way, pray that God would open a door for the Word to get through to those they are trying to reach."* One commentator reminds us that it is interesting what Paul did not ask us to pray. (Barclay's Daily Study Bible (NT)) He did not ask that we pray that he might be released from prison, or that they might remove his uncomfortable chains. He did not ask to be spared from execution. He didn't even ask that his daily necessities be met or for the support of the Colossians. Paul asked for prayer that he might carry out the task that God gave him, to declare the mystery of Christ... *4 that I may make it clear, which is how I ought to speak.*

Paul made a request that was in line with what he asked in verse 2 and consistent with our interpretation. He was asking that God fulfill the mission through him. (1:25-26) Clear communication differs from culture to culture and even person to person. That is why we must rely upon the leading of the Holy Spirit. Paul wanted to do it to the best of his ability, to communicate it clearly, because that is how it should be done. He understood that the revelation of Christ as Messiah that paid our sin debt, both for Jew and Gentile, was a very important message. (Romans 16:25-26) He didn't want to teach cheap grace, nor did he want to teach something that was earned through works. Our understanding of what Christ accomplished on the cross comes mostly from Paul's writings, an answer to this prayer request.

Although not nearly as urgent or important as Paul's request, I ask that you do the same for my speaking and writing. I want to make the message of Scripture clear, and say it in a way that communicates it clearly. I would especially make that request for my upcoming book that teaches the divinity of Christ from the Gospel of Matthew. We know God wants people to know Jesus is divine so we can know we are praying God's will. Of course our will is involved too. We can hinder the answer to prayers by our unwillingness to yield to God's enabling power. However, we can even pray that God will help us yield to His Spirit and put His will above our own. (Luke 22:42)

Whatever your gift or calling, you can pray that you exercise it as you ought. You can pray that you exercise it in a way that glorifies God. You can pray that others see Jesus in your service. That, we know, is God's will.

We prayed for a year and a half that my son Daniel would find a doctor that understood what was wrong with him. We didn't know for certain that was God's will, but we thought that was how God was leading us to pray. He found the only doctor in the world that was aware of the particular protozoa that had colonized his blood stream. He isn't completely well but he is much better and now has hope of being free from headaches and fatigue. We continue to pray for his complete healing if that will glorify God.

As a church, we are praying the prayer from the beginning of this letter to the Colossians. We pray that God will strengthen us according to His glorious might for all endurance in every circumstance and patience with every relationship, with joy, giving thanks to the One who called us to share in the inheritance of the saints in light. (1:11-12) We know it is His will because it is according to His Word.

Paul's next instruction was to *5 Walk in wisdom toward outsiders, making the best use of the time.* The world is always looking for excuses to discount Christianity. The enemy of our soul is always looking for ways to discredit your testimony of what Jesus has done in you. That is why this command is important. We should live in a way that is as non-offensive as possible. (Luke 17:1) We even give up some of our freedoms in Christ so as not to stumble others who are watching. (Romans 13:13)

Walking in wisdom means that we look to God for how to act in relationship with others. We should be sensitive to what is offensive to them, and yet never compromise the Gospel message. I cringe at times when I hear people think they are being a bold witness when in fact they are being an offensive witness. I have had people ask me to keep so and so away from them because they keep trying to cram Jesus down their throat. One of my best friends used to complain about Christians always telling him he had to get saved today or he may go to hell. Those Christians were sincere and their message was true, but that friend was won by patient love rather than zealous human preaching.

The wisdom that comes from above is peaceable, gentle, and open to reason, wrote the Apostle James. (James 3:17) The message that may be needed for Pharisee is not what is needed for a "sinner". Walk in the wisdom of the Holy Spirit to glorify God. It costs us more to invest our time in the lives of others, but love takes time and bears fruit.

Make the best use of the time. This is something God instilled in my life from an early age. If we have but this short life to invest in eternity, what are we doing sitting around twiddling our thumbs? There is so much that we

162

could be doing. At the same time we need to learn God's balance of rest and enjoyment. God doesn't drive, but He does lead continually, and sometimes He leads to still waters. (Psalm 23:2)

I just came back from a time of refreshing. It took me a long time to learn that that too can be the best use of our time. He created a Sabbath rest (Genesis 2:3) because He loves us and knows that we are more productive for the Kingdom of God when we take those times of rest. Best use of time sometimes means down time. Are you investing for eternity?

The phrase "best use of the time" in Greek literally means to redeem, or buy back, time. Opportunities come our way by the hand of God. We can buy them up by using them to advance the kingdom, or we can lose them forever. God has planned these gracious opportunities to bless us with a chance to work with Him. (Ephesians 2:10) Buy them up! Don't let them pass. Invest in them for His sake and for your eternal future.

Paul's final instruction goes right along with walking in wisdom. *6 Let your speech always be gracious, seasoned with salt, so that you may know how you ought to answer each person.* Much of the wisdom we need with outsiders is connected with the way we express ourselves. But even with fellow believers, our speech should always be gracious. We can use graciousness as a gauge to measure whether or not we should say what is coming to mind. Of course, if you have the mind of Christ, (1Corinthians 2:16) it will always be gracious. There are so many ways to say things; always choose the more gracious expression. C.F.D. Moule commented on this passage. "The Christian must commend his message with the charm and the wit which were in Jesus himself. There is too much of the Christianity which stodgily depresses a man and too little of the Christianity which scintillates with life." "Scintillates with life" – what a great way to express what Paul was conveying.

You might ask if some of the sharp rebukes that Jesus gave the Pharisees were gracious? (Matthew 23:27) Sometimes the truth expressed in love can be very pointed and clear. Where is the grace in that? It is much more gracious to speak the truth than to remain silent when the truth needs to be told. It is more gracious than saying something that is flattering but is a lie. (Proverbs 27:6) When you read gracious, don't always think of easy or acceptable. The conviction of the Holy Spirit is an expression of the grace of God in our lives! (John 16:8)

The other expression is "seasoned with salt". Salt gives flavor and leaves us wanting more. Think about what you are about to say and let the Holy Spirit flavor it. There is a little Mexican treat called a saladito. It's a dried plum that is thoroughly salted. It leaves you with pucker on your face but wanting more. Holy Spirit filled expressions can be like saladitos. Not everyone likes them. Not everyone likes what the Holy Spirit has to say, even when it is an expression of love. Yet, that is how we are supposed to speak. Every individual is different and what one person needs to hear is not what another needs, however, full of grace and seasoned with salt applies to how we should speak to everyone at the leading of the Holy Spirit.

Paul's closing instruction to the Colossians and to us is to have a life of prayer, pray for the kingdom to advance, for your gifts to be used, walking in wisdom, using the opportunities God presents, and speaking flavorfully with grace. Can we do it? Only if Jesus is our life! We search for the perfect witnessing formula. It would be easy if I could give you a 1,2,3 on relating to those who do not believe, but the Biblical answer is to die to self and live in Christ. Devote yourself to prayer. To walk in Jesus is to walk in wisdom. Let the Holy Spirit lead you to make the most of your time as you speak to others with His grace and flavor that scintillates with life!

Questions
1 What kind of prayer was Paul commanding?
2 How can we be watchful in prayer?
3 Why does Paul keep telling us to be thankful?
4 What were Paul's two prayer requests?
5 Will you pray this for those who preach the Word?
6 What is the mystery we declare?
7 What price was Paul paying?
8 What is the next imperative command?
9 What is the connection with the first command?
10 How do we make the best use of our time?
11 What is the description of believer's speech?

Portraits Colossians 4:7-18

Paul closed his letter to the Colossians with greetings from the people who were with him. He begins with Tychicus who was probably the bearer of the letter. *7 Tychicus will tell you all about my activities. He is a beloved brother and faithful minister and fellow servant in the Lord. 8 I have sent him to you for this very purpose, that you may know how we are and that he may encourage your hearts,* Colossians 4:7-8 (ESV)

There are three descriptions used for Tychicus. Let's look at each one. First, he was a beloved brother *(agapetos adelphos)*. Greek sentence structure is very flexible, so the order in which things are placed usually gives a sense of the writer's emphasis. Paul valued Tychicus, first of all, as a beloved brother. As the family of God, we have a lot of brothers and sisters! (Mark 10:29-30) But certain ones are especially beloved. We connect on a deeper level and can really share our hearts with these beloved ones. (Proverbs 18:24)

I hope you have a number of beloved brothers or sisters. There is never any concern that what you share with them in confidence will be broadcast. If you disagree, your love for one another is not threatened. You never have to wonder about their motivation. They love Jesus. They genuinely love you. That's their bottom line. You can't help but love them because love begets love. (1John 4:19) Just as we love Jesus because of his love for us, we love them because we see His love in them. (2Corinthians 5:14)

Tychicus was also a faithful minister. The term is used for deacons. It means those who serve. It had come represent an office in the church that originated in Acts 6. (Acts 6:3) The people chose men who were full of faith and the Holy Spirit to handle the physical affairs of the church. The first martyr was the deacon Stephen. (Acts 7:59) Man could he preach! Deacons differ from pastors simply in that their service is more physical in nature though their qualifications are almost the same as that of the elders. (See 1Timothy 3:8-13)

By calling Tychicus a faithful minister, Paul was saying that he carries out his service to the church with dependability and sincere conviction. He had probably been supplying Paul's daily food in prison. Roman prisons did not feed their prisoners. That was up to family and friends. Because Paul was in prison for having a Lord higher than Caesar, those who visited him risked being asked where their loyalties lay. Could they call Caesar lord? Tychicus risked imprisonment to meet Paul's needs. That is a faithful minister! (1Corinthians 4:2)

Finally, he was also called a fellow servant. This Greek term is literally translated, "a slave with me". In other words, Paul saw himself as a slave of Jesus. Jesus was his master, and he was glad to be in His service. It was a privilege to take orders from Him. (Romans 1:1) Tychicus was a fellow slave. They both served without question their Master who is also their Maker.

I don't know if you could use any higher expressions for a brother or sister in Christ than these: beloved brother, faithful minister, and fellow servant. Paul obviously held Tychicus in very high regard.

Could these be applied to you? Are you a beloved brother or sister to others? It is usually only about a dozen or so people that you can really be a beloved friend at any given time, simply because it is an investment of time. They pass in and out of our daily life but will remain beloved to us forever. Some will go before us into heaven. Are you being a beloved brother to someone? (1Peter 1:22)

Are you a faithful minister? You don't have to be a deacon or deaconess, but are you faithfully carrying out the call that God has on your life? Pastors appreciate the faithful ministers because they are the ones that make the church function. No matter what their calling, the faithful ones can be counted on for consistency and sincere devotion to the kingdom of God. I don't mean that they do what I ask, but they do what God leads and that always builds up and strengthens the church. (Ephesians 4:15-16)

Are you a fellow servant of Jesus? That is someone who has died to their old nature and lives to glorify God each day. That kind of person is always seeking God's will. They put their own needs last and live to serve, following the example Jesus set at the Last Supper. (John 13:14-15)

8 I have sent him to you for this very purpose, that you may know how we are and that he may encourage your hearts, Colossians 4:8 (ESV)

Tychicus had purposes other than carrying the letter. He was to share the testimonies from Paul's ministry. Paul wrote them very little about what he was enduring or of his accomplishments. His main concern in writing was to help them stay on track spiritually and not be deceived by the slick talkers. Tychicus would be filling them in on how things were going with Paul.

He was also to encourage their hearts. Paul had prayed that God would encourage their hearts (Colossians 2:1-2), but he put feet to his prayers by sending Tychicus with this letter. Tychicus was probably going to encourage their hearts by reminding them how they were loved and prayed for as well as by the testimonies of what God was doing through Paul's ministry in other parts of the world. When we hear about people coming to Christ, churches being formed, lives being transformed, we are encouraged to see the kingdom of God advancing.

Maybe you've been praying for someone to be encouraged. Have you considered putting feet to your prayers? I'm so blessed to have a number of you stop by and tell me how you have been praying for me through times of difficulty. Just to hear that you are with me in the battle and believe in the calling on my life is such an encouragement. Who do you know that needs encouragement? Have you been praying for them? Do you need to put feet to your prayers, or perhaps a phone call or card? (Hebrews 3:13)

I'd venture to guess that Tychicus was also supposed to make sure Onesimus stayed faithful to his conviction to return to his master. *9 and with him Onesimus, our faithful and beloved brother, who is one of you. They will tell you of everything that has taken place here.* Colossians 4:9 (ESV) Onesimus is also described as being faithful, and as a beloved brother. Notice the deacon term did not apply to him. Nevertheless he was faithful in following Christ. Nor was he a fellow slave of Jesus yet. That is a state of spiritual maturity. He was still a babe in Christ. But they can both share testimonies regarding the place of Paul's imprisonment.

10 Aristarchus my fellow prisoner greets you, and Mark the cousin of Barnabas (concerning whom you have received instructions— if he comes to you, welcome him), Colossians 4:10 (ESV) He was from Thessolonica and was currently a prisoner with Paul, most likely because of his stand for Jesus. It wasn't the first time he'd been in trouble for hanging around a radical like Paul. He was the one that the mob in Ephesus dragged into the theater when the idol makers were upset with all the conversions and downturn in their business. (Acts 19:29) He was also with Paul on the ship that ran aground on the isle of Malta, perhaps as a prisoner with Paul or perhaps serving him by supplying his necessities. (Acts 27:2) Some brothers are there with you no matter what difficulties you are going through.

I have some that have been with me through a few shipwrecks and riots. It's part of becoming beloved brothers. I hope you have some too. If not, reach out and be that to someone, and you'll find they will be to you as well.

John Mark is a story of redemption. He left Paul and Barnabbas in the middle of their first missionary journey. (Acts 13:5, 13 under the name of John) Paul decided he didn't want to take Mark on the second mission because of his failure. Barnabbas thought he deserved a second chance. Paul and Barnabbas couldn't agree so they went their own ways, Barnabbas taking Mark with him. (Acts 15:39-40)

Now, much later in Paul's ministry, Mark had proved himself and was again working with Paul. Paul made special note to tell the Colossians to receive him, probably because they had heard about his past failure. John Mark was one of the few that stayed by Paul's side before he was executed. (2Timothy 4:11) He went from backslider to most faithful servant during the long ministry of Paul.

Paul also mentions Justus of whom we know very little. (Acts 1:23; 18:7) He says that these men are the only believing Jews that are ministering with him. He has a pretty small team considering the size of his ministry. It was very hard and risky work Paul was doing. He'd been stoned, beaten, scourged, shipwrecked, and was currently in bonds, and he wonders why there aren't more believing Jews with him?

When you saw the things that Paul saw, and when your life was so radically transformed from Christian killer to Apostle of the early church, it was hard to understand why more fellow Jews didn't jump on board in spite of the cost. Would we have volunteered to serve with Paul if we saw the potential risks involved? Do we put security before the will of God today?

It's always a blessing to have people from your background in ministry with you as it is easier to relate with them. Paul called them a comfort to him, and yet he loved these Colossians enough to send two of the brothers off to encourage them.

12 Epaphras, who is one of you, a servant of Christ Jesus, greets you, always struggling on your behalf in his prayers, that you may stand mature and fully assured in all the will of God. Colossians 4:12 (ESV) We met Epaphras earlier in the letter. (Colossians 1:7) He was the evangelist that started the church. He also started the churches of Hierapolis and Laodicea. He was truly a slave of Jesus. He is staying there with Paul, perhaps jailed as Paul's servant. They used their prison time "struggling on your behalf in prayers". The thrust of his prayers was mentioned in the first chapter, the Colossians' maturity in the faith, and that they be fully assured in all the will of God. That is what we are praying for our church as well. (Colossians 1:9-12)

Are you continuing to pray that prayer, that we be filled with a knowledge of God's will, walking in a manner that is fully pleasing Him, bearing fruit, growing in the knowledge of God and being strengthened with God's glorious might, for all endurance and patience with joy, giving thanks to God...? If these men of God struggled on their behalf in prayer, can't we do the same for the church of which we are a part? Sounds like some serious praying, like devoting yourself to prayer. (4:2) Epaphras will forever have the testimony that he worked hard for the churches of the Lycus Valley.

14 Luke the beloved physician greets you, as does Demas.
*Colossian*s 4:14 (ESV) Luke is probably the stenographer and Paul's

personal physician, caring for his thorn in the flesh. He too will be with Paul to the end. (2Timothy 4:11) Without Luke we'd be missing a large chunk of the New Testament and much of our knowledge of the early church. His work has literally influenced billions!

And then there is Demas. We have been challenged by some amazing servants of God. Their testimony has lived on to encourage us to be all out in our service to God. But now we come to a warning message. In the letter about Onesimus called Philemon, Paul mentions Demas as a fellow laborer. (Philemon 1:24) That was a short time earlier. In this letter there is no comment. In Paul's final letter, he mentions that Demas left him because he loved the world. (2Timothy 4:10) He was a picture of the seed that fell among thorns, and the cares of this life choked him until he became unfruitful. (Mark 4:18-19) What a warning!

Paul also sends greetings to a woman whose home is the gathering place for a church. Some Greek women did very well in business and had homes large enough to hold the weekly gathering of believers in the area. Archippus also had a church in his home. (Philemon 2). 17 *And say to Archippus, "See that you fulfill the ministry that you have received in the Lord."* Colossians 4:17 (ESV) My guess is that he had been appointed as an elder of the church in his home. As the owner of a large home, he would have had a lot of business to attend to, and yet the people were to remind him to fulfill the ministry he had received from the Lord. I see increasing numbers of people leaving a successful secular carrier and enter into ministry fulltime.

Paul authenticated the letter by writing the last lines in his own hand, probably large Greek letters because of his eye condition. (Galatians 6:11)

Paul closed the letter with a strange request. *"Remember my chains."* (Hebrews 13:3) He would have been chained to a soldier that kept watch over him. The mention of the chains is not for sympathy but rather a claim of authority. He has the right to tell us to suffer for Christ and count it gain because he is living it. Can we effectively tell others to carry the cross of Christ if we have not done so ourselves? (Matthew 16:24)

In these closing greetings, we've caught a glimpse of a number of lives. We've seen portraits of their testimonies. Some were incredibly strong men of faith that were sold out to Jesus. One had failed, but thanks to the grace of God had proved himself committed and stayed faithful, even serving Paul in his last days. Another loved the world more than he loved Jesus and walked out on ministry.

Someone shared the thought that the events of our life are like portraits hanging in our life's gallery. When others walk through the gallery of your life what will they see? What do you want to see there? Today and tomorrow and the next day will add to the portraits. Which one of these that we have seen in our text today will our gallery look like? Each day we decide what that day's portrait will be in the choices we make. Set your course and persevere!

Questions

1 What are the portraits of Tychicus?

2 Describe the three main expressions?

3 What was his assignment?

4 How can you put feet to a prayer to encourage someone?

5 Describe the portrait of Aristarchus.

6 And Mark?

7 And Epaphras?

8 And Luke?

9 And Demas?

10 And Archippus?

11 What kind of portraits do you want in your life's gallery?

Other books by Pastor Paul Wallace
In ebook on Kindle and paperback on Amazon

Through the Bible Daily Devotional
Through the Bible Again Vol 1 and 2
Jesus Concealed in the Old Testament
John's Rabbi
Divine Messiah?
Preaching Through Genesis
Preaching Through Exodus
Preaching Through Isaiah
Preaching Through Zechariah
Preaching Through Matthew
Preaching Through John
Preaching Through Acts
Preaching Through Romans
Preaching Through Ephesians
Soon to be available:
Preaching Through Luke

Made in the USA
Lexington, KY
24 August 2019